Meaning in Movement, Sport and Physical Education

Meaning in Movement, Sport and Physical Education

Peter J. Arnold
Head of Education Department
Dunfermline College, Edinburgh

With a Foreword by Dick Jeeps, CBE,
Chairman of the Sports Council

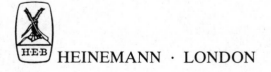
HEINEMANN · LONDON

Heinemann Educational Books Ltd
22 Bedford Square, London WC1B 3HH
London Edinburgh Melbourne Auckland Toronto
Hong Kong Singapore Kuala Lumpur New Delhi
Nairobi Johannesburg Lusaka Ibadan
Kingston

ISBN 0 435 80033 7 (Cased)
        0 435 80034 5 (Paper)
© Peter J. Arnold 1979
First published 1979

British Library Cataloguing in Publication Data

Arnold, Peter James
    Meaning in movement, sport and physical
    education.
    1. Man – Attitude and movement
    2. Human mechanics
    I. Title
    612'.76   QP301

    ISBN 0–435–80033–7
    ISBN 0–435–80034–5 Pbk

Set, printed and bound in Great Britain by
Fakenham Press Limited,
Fakenham, Norfolk

Dedication

To my mother ... to whom I owe
more than I can say

Acknowledgements

In completing this book I am conscious of the debt I owe to numerous people without whose assistance it would have proved infinitely more difficult to write.

To the Principal, Mollie Abbott, and Governors of Dunfermline College I am indebted for allowing me a year's seconded leave when it mattered most. To the college library staff, upon whom I made regular and constant demands, and to colleagues with whom I attempted to clarify my thoughts I owe a great deal.

With regard to what is written I would like to express my thanks to B. L. Curtis for a number of helpful comments and suggestions. It is, however, to R. K. Elliott that I owe most, for it was he who read and made detailed comments upon the bulk of the mid sections, often suggesting improved forms of expression, besides putting me in touch with some phenomenological texts which proved to be invaluable. Needless to say after much help I must take full responsibility for any obscurities or misunderstandings that remain.

Not least I must thank my wife, Jane, without whose forebearance and ability to type in the midst of a young family, little would have been accomplished.

Contents

DEDICATION   *page* v

ACKNOWLEDGEMENTS   vi

FOREWORD BY DICK JEEPS, CBE, CHAIRMAN OF THE SPORTS COUNCIL   x

PREFACE   xi

1 The Person as an Embodied Consciousness

The Phenomenology of the Animate Organism   1
The Concrete Experience by Consciousness of My
Own Animate Organism (2). My Body is Mine only
in so far as it is me Acting (2). My Body is an
Ensemble of Powers (3). My Body is the Primal
Condition or Orientational Centre of the
Physico-Cultural World (4). My Body is a
Synthetically Organized System of Organs (4).

The Lived Body   5
Four Modes of Lived Body Experience (7). Mode
One – The Lived Body as Self-Referential (7).
Mode Two – The Lived Body in Reference to
Others (8). Mode Three – The Lived Body and
Human Space (11). Mode Four – The Lived Body
and Human Time (13).

2 The Phenomenology of Action and Meaning

The Concept of Action   15
Project and the Process of Protection-Retention (15).
Actional Movement as Meaningful Lived Experience   20
Discrete and Non-Discrete Experience (20).
Summary (21).

Peak Experiences as Meaningful Phenomena   22

Three Categories of Subjective Movement Meanings   25
Primordial Meanings (26). Contextual Meanings (32).
Existential Meanings (38).

*Quotations Demonstrating Range and Complexity of
Existential Meanings*   43
Freedom, Autonomy and Aloneness (43). Self Mastery
and Self Fulfilment (45). Challenge and Excitement
and Power (46). Achievement and Perfection (49).
Unity with Self and Nature (50).

3 **Movement as Social Interaction and Communication**
General Introduction   53
Social Interaction (53). Communication (54). A Note
on Non-Verbal Communication (55).

Movement Communication, Meaning and Expression   56
Movement and Meaning (61). Inferential Interaction,
Code Communication and Expression (63).

*Movement Interaction and the Phenomenology of
Inter-Personal Perception*   65
Knowledge 'about' Inter-Personal Perception (67).
The Life World (69). The Phenomenology of
Inter-Personal Perception (71). Movement and
the Phenomenology of Interactional Relationships (77).

4 **Perceiving and Knowing in Movement**

The Existent as Knower   86
Actional Movement as Practical Understanding (87).

Moving as a Perceptual Form of Consciousness   88
The Sensory Basis of Perception (89). Kinaesthesis
and Kinaesthetic Perception (90). Kinaesthesia,
Action and the Self (91). Feeling, Thought and
the Limitations of Language (93).

Conceptualizations about the Moving Experience   94
Movistruct, Movicept and Movisymbol (95).

Movement: A Unique Amalgam of Knowledge Types   102
Movement in Relation to Types of Knowledge (104).

5 Movement as a Source of Aesthetic Experience

*Aesthetic Perception as a Distinctive Mode of
Consciousness*   120
     Kinaesthetic 'feelings' as Intentional Aesthetic
     Objects (121).

Movement Activities: 'Artistic' and 'Aesthetic'   124
     The Artistic in relation to Ends and Means (124).
     Aesthetic Experience: the Performer and the
     Spectator (126).
Dance: A Paradigm Artistic Movement Form   137
     The Dancer as an Artistic Performer (137).
     Creating and Becoming in Dance (142).

Aesthetic Aspects of Sport   143
     Sport and Art (143). The Nature of Sport (144).
     The Aesthetic Perception of Sport (147).

6 Education, Movement and the Curriculum

*The Place of Movement in a Curriculum of General
Education*   162

*Education and the Three Dimensions of the Concept of
Movement*   168
     Dimension 1 – Education 'about' Movement (168).
     Dimension II – Education 'through' Movement (170).
     Dimension III – Education 'in ' Movement (176).

REFERENCES   181

GLOSSARY OF PHENOMENOLOGICAL TERMS   189

AUTHOR INDEX   195
SUBJECT INDEX   197

Foreword

by Dick Jeeps, CBE, Chairman of the Sports Council

Although Dr Arnold and I were at school together his view of human movement is a good deal more philosophical than mine. Perhaps he was the more attentive pupil! But what astonishes me is how he can study, analyse and probe the curious but universal physical activity we call sport and yet come so close to the truth of it which I have found purely as a practitioner.

He writes: 'The *envisaged project* or plan, as it exists in the imagination, only becomes operational or an *actual project* when carried out in performance ... otherwise it is but a form of thinking without acting.' This very neatly answers the question, occasionally put to me: 'Did you always mean to captain England at rugby – or did it just happen?'

You play rugby (or any other sport); you play well and you play badly; and if you are interested in success rather than failure, when you play badly you find out *why*. You put your body through training routines, you think hard about the game, you *plan* to do better. And if mind and body pull out the necessary speed, rhythm and know-how, there should be no limit to what you can achieve.

Another theme in this book, which I have found wholly absorbing is equally as stimulating to the intelligence: 'It is in such spontaneous activity as play that the person is freed from his usual constraints and pressures and is able to immerse himself in movement for their own sake....' This is precisely the message of Sport for All, the campaign to encourage more people to take part in sport, that the Sports Council has been putting across for some years now.

Then again: 'The agent thinks and chooses *as* he performs....' Surely this is the secret of good and satisfying play at whatever level, of the value of activity as against non-activity? Don't just think and dream about doing something – face the challenge and *do* it.

There are countless references to sport and its performers in this book, from hurdlers, gymnasts and water sportsmen to the players of most ball games. Young aspirants should all read Dr Arnold for he has much to teach them.

Preface

In general it can be said that movement has a variety of meanings and these are usually made clear by the context in which the word is used. Thus we can speak of the symphony's third movement; the Tachist movement in Art; the movement of the earth round the sun; or the upward movement of shares on the Stock Exchange, without anybody becoming unduly perplexed.

Movement in the way I have explored it, however, is not sufficiently well established yet in ordinary language to make its meaning clear by looking at its use in context. This is partially because there is ambivalence about its meaning even in those specialized communities who use the term, and partially because only recently has enough been done in the re-structuring of old thought processes to present the term as a new concept.

The concept of movement as it has been explicated is concerned predominantly if not exclusively with human motion. Although it can in principle and sometimes does in practice incorporate the 'physics' of snooker or the 'biology' of a cat jump, centrally it is to do with the intentional physical activity of people. Movement then should not necessarily be regarded as being commensurate with *human* movement. Nevertheless for the purposes of this book movement will be discussed as if it were.

The various systematic frameworks of organized knowledge within which human movement can be discussed are varied but not mutually exclusive. Within a 'bio-mechanical' framework, for example, it is possible to look upon movement as being subject to certain universal laws and principles as well as being partially bound by particular differences in human morphology. It can be made clear too that there is more to movement than those expressions of capacity that are readily observable. Similarly within a particular 'socio-cultural' framework movement is often reflective of the occupations, religion, art and technology that characterize it. Attitudes, sentiments, feelings, beliefs, and an appreciation of sex differences are no less important factors in an understanding of the movement of man than are the various and variable ways by which he is able to use his body as means of communication.

Words and phrases such as play, recreation, games, sport and physical education may all mean different things to different people but movement, in my view, is the only reasonable and sufficiently uncomplicated label that can be used to conceptually embrace this interrelated family of terms and activities.

As I have tried to make clear in the last section to do with education, movement involves more than its academic study. Although a number of important and interesting things can be said *about* movement such as 'muscles exercised gain in size'; 'skills are specifically acquired'; 'the family is the earliest and most vital influence upon the child's attitudes towards physical activity'; 'play is a universal phenomenon' they take us only so far in our understanding of it. To more fully appreciate what movement means it is helpful to look at movement as a means of fulfilling ends that lie outside itself. In this sense it can be seen as an instrument in the service of the person or outside agency being used to bring about certain specified objectives. Thus movement in the form of sport can be made to serve political purposes; the interests of health; or even greater economic productivity. When movement becomes a vehicle in the furtherance of some extrinsic end it can be regarded as a medium *through* which intentions and purposes are being lived out for the sake of something else. It will be seen that the ends which movement can help fulfil can be regarded as 'good' or 'bad' according to one's moral standpoint.

A third way to gain an insight into what movement entails is to actually engage *in* movement activities for their own sakes as a worthwhile part of our social–cultural heritage. Here instead of objectively looking at movement from the 'outside' as a scientist might with the idea of saying something about it; or alternatively, as a utilitarian might, with the idea of seeing how it can serve practical purposes in some way, it can be viewed and experienced as a group of physical activities that have inherent value and therefore pursued as being worthwhile in themselves. It is this last perspective with which I have been predominantly concerned in this book. Whenever possible I have attempted to take up the viewpoint of the mover as agent and performer. This as far as I know has not been attempted in any adequate way previously. This approach to movement, it seems to me, is very much needed as, especially in Britain, it has been almost totally neglected. That this is so is probably because of a preoccupation with scientific method.

It will be appreciated that any philosophy to do with movement and education that pretends to have some relevance to human experience, its description, interpretation, or evaluation, must at some time come to grips with the question of what man is and to what purpose, if any, he exists.

Upon our understanding of the concept of person and what it means to be human there depends not only matters of practical concern, such as the conduct of our lives and our behaviour towards other people, but also matters of theoretical concern, such as what should ideally constitute the nature of education.

Whether we conceive of the subject of philosophic inquiry as language or knowledge, action or being, the person is involved in his capacity of talker or thinker, agent or existent, and is our most immediate and familiar instance of any and each of these functions.

It seems to me that the attempt to define the scope of philosophic enquiry as an impersonal, 'objective' mission is not only in danger of cutting itself off from life's concerns but of remaining a barren, sterile and esoteric activity that in the last resort is de-humanizing. I think some linguistic approaches to philosophy get close to this. Nonetheless language and the scope it offers must remain the only way forward, but with the recognition that it has its limitations; and in relation to the process of moving is only valuable in so far as it can evoke or describe the 'lived-body' event. It can never be a substitute but only when handled sensitively and based upon experience, an illuminator. It is in this spirit that I have written this book and it is perhaps because of this that much of what is said will be considered controversial and by some no doubt wrong. If, however, what I have written provokes a more serious consideration of the meaning of movement and its place in human life and education then I shall be amply satisfied.

Peter J. Arnold
Edinburgh, July 1979

1. The Person as an Embodied Consciousness

It is a central tenet in phenomenological and existentialist thought that to be in the world is to have a body or be a body, or, as Marcel expresses it, to be incarnate. In the world my body is, so to speak, the territory that is wholly mine. It is only through existing in bodily form that I am what I am. It is through the body that I perceive myself, other persons and things that make up the world. It is through the agency of my body that I am able to act upon them and conversely it is by virtue of my being bodily that they are able to act upon me. When I make the claim that I am a body I mean that it is constitutive of my conscious being in the world. Without my living body I would not exist. It is to this general thesis of bodily being that the term embodiment is given. The concept of embodiment as it has been explicated by Marcel,[1] and others like Sartre[2] and Merleau-Ponty[3] not only redresses the neglect of the body in the tradition of Western philosophic thought but emphasizes that the person is unified and not dual in nature. It is the task here, calling mainly upon the thoughts of the writers mentioned above, to say something further upon the incarnate subjectivity of the embodied person.

In the present context the notion of embodiment is important for two reasons. First, as has been indicated, it is the *sine qua non* of my existence and therefore of my consciousness. Secondly, it is my mode of experiencing the world, and therefore a prerequisite for discovering who I am. Embodiment allows me both to recognize my existence and at the same time permits me to explore my essence. It is therefore concerned with both self and identity and because of this worthy of being considered further.

The Phenomenology of the Animate Organism

A further understanding of the term embodiment is perhaps best attempted by making reference to what Zaner[4] has called the phenomenology of the animate organism. It can be conveniently discussed under five main headings:

(i)   the concrete experience by consciousness of my own animate organism;

(ii) my body is mine only in so far as it is me acting;

(iii) my body is an ensemble of vital powers;

(iv) my body is the primal condition or orientational centre of the physico–cultural world;

(v)   my body is a synthetically organized system of organs.

1   The Concrete Experience by Consciousness of my Own Animate Organism

The point here is that each of us has a sense of bodily continuity. Embodiment is not a once and for all cognitive grasp that I am a bodily being. Rather it is something that is experienced as an on-going fact in the day-to-day flux of my psychic life. It is I who experience myself as flesh and blood, that is being biologically alive and real. My body is known to me not only by a general sense of corporeality but on occasions, in the words of Husserl, the 'bearer of localised sensations'. When I choose to I can attend to such taken-for-granted functions as breathing, swallowing and pulsating and be witness to my own physicality.

Sensations and feelings are a part of what I am as a consciously embodied existent. For each individual the taste of a savoury dish, the smell of spring wheat, the comfort of a warm sweater, the sound of a fog horn at night, the thrill of the big dipper, the agony of a sensual pain are different intentional acts. They are a part of my 'psychic' body as Sartre[5] would say. Every thought, every movement is sluggish when I feel sluggish. My whole body is affected by the state I am in. It is in recognition foundation experiences such as these that leads Marcel to say 'I am my body only in so far as I am a being who *feels*.'[6]

It is by my attending to the concrete experiences of my animate organism that I become more conscious of my own embodiment.

2   My Body is Mine only in so far as it is me Acting

By virtue of what do I experience *my* body as mine? There are a number of possible answers to this question but one of the most convincing as we have just seen is: By virtue of the feeling I have when I engage in bodily action. When I move kinaesthetic flow patterns accompany what I do. As I do I necessarily feel. It is because that movement is necessarily bound to the feelings that accompany it that it is possible to speak of their 'mutual founded-ness'.[7] The fact that I always feel my body as mine when moving is another exemplification of the concept of embodiment.

It is in voluntary movement especially, such as the swinging of a golf club, that I am most able to take account of the kinaesthetic feelings that are an 'inner' and integral part of the backswing and downswing of the action sequence. Every phase of the movement is checked against its own intentionality with regard to space, time and effort. The kinaesthetic flow patterns (based upon specific types of coenesthetic or proprioceptive data) are experienced or 'felt' as an immanent part of the flow of action that is mine. Because feeling and acting are mutually founded I am able to feel my body as mine by virtue of the actions I make.

From what has been said in this section it will be seen that 'movement' consciousness is of the order of 'I do' and not of 'I think that'.

3 My Body is an Ensemble of Powers

Apart from experiencing myself in my 'functioning corporeality' and as a feeler of the actions I undertake I am an ensemble of powers that when exercised help me to actualize myself.

I do not know what powers I have until I employ them. Until this occurs they only exist potentially. Like everyone else I know I have some degree of strength, stamina and speed but it is only when I test them out by running, jumping or throwing and so on that I experience them as 'mine'.

In the performance of acquired skills I utilize powers that have been harnessed for some specific purpose. It is as well to remember, however, that when I am caught up in an on-going performative project, although my bodily powers are being utilized, I do not think of them as a means towards an end. Rather in the absorbed 'heres' and 'nows' of the action my ensemble of powers are experienced as that which I am.*

This aspect of embodiment then, which is brought about by the actualization of my physical powers, is 'concretized' in my stream of consciousness by what I do in terms of moving. Moving therefore is a form of praxis which is of a quite different order from the theoria of 'I think that'.

---

* It is perhaps in childhood when such bodily powers as co-ordination, balance and control are assimilated into such newly acquired movements as hopping and skipping that they are most uncomplicatedly experienced as being 'mine'. Each accomplishment too, at this stage, is a further step towards identity for, to the child, *what* he can do, especially in relation to others, is associated with *who* he is.

4   My Body is the Primal Condition or Orientational Centre of the Physico–Cultural World

.My body in the world is the given of givens. It is my orientational centre or 'that by means of which' I am able to gear in on the world and make sense of what is about me. All 'objects' in the world have a certain distance from me. I am always 'here' and they are always 'there'. This state of affairs, however, is not fixed but changeable. Either they can approach or move away from me; or alternatively I can change my standpoint and be 'here' rather than 'there'. 'Each step I take', observes Stein, 'discloses a new bit of the world to me or I see the old one from a new side.'[8] In so doing my embodied consciousness is always present. For Sartre to 'be-in-a-world' and 'to have a body' are synonymous.[9]

My embodied being in the world brings me into contact with the things that are a part of the world. It is by means of my body that I am able to relate to other embodied beings, for example, and enter into relationships with them. I am not only able to touch, kiss and make love but communicate with them on myriad other matters of mutual concern. Each successful excursion into the world adds an imperceptible richness to my personality and establishes my identity more firmly. My body is both a member of the world of objective things and a constituent of the subjective reality which is myself. It is through my embodied consciousness that I am able to encounter the world in its physical and cultural forms and personalize it.

5   My Body is a Synthetically Organized System of Organs

My body is not only my orientational centre in the world but is a synthetically organized system of organs which are functionally correlated.

What is referred to in traditional philosophy and psychology as 'sense data' (visual, tactile, auditory, gustatory, olfactory and kinaesthetic) and looked upon as 'physical processes', I experience as 'live-body events'. They are part and parcel of my animate organism. Although each of them can operate independently, more often than not they work in conjunction with one another in an interrelated and harmonious way. As a tennis player, for example, I see the ball coming, I approach it, I hit it, I hear it rebound off my racquet. As a connoisseur of good wine I smell it, move it to my lips and taste it. In each case my animate organism is experienced as one synthetic corporeal system. By means of its related elements the animate organism is experienced as a unified whole. It is of interest to note that in many instances of functional correlation it is the kinaesthetic sense that provides a common denominator. On this point and in relation to what has been said, Merleau-Ponty has this to say:

> Movement, understood not as objective movement and displacement in space, but as a project of movement or 'virtual movement', is the foundation of the unity of the senses ... my body is precisely an already constituted system of equivalences and intersensorial transpositions. The senses mutually translate one another without need for an interpreter, mutually comprehend one another without needing to pass by way of the idea. ... With the notion of corporeal scheme it is not only the unity of the body which is described in a new manner, but also through this notion the unity of the senses and the unity of the object.[10]

In conclusion then, the animate organism becomes constituted for me as mine in such a way that it both *is* me, and *expresses* me. It is the embodiment of my consciousness and my mode of being in the world. The phenomenology of the animate organism, in accordance with what has been said above is 'the descriptive–explicative analysis of the continuously on-going automatic embodiment of consciousness by an organism singled out as peculiarly "its" own, and at higher levels, graspable by me as "my own".'[11] Put at its most simple, embodiment is the incarnate location of all that occurs to me.

The Lived Body

In discussing the concept of embodiment by reference to the phenomenology of the animate organism an attempt was made to characterize what it is to be a bodily being. The task now is to look at some other dimensions of the embodied person in terms of the lived body engagement in the world. But first, in general terms, what does the phrase 'lived body' denote? It refers, according to Schrag[12] to 'a structure of human subjectivity. It indicates the experience of my body as it is disclosed to me in my immediate involvements and concerns.' Now although the lived body can be experienced in a thousand and one different ways in everyday life it is *in*, *by*, and *through* movement in its various forms that it can be and often is most poignantly felt. In addition then to movement being one of the most important characteristics of *living beings* it is also a rich source for gaining lived body experience. This has important implications for self development and the formation of identity because, as has been shown, both are affected by the way in which we experience and react to our own incarnate beings.

It is in such spontaneous activity as play that the person is freed from his usual constraints and pressures and is able to immerse himself in movements for their own sake. Muscular sensuousness for the individual can become both a source of pleasure and a value without need of justification. In the *élan vital* of childhood there is always a spark of authentic existence that in adulthood seems to get buried more and more under the demands, routines and habits of our exigent lives. Because feelings of *élan vital* and *joie de vivre* are most readily associated with childhood and play it should not be thought, however, that they are confined to them. Take, for example, this passage from Bannister's book, *First Four Minutes*:

> In this supreme moment I leapt for joy. I was startled and frightened by the tremendous excitement that so few steps could create. I glanced around uneasily to see if anyone was watching. A few more steps—self consciously now and firmly gripping the original excitement. The earth seemed almost to move with me. I was running now, and a fresh rhythm entered my body. No longer conscious of my movement I discovered a new unity with nature. I had found a new source of power and beauty, a source I never dreamt existed. From intense moments like this, love of running can grow. ... This attempt at explanation is of course inadequate, just like any analysis of the things we enjoy—the description of a rose to someone who has never seen one.[13]

It is in such 'peak moments' of our existence that our bodily selves take on a heightened awareness which give them, in our living biography, special meaning and significance without them ever perhaps being, or even capable of being, expressed in words.

The lived body, in contrast to the physical body of 'l'homme machine', is not an independent morphological substrate but the body which embodies *me* in my dealings with the world. It is as Pügge[14] observes 'something never completed but ever newly arising, to be understood as a phenomenon crucially determined by the given situation and its meaning, changing from one to another form, personal and yet belonging to the world'.

In general terms then the notion of the lived body is both positive and dynamic. It requires of the person that he be consciously engaged and doing something. It is by no means confined to physical activity but it would perhaps be true to say that it is more completely experienced in such movement forms as sport and dance where the embodied person is often most acutely aware of himself as an alive and animate being.

Four Modes of Lived Body Experience
Lived body datum is experienced as fusion. The person lives through the mass of psycho-physical occurrences in his stream of consciousness as an embodied individual. It is only by reflection that it is possible to discriminate between some of the major modes that at the time were experienced as a synthetic totality of oneness. This should be remembered in discussing (following Schrag)[15] the four modes of:

   (i) the lived body as self-referential;
  (ii) the lived body in reference to others;
 (iii) the lived body and human space;
 (iv) the lived body and human time.

Mode One. The Lived Body as Self-Referential
When examining the notion of embodiment the point was made that I experience my body as peculiarly and distinctively 'mine'. It was agreed that my body both is me and expresses me. Since my body is indissolubly linked to what I am, it is for me a matter of self reference as well as a mode of orientation in the world. As I concretely live my actions I come to know them as 'mine' because of the immanent experiences that make them so. In throwing the ball I come to have direct and concrete experience of my arm as it coils up, springs out and releases the ball. What I live out is not the movement that the physiologist researches into or the kinesiologist bio-mechanically explains, though I may be interested in this. What makes my throwing of the ball a lived body event is that it is *I* who experience it and as a matter of self reference it is my *right* arm and not my left that does it. Just as the tap dancer expresses himself with his feet, the pianist with his fingers, so the fielder does with his arm. Apart from the lived body providing specific and concrete data to my self it can, when seen against the background of my existential projects, be a source of meaning and significance. My throwing of the ball, for instance, in itself, can be meaningful for me but in the context of a cricket match and all that this implies in the way of rules and ritual and so on, it can add to whatever *primordial meaning* was already there. In other words if my lived body cricket ball throw was done in the situational framework of the cricket game then *contextual meaning*, which is socially given, would be added to the *primordial meaning* which was immanent in the action itself and which is of importance to the physical self. Furthermore if my cricket ball throw happened to be dramatically successful, in that I saved the match, by knocking down the stumps just as the last batsman was about to

score the winning run, then *existential significance* would be added to the two orders of meaning mentioned above. A cherished if relatively minor project would have been fulfilled. For me and for ever it would remain a savoured moment. A moment in which I had actualized myself as a fielding cricketer!

Lived body experiences as self-referential datum are of course not always so indelibly impressive as the one just cited but the point is that they are invariably self-identifying markers whose effect is complicated by the situational components in which they take place. As Schrag observes, 'the lived body is always related to an environment and social horizon, but in this relational complex it always appears as that which refers to itself as the locus of its relatedness'.[16]

The hand is well able to illustrate this point. It plays perhaps a particularly privileged role in the disclosure of meanings in my world orientations. It is through the use of my hand that I project meanings and transact my business. With my hand I point, pick up, feel things, gesticulate, ask for silence, write, make things, hit, catch, throw, and grasp others in friendship. It is through the activities of the hand, maintains Von der Wahrheit[17] that the activities of thought are explicated. All these possibilities for the hand arise from the unity that is me.

Perhaps enough has been said to indicate that it is through my lived body experiences that I come to know myself and take up my orientation in the world. It is in and through my body that I both become and individualize myself as an embodied person.

Mode Two. The Lived Body in Reference to Others

In addition to my body being lived in its existential immediacy and apprehended as my own it is also apprehended by the other. The world of everyday life brings me into contact with others and it is with them that I interact. Although we are independent selves we are both members of the human community that exists for each of us. This standing in relation to the other provides two identifiable forms of awareness—the body of the other as known by me and the reapprehension of my body as known by the other. Although, when in the presence of the other, I experience my body as mine it can be also coextensive with my experience of the other, and what I take to be the other's view of me. The other thus becomes a factor in my world and to some extent affects my image of my self.

Although I can get to know the other as he can get to know me by speaking to him we are concerned here with the lived body as it relates to the other in terms of movement. Sartre[18], in addressing himself to this problem, distinguishes three dimensions:

   (i) the body as being for itself;
  (ii) the body as being for the other;
 (iii) the body as body-known-by-the-other.

Imagine the mountaineer. In the *first dimension* the mountaineer having made his plans the day before and expressed the wish to reach a different summit with his friends, will come to disregard them. In the climb he ceases to pay attention to the equipment that he uses, the technique that he adopts, the people he is with. As the climb develops and he becomes absorbed by the mountain he 'ignores his body' which he has trained previously for days on end. Now, psychologically speaking, there is only the mountain. His attention is totally taken up by it. As he forgets his body so the body can realize itself as a living entity. 'The qualities of the body: its measurements, its ability, its efficiency and vulnerability can only become apparent when the body itself is forgotten, eliminated, passed over in silence for the occupation or for the landscape for whose sake the passing is necessary.'[19] It is, so to speak, only in the movement project itself that the body exists.

The *second dimension* of the body comes when it exists for the other. The change here is that as the mountaineer climbs he comes unknowingly under the eye of the other, perhaps one of his companions. The observer sees the very things the climber himself has transcended: his boots, the stick that supports him, the movements that he makes, the grazed and bleeding knuckles. The body and the rugged landscape with which it contends and against which it is seen, is for the observer a living 'object', a 'functioning organism'. Apart from the mountaineer being seen by someone else he can himself constitute his body in this second dimension. This may happen, for example, when he tends to his blisters and his bruises. His wounded parts are examined and touched *in order* to tend to them; or, *in order* to continue on his way. He looks at his body, as it were, with the eyes of an 'objective' medical practitioner.

The *third dimension*, and the one which is most important in terms of the lived body in reference to others, comes into being when the mountaineer becomes aware that I am regarding him. Leaving aside the improbable but possibly rare case that the matter is of indifference to him, there are two further possibilities: one negative, the other positive.

Sartre, in discussing this third dimension of the body, confines his analysis to the negative case and thereby conceives of it to be destructive. He depicts the mountaineer as disliking the regard of the other. As a result he begins to feel hindered, because he knows that the other looks at him critically. As a result he loses his absorption, his 'passing beyond' himself, and becomes uncomfortable, annoyed, vulnerable and defenceless. He miscalculates, makes mistakes and becomes ashamed of the faultiness of his attempts. The feeling that takes hold is not unlike that which comes upon the writer of a letter when he knows that someone from behind is looking critically over his shoulder at his composition. Such feelings are not uncommon. Certainly in athletic communities such feelings are well known. They are experienced particularly perhaps by those whose skills have been only partially consolidated and who find themselves, for one reason or another, in view of the other's eye. Such feelings I have assuredly experienced as a noviciate on the golf course!

Yet, Sartre, in leaving his analysis at this point, presents only half the picture. There is also for some people and on some occasions a positive side to knowing that one is being observed. Looks can be received as 'loving' as well as 'critical'. They can be encouraging and supportive as well as condemning and undermining. It is well known that individuals and teams rise above themselves when well wishers are present and may be cheering them on. Van Den Berg is surely right when he makes the assertion that 'Innumerable are the declarations of sportsmen that their achievements exceed their expectations owing to the eyes of thousands that are directed upon them'.[20] Certainly Mary Peters made a point of testifying to this experience, following her pentathlon gold medal victory in the 1972 Olympics. It was the abundant goodwill of the British contingent, she observed, that sustained her in her ordeal and so great was it felt in the high jump event that it helped in 'lifting' her over the bar. In professional sport supporters' clubs exist for this very purpose and there is little reason to doubt that their presence at matches is other than welcome by the players to whom they give their allegiance.

Sartre's analysis of the body as body-known-by-the-other is distorted by his one-sided and negative treatment of it. The look is the malicious look from behind. It is the alienating look of the critical stranger. Such, as has been indicated, is not always the case. There is in addition, the look of understanding, of sympathy, of friendship and love.* In the loving look of the other it is possible for me to gain the feeling that the other is on my side and that far from being disruptive of my movement can aid it in the support and confidence

* A good exposition of the subtlety of what is entailed here is given in J. B. O'Malley's *The Fellowship of Being* (Martinus Nijhoff, 1966), pp. 95–137.

it gives. This is possible whether on the mountain, the games' field, the athletic track or simply coping with day-to-day projects. In the words of Van Den Berg:

> Under the encouraging stimulating look I know what I do and *that* I do it; every action that I perform is action of my hand, my arm, my body. The accepting look of the other gives me the almost exceptional right to be myself as a *moving* body.[21]

Mode Three. The Lived Body and Human Space
Human space is not objective space. It is not quantitative and measurable but is experienced as an existential quality of the lived body. Human space is concerned not with abstract distance and impersonal vector points but with 'personal placement in a perceptual reality defined by the individual'.[22] In other words as an individual I experience my spaciality in terms of my personal projects and bodily actions. As a student of discus throwing, for example, I am interested in mathematical space as it relates to such considerations as the constraining parameters of the circle and the theoretical release angle and so on; but as a performing athlete I perceive my movements in space as expressive of my particular mode of being. In the act of making my turn I have to get my feet spread into position whilst leaving my trunk, shoulders and arm *behind*. As I begin my throw my right leg drives my hips *upward*, *round* and *forward*, my shoulders hang back with my arm trailing as if it were quite inert. Then as I rise and grow tall over my left side my trunk uncoils and comes round to where I am aiming. My right arm, as if impelled by the stretched muscles snaps into life, sweeping and pulling round until finally I squeeze the discus from my hand attempting to run its perimeter across my forefinger to impart some spin. I immediately reverse on to my right leg, dropping down to prevent myself from pitching forward out of the circle.

The point then is that no matter what knowledge I have of quantifiable space as an abstract continuum of points I live the movements of my body in personal terms. The space which I occupy, and in which I apprehend my body, is in and through my practical projects, whether they be of the 'closed' skill variety such as discus throwing or those that relate to the day-to-day business of living. The fact is that, no matter what our theoretical convictions are, spatiality is fundamental experience common to all human beings whether or not they are conscious of it or are able to articulate about it.

It was in an effort to bring about a distinction between the impersonal abstract space of mathematics and the personally orientated space of the lived body in relation to a particular situation or context that Merleau-Ponty[23] coined the phrases 'spaciality of position' (spatialité de position) and 'spaciality of situation' (spatialité de situation).

Apart from there being differences between measured and objective space and human space in general terms in the sense that the first is abstract and impersonal and the second is directly experienced and personalized, there are at least three further distinguishing characteristics about human space that should be noted. The first is that as the body moves through space there are certain phases in the sequence that are marked out by the person as being 'markers' or 'checks'. A spacially aware discus thrower will know whether or not he has missed placing his feet correctly when turning or if his arm has got ahead of his body at release. The second characteristic of human space and one that is related to the first is that it has dimensions of different and specific value. Ellenberger[24] has referred to this feature of human space as 'anisotropic' because again it contrasts with the impersonal tracing points of mathematics. To golfer A, for example, the beginning of his downswing may be of particular importance; to the ballet dancer B the use and carriage of the arms when pirouetting may be of special concern; to gymnast C the orientation of the flight on to and half twist off the horizontal bars may be a preoccupying value in a flowing sequence of movements. The point then is that human spaciality recognizes that a psychological being lies behind the publically presented pattern of movement and that the values put upon what may appear to be the same vary from one individual person to another. A third characteristic of human space is that in addition to there being differences between individuals there can also be variations within individuals at different times and on different occasions. May,[25] working within psychiatry, for example, cites that space can be affected by mood. It can become conditioned or 'attained' by a person's feelings and emotions. Depending upon one's state, space, as is known in everyday life, can be 'expansive' or 'contained'. Love, for example, produces a feeling of nearness to the loved one even though he be a thousand miles away. Happiness enlarges space whilst sorrow and despair empties it.

Human space in relation to the lived body and movement has three directional axes—the horizontal, the frontal and the vertical. In terms of my *proximate space* or the space which is immediate to where I physically am, I am able to step forwards and backwards; stretch sideways to the right or left; or reach up or crouch down. In terms of the icosahedronal form I am basically able to become spatially aware in eight areas—forward high to the right and to the left, forward low to the right and to the left, backward high to the right and to the left, and backward low to the right and to the left. It is within these zones that I am able to perform my basic daily tasks, be they writing a letter, washing up, weeding in the garden or reaching for a file as I sit at my desk. It is such words as above, below, left and right, over, under, through, into, towards, away from, too far, too close, around, up against, that enables me to describe something of my spatial awareness.

My *projectional space*, or the space through which I have to transport myself in order to fulfil tasks which cannot be achieved by remaining where I am, are also performed within the three directional axes. To the hurdler space is not experienced in terms of mathematical distance but in terms of the lived body actions it takes him to get from one obstacle to another in order to make his clearances efficiently. Invariably in projectional space, whether actions are done independently of or in relation to others, as in team games, the related question of time arises.

Mode Four. The Lived Body and Human Time

Accounts of space and time in existentialist philosophy are given from the standpoint of the spatiality and temporality of the existent, and it is the job of the phenomenologist to disclose the spaciality and temporality of the lived body. In discussing human time therefore we are not so much concerned with the quantitatively homogenous unities of the clock or the chronometer but with the time of 'inner duration'. Although it is necessary to examine spatiality and temporality separately they are of course constituting factors of human notion as action. The one cannot exist without the other. As I move through space I find it takes time to do so. As I rise from my chair I can move either slowly or quickly; jerkily or smoothly. I can accelerate, decelerate, stop and continue. In the actions of the lived body tempo–spatio phenomena are always correlated. The two are simultaneously present in the bodily actions of the living synthetic unity that is the person. The present NOW of the person's action stems from his past NOWS just as it moves towards his future NOWS. In other words, temporality is biographical. It refers to the conscious experience of the person. Just as spaciality is peculiarly mine so too is temporality. It is subjectively real and qualitatively unique. If they were not we might all learn to become jugglers, dancers or musicians and have identical sets of experiences to report. This does not happen.

In the project of discus throwing I become not only spatially aware of the related bodily parts, whether they are 'here' rather than 'there' but temporally aware as I find or break the rhythm of my turn. Others may suggest or observe the rhythmical sequence of my actions but it is I only who feel them. Only I have access to myself as a lived body and feel as mine what actions I make.

2. The Phenomenology of Action and Meaning

The Concept of Action

Action, in contrast to reactive or reflexive behaviour, is character-ized by its conscious, voluntary, ongoing and intentional nature and as such may be regarded as a sub-class of movement. In the present context it will be considered as a form of purposeful human motion in which the self as agent is participating. It is therefore to be seen as a positive and dynamic concept which is principally concerned with the subjectivity of the performer. Since actions are initiated and carried through by the agency of the person they can only be fully comprehended by him. It is he who perceives, interprets, judges. It is he who is confronted by situations and has to deal with them in the light of his particular biography. It is he who lives through, shapes and times the movements he makes. It is he who constitutes what meanings these movements have for him. In short, action in human movement is concerned with the perspective of the performing agent and not with what interpretation may be put upon it by others. It is social only to the extent that the agent may engage in the same activities as others, follow the same rules as they do, and be observed and influenced by them. Phenomenologically speaking, action is not so much concerned with external criteria, important though these are, but with the agent's inner processes as he attempts to fulfil a self-chosen project. It is in an effort to clarify some of these processes in relation to movement and meaning that this section has been written. Later, when dealing with communication, further attention will be given to the notions of intention and voluntariness.

Project and the Processes of Protension–Retention
Action is conduct which is based upon some sort of preconceived project no matter how vague or how well formulated that project may be. Until such time as the envisaged project is actualized in

performance, however, it remains but a phantasy. It is but a form of thinking without acting. A dream that remains a dream. Only in action can the dream be transformed into practice and the envisaged project made realizable. The actual outcome of a project as envisaged can never be guaranteed but if it is realistic or viable there is a good chance of it being fulfilled. In the everyday world there is an implication that the project entails a compatability between ends and means and that a person who engages upon a project hopes to realize it. This is as true of movement and sport as of many other life concerns. What has so far been said is that the *envisaged project* or plan, as it exists in the imagination, only becomes operational or an *actual project* when carried out in terms of performance. It is only when the project becomes an actual and unitary process of thinking, feeling and doing that action can be said to be *ongoing* and dynamic. When this occurs the agent can be said to be involved or immersed *in* it.

When the actual project gets underway the mover as agent becomes 'geared into' the world. His self becomes related to the world as he experiences it, be it object in the form of a mountain, medium in the form of water, or person in the form of an opponent. As an agent in the world engaged upon a project he will have to consider as we have seen such factors as space and time. Movement action without either is inconceivable. Even when involved in relatively simple projects such as passing a rugby ball the agent has to anticipate his performance in relation to spatio–temporal determinations such as 'here–now' and 'there–then'. His personal biography as a 'performer' is always potentially able to assist him in the fore-reading of the future in relation to any particular movement project. This raises the question of *protension* or what the agent 'foresees' or expects to experience after the present experience. Protension, according to Husserl, is related to *retention* which refers to the remembrance of an experience which has just passed. Let us see how these two terms apply to the agent in action.

It has been suggested that every action necessarily involves anticipation of the future. In other words action is 'future-directed'. Husserl is most clear on this point:

In every action we know the goal in advance in the form of an anticipation that is 'empty', in the sense of being vague, and lacking its proper 'filling in', which will come with fulfilment. Nevertheless we strive toward such a goal and seek by our action to bring it step by step to concrete realisation.[1]

Let us take again the rugby ball passer. In action the player is able to anticipate about 'when' to pass the ball. As he moves across the field others move towards him. He has in the midst of the intended project continually to think and adjust in the light of what is happening to a mass of variables—the state of the pitch, the weather, the position of his team-mates, where the covering defence has got to, etc. It is only when one experience replaces another in the midst of action that it can be reflected upon and retained as having happened. It is only when the past NOW has been 'filled in' or made 'concrete' (retention) that he is able to modify his action by attempting to anticipate the future or next NOW (protension) as it leads to or away from the fulfilment of his goal (project)—the successful passing of the ball.

The point, then, is that actional movement, especially perhaps in such activities as games-playing, requires of the agent an endless number of adjustments, choices and decisions to be made whilst the action is ongoing. The dynamics of intelligent action are never-ending because the processes of protension–retention are going on throughout the action as it unfolds towards its ultimate fulfilment. The eight-hundred-metre runner may set out with a predetermined plan but if he is intelligent he will continually be assessing and re-appraising what needs to be done in terms of what the project demands as he engages in the action leading towards its conclusion. As an experiencing being, the agent is at the centre of his environment. His position in action is always HERE and NOW and is the hub of his spatio–temporal orientation. Future and past are personal tenses of time that are always related to the present of an experiencing being. In actional movement the present 'now' is always relinquished in favour of a future one. The process of protension–retention recognizes in this that the agent continues to think, plan, experience and make judgements in the course of the action. In this sense action is *dynamic*.

Non-actional movement or movement which occurs without a project and therefore unpremeditatively, such as twitches, jerks and reflexes are best described as forms of behaviour. It follows too that movements 'caused by' the application of external stimuli such as those used sometimes on mental patients in hospitals would in no way qualify as action. *Habits*, on the other hand, such as taking a particular route to work might well; especially if they were learned or carried out within the framework of a project, even if the protensional–retentional processes are diminished.

What is often regarded as a central case of action is what is sometimes called *'rational action'* or action that attempts to actualize a project that has been worked out with the utmost clarity against a background of alternatives. It is, in other words, in terms of movement a performance which has been preceded by 'a dramatic rehearsal in imagination of various competing possible lines of action',[2] much as a chess player might undergo before deciding upon what move he will make. In general terms rational action presupposes a choice between two or more means towards the same end, or even of making a selection between alternative ends. As will be appreciated, however, movement situations, especially sporting ones, are often very unpredictable. Plans, of course, can be previously mapped out and serve as guide lines, but because as the project unfolds—be it small, like an accurate pass in rugby; or big, like a full-scale assault on the Eiger—circumstances change, so too must the actual project as it is lived out in reality. In sport then, because of its motile and uncertain nature, rational action is logical and deliberate only in so far as one experience is replaced by another and the project as envisaged is alterable as the action 'opens up' to the moving agent. In everyday parlance this may come down to a decision about strategy and tactics in the light of what *has* occurred and in view of what the agent's goal is or becomes. Although the end may remain the same the means or intermediate objectives may necessarily have to alter. If the situation requires it then it would be rational to put into effect in the performance that which is likely to bring the sought after end or result. Failure to respond, or to proceed blindly as if nothing had occurred to change circumstances when they have changed, would be out of keeping with the notion of rational action. Perhaps especially in movement, rational action requires a consideration of what possibilities are open as the actual project develops and takes its course. In so far as the successful completion of the project is concerned the agent may choose 'rightly' or 'wrongly' but the notion of rational action at least presupposes a consideration of alternative possibilities.

Action is Choice. Let us refer once more to the case of the middle distance runner. His initial project is to win the race by leading from the front. As the race develops he finds he is unable to maintain his lead. He realizes that he has underestimated the abilities of his opponents. The plan he started off with has failed. As the race unfolds he must now think of other means of winning. He decides to try to break up the rhythm of the runners by short irregular bursts of speed. This works at first but he realizes his own strength has been sapped. He re-appraises his position. He asks himself whether he can still win in view of his own limited finishing speed, taxed energies and the undoubted speed of team-mate X who has already taken a commanding lead. He sees that he cannot. In the interests of team victory he determines he will try for second place. He lies back and decides to attack the others coming off the last bend. In the course of the race the project as originally formed has been altered. First the means then the end were changed. Nonetheless what he did in view of the circumstances that 'opened up' was rational.

The mover in action chooses to move *this* way rather than *that*. He can from the range of possible directions open to him only choose one of them. If he takes up one possibility he negates others. Choice at one moment in time is no longer the same as that which exists a moment later. When a 'wrong' choice is made it may or may not be open to rectification. What is done at a given moment cannot be undone. Each move in space and time can only be lived through once. 'Action is choice' means therefore that although in the *envisaged project* plans can be made in advance, when it comes to the *actual project* as it dynamically unfolds, choices have to be made in the light of changing circumstances *as* the agent performs. *In* actional movement, thought does not precede movement in the sense of the agent thinks *then* acts. Rather it is the case that the agent thinks and chooses *as* he performs. Choices that are made arise from and are an ongoing part of the action itself as it unfolds to actualize the possibility of the project, whatever that may be.

Act and Action. Action differs from act in that the former is concerned with the *process* of the unfolding project as a sequential flow of purposeful movements in the course of being constituted whereas the latter is concerned with the *product*, result, or completed unit upon which the agent can look back in appraisal or upon which others can attempt to look 'objectively'. Action is to do with *what is happening* towards (or away from) the fulfilment of the project; the act is to do with *what has been done*. The one is to do with the project in progress; the other with its accomplishment. Whereas the act as a completed performance can be looked at impartially and 'given meaning', so to speak, by others, action is 'agent-bound' and the meaning that emerges for the agent is not necessarily the same because it is constituted by him out of the lived experiences through which he has passed. When the phrase *unity of the action* is used it refers to all those experiences that *the agent* has passed through between the initiation of the project and its completion. It is therefore distinctively subjective in character and is not to be confused with the act as it might be 'objectively' interpreted by someone else.

In looking back upon what has been discussed two key points

have emerged. First, that phenomenologically speaking, the concept of action is tied to that of agency; and secondly, that meaning *in* movement relates to that meaning which is constituted by the performer.

Actional Movement as Meaningful Lived Experience

It is possible to make a distinction between living with the stream of experience and living within the world of space and time. Bergson,[3] for example, contrasted the *inner stream of duration*, the durée—a continuous coming-to-be and passing-away of heterogeneous qualities—with *homogeneous time*, which has been spatialized, quantified and rendered discontinuous. In 'pure duration' there is no divisibility but only a continuous flux and flow of psychic activity, somewhat like the shapeless and vacuous passage of a dream. What occurs, so to speak, has not been 'taken up'. It has not yet been captured in the net of reflection. What is made of experience will vary according to whether we surrender ourselves to the flow of duration or stop to reflect upon it as it passes us by.

Discrete and Non-Discrete Experience
In my experience as durée I do not have any clearly differentiated experiences at all. I simply float upon, as it were, a series of un-differentiated waves of experiences that follow on from one another without particular reference to space or time. I just 'grow older' in experience as duration in a way which is uni-directional and irreversible. I am, whilst immersed in this stream of experience, both unaware of my growing older or of any difference between past and present. The very awareness of the stream of duration, however, presupposes a turning back against the stream and this brings about a special kind of attitude towards it. In other words a modified form of awareness develops which in general terms can be called a *reflection*. It is as a result of reflecting back that a NOW becomes constituted as a past NOW. It becomes in fact a *remembrance*. Husserl[4] in describing this process, makes a distinction between a 'primary remembrance', or *retention* as the after consciousness of the primal impression; and 'secondary remembrance', which is a form of recollection or *reproduction* of a past NOW after a considerable lapse of time. Since reproduction does not grow out of actional movement as it immediately unfolds in the project, it is never quite as pristinely clear as the primal impression of remembrance. In

terms of temporal contiguity it may in fact be considerably removed from the lived experience of the action. Reproduction, then, may not be a part of the process of actional movement as retention always is. It may not occur, if it occurs at all, until after the action is over. The main point, however, is that it is by my act of reflection, when I turn my attention to my living experience that I 'break up' my durée or stream of pure experiential flow, and mark out some NOWS from others. Thus portions of my experience get apprehended, distinguished and brought into relief in my reflective consciousness. It is in this breaking up of the durée that I am able to separate out my *discrete experiences* from my *non-discrete experiences*. Experiences which were previously within the flow of duration now become *objects of reflective attention*. Husserl[5] once again makes clear how through the act of attention this shift comes about in relation to the lived experience.

We must distinguish the pre-empirical being of the lived experiences, their being prior to the reflective glance of attention directed toward them, and their being as phenomena. Through the attending directed glance of attention and comprehension, the lived experience acquires a new mode of being. *It comes to be differentiated*, *'thrown into relief'** and this act of differentiation is nothing other than being comprehended, being the object of the directed glance of attention.

The nature of discrete experiences is important in the present context for it is seminal to a proper understanding of the phrase 'meaningful experience'. This is so because as Schutz[6] observes: 'the concept of meaningful experience always presupposes that the experience of which meaning is predicated is a discrete one'. It is because reflection involves a turning back against the stream of experience that it becomes clear that only a *past* experience can be called meaningful. Meaning therefore refers to an experience that is over and done with, and that I am conscious of it in the form of a retention or a reproduction. A natural corollary to this is that only those experiences which are recoverable are rationalizable but this does not mean that those that are not recovered are not lived through. Actional movement, however, in view of what has been said, is not only lived through but experienced as meaningful as well.

Summary
By way of summary and clarification it can be said, following Bergson and Husserl, that there are a number of different planes to

* My italicization.

our conscious life, varying from the dream on the one hand to action on the other. For an experience to be constituted as meaningful it is necessary to attend to it by an act of reflection. It is therefore incorrect to say that experiences *have* meaning, for meaning does not lie *in* the experience. Rather experiences *become* meaningful as a result of being grasped reflectively. Until the experiences I have in the durée are recovered in retention or reproduction they remain undifferentiable. Lived experiences then *per se* are not meaningful for merely having been lived through. Life considered simply as duration would not be meaningful for it has not been attended to and reflected upon. Although the lived experience of the durée is the very source of the experience it is only in the reflective glance, that singles out an elapsed experience, that meaning is constituted. The difference between movement as durée and movement as action is the difference between human motion as non-discrete experience and human motion which has been reflected upon by an agent made discrete and constituted as meaningful in terms of both his performance and the project which he is attempting to fulfil.

'Peak' Experiences as Meaningful Phenomena

'Peak experiences' or those 'moments of highest happiness and fulfilment' as Maslow[7] describes them are of particular interest to the present theme because it would appear that movement and sport seem to produce conditions that are conducive to them. They may be regarded as discrete experiences which are intensely felt and meaningful, and which are recollected as joy-giving high spots which stand out like mountain tops in one's past experience. Far from being mundane they are extraordinary, savoured over and recalled without much difficulty. To the people who have them, no matter whether to others the occasion of their occurrence is big or trivial, they are especially meaningful and therefore in terms of their subjective selves important. Peak experiences can come to the child who has just taken his first few strokes at swimming no less than to the adult who has won an Olympic gold medal.

Peak experiences, of course, can come about in a variety of situations be they to do with love, parenthood, religion, aesthetic perception, intellectual insight, orgasmic functioning or poetic endeavour. They can come to the musician, potter, or poet just as to the housewife, white collar worker or policeman. There are no classes to which one has to belong or any rules which can guarantee success. There are, however, according to Maslow[8] a number of features that peak experiences frequently possess. Among these are: that perceptions tend to be poignant and unitary and not as in ordinary perception belonging to a class or certain category of things. In this respect they are often idiosyncratic and highly 'personalized'; that the experience is found to be self-validating and carries with it the feeling of intrinsic worth. It is in other words on reflection regarded as an 'end' experience rather than a 'means' experience; that the experience brings with it a characteristic disorientation in space and time; that the experience is invariably regarded as good and desirable, never evil, painful or undesirable; that the experience is sometimes spoken of as the kind that encompasses the whole being and in this respect is often akin to what has been described as a mystic experience about which there is sometimes talk of oneness and unity with the world. During such periods cognition of what is taking place is much more passive and receptive than it normally tends to be. This is in accord with what people mean when they sometimes say it came to them rather than that they sought after it; that experiences are sometimes accompanied by wonder and awe. All in all the phenomenon of the peak experience is a striking and satisfying departure from the ebb and flow of a person's normal conscious life. As such it is an important phenomenon and, as will be shown later, related to the notion of self-actualization. Although the peak experience is both exceptional and meaningful its frequency between one person and another varies enormously. In principle one person may experience several of them in a relatively short period in a variety of situations; another person may not have experienced one at all.

Such then is the general nature of the peak experience. The question however, for us, is 'Does the medium of movement and sport provide conditions and circumstances that are conducive to their occurrence?' Ravizza,[9]* one of the few people to examine the phenomenon of the peak experience in relation to participation *in* sport rather than those that derive *from* sport in the form of public acclaim, receipt of medals and so on, concluded that 'sport possesses a meaning and purpose' that goes beyond what is commonly associated with it. He claims that the 'sport environment provides an ambience which is conducive to the peak experience'. Why this is so seems to be entailed by the comment that sport provides man 'with a freely chosen opportunity to focus all his energy upon a specific task within specific rules and regulations of that sport. The performer intent upon his project "does not have to worry about the usual

* See also Ravizza, K., 'Potential of the Sport Experience' in Allen, D. J. and Fahey, B. W. (Eds), *Being Human in Sport* (Lea and Febiger, 1977), pp. 61–72.

mundane problems of daily existence, but instead . . . is able to go all out, to totally immerse himself in the activity, and experience his unique self at the outer limits . . .".' Characteristic of the experiences the participants deemed as 'peak' were:

(i) *Uniqueness* (and clarity when asked to remember it). 'There is no way this could happen twice.'

(ii) *Transience of self* (sense of harmony, oneness with object or environment). 'There is no distinction between myself, the bicycle, track or anything' (cyclist).

(iii) *Total immersion* (state of concentration and absorption). 'I am not aware of the external (crowds, etc.). My concentration is so great I don't think of anything else' (Lacrosse player).

(iv) *Euphoria in perfection* (everything as it should be). 'Everything is right, everything is in line, everything is clicking, nothing is opposing me' (American Football player).

(v) *Control* (not fought for, is just present). 'I was in control of the water and my total bodily actions' (swimmer).

(vi) *Loss of fear*. 'Many times I am afraid while skiing, but this time I flew through it without being afraid as usual' (skier).

(vii) *Effortlessness* (absence of pain and effort). 'But this time I hit him right and everything went perfectly. Just right . . . effortless . . . I hit him and he just flew' (American Football player).

Other findings about the nature of peak experiences whilst the agent is engaging in sport is that they are temporary and of relatively short duration; are non-voluntary and cannot be induced at will; are not necessarily associated with winning as an overall outcome of the project. Lastly, and this is perhaps a pre-condition for their occurring at all, a need for the basic skills in any particular activity to have been mastered.

Peak experiences in movement and sport may be regarded as being outstandingly meaningful. They represent examples of supreme discrete moments in the conscious life of the person. It is important to stress that peak experiences themselves are not observable nor are they always communicable, especially by those who are poor at expressing themselves. Only the linguistically gifted can adequately convey something of the 'peak' previously experienced. Here, from Ravizza's study, is one such. It concerns a skier.

Everything was so perfect, everything so right, that it couldn't be any other way. . . . I used to think of it as me and the mountain for it was a solitary encounter. At first it was me and it was as if there were two of us and it was both of us. I did not attempt to master it, beat it, finesse it or cheat it. The closest thing I can say about it was that there seemed to be tracks in the snow that my skis were made to fit in. . . . It was no longer me and the hill, but both of us, it was perfect, I belonged there.[10]

About the end of his run he stated:

I felt like I was radiating in every direction, not with pressure but with joy. I felt a tremendous amount of heat. I was totally filled up with joy like a helium balloon, and it was fantastic.

Three Categories of Subjective Movement Meanings

It has so far been said that experiences become meaningful as a result of them being grasped reflectively and further that some experiences can become 'peak' in that they are felt intensively and are remembered as being moments of great happiness and fulfilment. It will now be possible, still talking from the subjective perspective of the moving agent, to explicate three categories of meaning which will enable us to provide in part an answer to the question 'What does meaning in movement mean?' It is, of course, in no way suggested that all meanings that arise from the various forms of movement are limited to being passive or private. On the contrary movement as communication, as will be shown later (pages 63–64) is very much concerned with meaning as being intended, public and shareable. This inter-personal sense of meaning, how-ever, is not the concern here. In this section attention will be confined to what meaning means from the standpoint of the agent as a performer of movement actions and as a completer of acts, regard-less of whether or not they are intended to or do convey meanings to others.

The three categories of meanings that are present, if not always to the foreground of consciousness, are best designated as follows:

   (i) Primordial meanings;
   (ii) Contextual meanings;
   (iii) Existential meanings.

Each will be described in turn.

1 Primordial Meanings

Primordial movement meanings are those meanings which are basic and underlying to our everyday existence as movers. They refer to those experiences which are brought to a new level of consciousness by receiving attention and which then in themselves become meaningful. Primordial meaning, then, is not just a question of being aware of what is being experienced when moving but of attaching some *value* to that awareness. Essentially it is something which is *felt* to be 'good' in itself and which can be appreciated for its own sake regardless of whether or not it may also be experienced in relation to a larger project. Thus the swimmer practises his turns not only because they might be of use to him in a race as a *means* but because the action of turning *per se* is experienced as meaningful. Similarly the walker walks not only because it is a means of getting from A to B but because there is a certain inherent appeal in walking as an activity in its own right. The motion itself is intrinsically rewarding and quite apart from its utility value is likely to lead to its recurrence as something the performer finds worthwhile.

It is likely that primordial movement meanings stem from particular combinations of kinaesthetic flow patterns which are recognized by me, the performing agent as discrete units of sensory experience which give both pleasure and self-identity. The result is that certain movements I do become 'favoured' and are regarded by me the performer as peculiarly 'mine'. It is of re-assurance and comfort to me to know that over the years I have acquired a bank or stock of primordial movement meanings upon which I can draw whenever I am in need of kinaesthetic pleasure or confirmation that a part of what I am lies in what I can do. Some movements become so meaningful, like some arias to an opera singer, that to be denied them or not be able to perform or recollect them would be to detract from the being they have helped make me become. It would be like removing favourite melodies from a musical person's life.

In order to say something more about the nature of primordial meanings in movement and show that they can vary in nature I shall discuss briefly and in turn spontaneous movements and acquired skills.

Spontaneous Movements. It may at first seem a contradiction to speak of spontaneous movements as meaningful when earlier it has been said (page 22) that experiences become meaningful only as a result of being grasped reflectively. On further consideration, however, it will be seen that spontaneous movements are no less eligible to receive 'the backward glance' than other forms of voluntary

movement. What constitutes the greater problem is whether spontaneous movements can count as action. Even here there is no
obvious clear cut answer. A quick answer is that spontaneous
movements can count as action in one sense but not perhaps in
another sense. They would seem to qualify as action if once 'ongoing' they are subject to modification and are fulfilling a project no
matter how fleeting, transient or subject to change that project may
be. They do not readily count as action on the other hand, if one has
in mind *rational action* which, as has been indicated, tends to be
premeditated according to some envisaged and thought-out plan
and which even though subject to intelligent attention in the course
of its fulfilment is set upon achieving a predetermined goal or end.
Without prolonging the analysis the point to be made here is that
spontaneous movements can count as both meaningful experience if
reflected upon, and as action if only on the first, if weaker, sense of
that term. It should be made clear that spontaneous movements are
so called primarily because they are unpremeditated, voluntary,
relatively unconstrained and characterized by an element of fun. It
is in play activities, which are 'non-serious' and 'free' in nature,
besides being pleasurable, that they are most likely to occur. The
question then is 'Why are some spontaneous movements primordially meaningful?'

It was said that *primordial movement meanings* are basic and
underlying to our existence. They are in other words fundamental to
ourselves as existent beings. Because they are so fundamental their
importance to the person is overlooked by many students of human
nature. It is only in the spheres of rehabilitative psychiatry and
physical education that the value of spontaneous movement is in
some measure appreciated and encouragingly utilized. Writing in
the *Alphabetical Manual of Psychiatry*, Porot[11] claims that spontaneity is a function of the *élan vital* and is found in its most
flourishing state amongst children, weakened in middle age, and
progressively blunted in those who suffer from mental disorders.
Spontaneous movements such as those that occur in play activities,
are like love-making, fundamental to and characteristic of what it is
to be an embodied person. They are, when reflected upon and made
meaningful, the most authentic evidence a person has of what he is
because what they can reveal to the person is something of his own
uninhibited, vital, and unguarded self. They get behind the stifling
barriers of his calculated thought processes. In spontaneous action I
do not say I must do this then that. I simply perform like this! It is as
if on impulse I do what I want. Such departures from the constraints
and controls of my ordinary existence are illuminating discoveries of

what I am really like. My real self is actualized in the spontaneous movements that I make. They can be fun and enjoyable.* They can give me such feelings of elation and lightheartedness that I give way to them whenever I can. To me they are often both pleasurable and meaningful. To run suddenly along the beach, to leap for joy, to join in my children's play are intoxicatingly gleeful. They make me feel good. I value them as experiences and I enter into them whenever I can. In and through them I find out what I am really like. They constitute for me what it is to be alive and real. There is within them no 'bad faith'. It is only on considered reflection that I am able to conclude that spontaneous movement affirms itself as a positive here-and-now value. When it is over there is the next one to which I can look forward. The value it contains is immanent in the action. It is not subject to theorizing. It is simply something that happens and it is relishing when it does. To me my spontaneous movements are meaningful. On an ordinary routine day in the stream of experience they are on reflection like shafts of sunlight that express and reveal my innermost self. I catch myself out in new, un-thought-out and exciting antics. Spontaneity in movement seems to me to be profoundly human. To suppress and deny it is to curb what is there in the depth of our beings. Without their comings and goings I doubt if I should ever know myself fully as an animate organism.†

In humanistic psychology, which is concerned with both 'being' and 'becoming', spontaneity and creativity are regarded as helpful processes in self-actualizing. They are seen to be positive factors in the growth towards health and 'full-humanness'. Rogers,[12] writing of what a person would be like following optimal experience of psychotherapy, speaks of three major characteristics. He would:

(i) *Have openness to experience.* This is the opposite of defensiveness; all experience would be 'received' without distortion, whether it originated in the external world or inside the

---

* They can sometimes too, of course, result in acts of self-destruction and anti-social behaviour.

† For an interesting account of the relationship between expression and playfulness and their significance in existence see Kwant, R. C., *Phenomenology of Expression* (Duquesne University Press, 1969).

One passage from the above is particularly apt at this point. It is '... we should never forget that, if we rationally express matters that are not in themselves rational, there is a danger that the field of reason and the field of existence will be out of harmony and that our rational expression may become unfaithful to what we wish to express. Our rationalisation of the field of existence can disclose a far-reaching absence of "feeling" for what reality is.' (p. 81.)

person. It, in other words, entails an 'availability of experience to awareness'.

(ii) *Live in an existential manner*. That is the person would
become a 'participant in and an observer of the ongoing
process of organismic experience, rather than being in control of it. He would not display rigidity, tight organisation, or
impose on experience some structure'.

(iii) *Trust his feelings of what is right* in situations and allow them
to serve as guides to conduct.

It becomes quite clear when Rogers takes these and other characteristics and describes what a 'fully functioning' person is like, that
spontaneous movements both exemplify what he is saying and at the
same time provide a framework as to why they are primordially
meaningful, whether or not the individual existent *fully* realizes it.

He is able to live fully in and with each and all of his feelings and
reactions. He is making use of all his organic equipment to sense, as
accurately as possible, the existential situation within and without. He is
using all of the data his nervous system can thus supply, using it in
awareness, but recognizing that his total organism may be, and often is,
wiser than his awareness. He is able to permit his total organism to
function in all its complexity in selecting, from the multitude of possibilities, that behaviour which in this moment of time will be most
generally and genuinely satisfying. He is able to trust his organism in this
functioning, not because it is infallible, but he can be fully open to the
consequences of each of his actions and correct them if they prove to be
less than satisfying.

He is able to experience all of his feelings, and is afraid of none of his
feelings; he is his own sifter of evidence, but is open to evidence from all
sources; he is completely engaged in the process of being and becoming
himself; and thus discovers that he is soundly and realistically social; he
lives completely in this moment, but learns that this is the soundest living
for all time. He is a fully functioning organism, and because of the
awareness of himself which flows freely in and through his experience, he
is a fully functioning person.[13]

Skilled Movements. Skilled movements, like spontaneous movements, are capable of being primordially meaningful in that once
assimilated they become constituted as a part of my concrete existence in the sense that they are capacities that are experienced as
'mine'. To the extent that they are learned and repeatable and able
to be 'lived over' again they differ from spontaneous movements
which by their very nature are neither consciously acquired nor
repeatable to order.

Skills, unlike habits, can be regarded as miniature projects in which the agent remains sufficiently in control of them to make modifications and changes if and when they are required. Habits by contrast tend to be more automatic and less subject to the processes of protension and retention that are ongoing in the actions of a skilled performer. Whereas habits are relatively fixed, skills are relatively flexible; whereas skills are selectively applied in order to fulfil a project, habits sometimes emerge when least wanted; whereas skills are normally regarded as 'good' in the sense of having utilitarian value, habits can sometimes be 'bad' in the sense that they adversely impinge upon what the agent is trying to do.

It is often said that skills are *specific* and relevant only to the completion of particular tasks. Thus the skilled movements of the javelin thrower are not pertinent to those needed by the shot putter. Skilled movements, then, are those which relate themselves to particular projects. It makes little sense to talk about a skilful person in general but it does make sense to talk of a person being skilful at an activity or range of activities, be it violin playing, stock-car racing, punting, etc.

Invariably a skill is thought of as a learned ability to bring about predetermined results but what is often omitted is that it is charac-terized by a number of other factors such as speed, rhythmical timing, 'the suppression of flourishes', consistency, and ease of execution. Even these outward manifestations, however, do not explain why *some* movement skills for *some* performers are primor-dially meaningful. To understand this better it is necessary to take the perspective of the performer as agent and not as a body 'objec-tively' looked at by others. The skill as project-envisaged and project-actualized by the agent is what concerns us here. In other words we are once more concerned with another form of action.

As an agent it is I who has to learn and acquire some movements or patterned experiences whilst discarding others as I bear in mind their relevance for the project upon which I am engaged. It is I in this period of acquisition who make mistakes, take knocks, suffer disappointments, get angry, become fearful, undergo fatigue and am put under stress. These and similar experiences are a part of the process of learning. Finally, however, the *experiential pattern* or kinaesthetic flow cycle is assimilated and I am able to repeat it with reasonable reliability whenever I choose. It has in fact become assimilated and made a part of myself. I am able to regard it as one of *my* acquired capacities. It has in fact become something which I am able to employ in order to fulfil *that* project which brought me to learn it in the first place. The project is sometimes relatively 'closed', such as in discus throwing, where there is restricted applicability in a 'situation' of known requirements, and sometimes relatively 'open' such as in hockey playing where, in contrast to 'closed' skills, the range of applicability is greater and in a situation that is less predictable. The point, however, is that as with the swimmer's turn, some skills, once learnt, become not only specific and relevant to the fulfilment of a particular project in the world but are also 'mine' in that it is me who experiences them. Some skills thus take a life and value of their own quite independently of their utilitarian function. When skilled movements are held by the performer of them in this light they have primordial meaning for him. They are discrete kinaesthetically experienced patterns or gestures that are repeatable, held to be intrinsically valuable and are experienced as 'mine'. They can be concretely relived in real performance; simulated or 'ghosted' as cricketers sometimes do when they go through the motions of playing a stroke with or without the bat actually being in hand; or they can be recaptured as memories without the necessity of moving at all.

It has been suggested that there are at least two categories of primordial meanings in movement—those which are emitted spontaneously and those which are deliberately acquired in the form of skills. The latter when being learned can be looked upon as processes of becoming; once having been learned, however, they have become an acquired capacity which I now 'possess' and regard as mine. In the learning of *some* skills I invest a lot of myself in order to master them. Demands have been put upon me and I, with varying degrees of involvement, have met these demands. If and when these skills are mastered I feel that I have achieved something. Partially because of this, and partially because these skills in and of themselves provide me with distinctive and satisfying kinaesthetic flow patterns, they become for me primordially meaningful. They become values which I hold dear and am able to reproduce in one form or another whenever I feel inclined. I am still able to reflectively reproduce and get satisfaction from patterned experiences, such as the run up and throw of the javelin, in which I 'invested' heavily as a youth. I still 'possess' the muscular melody of the action even though for many years I have not actually performed it.

Skills once developed become capacities and sometimes these capacities become needs. A person who has just developed a skill wants to exercise it. To prevent him would be frustrating. 'Capacities clamour to be used', says Maslow, 'and cease their clamour only when they *are* well used.'[14] The newly-acquired skill, like the freshly-discovered accomplishment of the young child, is both eminently and immanently satisfying and is repeated time and time again simply because this is so. The motivation, so to speak, is intrinsic to the activity itself even though the skill might originally have been cultivated with the idea of making use of it as a means towards some specific end. The gymnast likes to practise his skills because they are in themselves satisfying quite apart from their use in competition.

In conclusion it can be said that skill learning is like entering upon a miniature if long-term project. It may therefore be seen as a form of action. Each experience that leads to its assimilation, whether patterned or not, if reflected upon, is meaningful. When established as a skill, however, the patterned experience can become primordially meaningful if it takes its place in a person's conscious life in a basic and underlying way and, whether fully realized or not, becomes a part of his mode of existence. A skill in fact is a part of a person's autobiography of consciousness and therefore affects the way he views the world, no matter how indirectly this may be.

3   Contextual Meanings

Primordial movement meanings, it was said, are a part of a person's mode of existence. Frequently but not invariably they take their imprint in consciousness in the learning of skills which belong to particular activities. When this is the case primordial movement meanings and contextual movement meanings can be said to correspond with one another. Contextual movement meanings, however, are not concerned with the experiences of different types of movements *per se* so much as with what meaning these movements have for the agent when performed in a specific type of movement situation. In other words contextual movement meanings are those meanings which are tied to and contained within *particular* movement frameworks. In order to prevent discussion from becoming boundless, attention will be confined to one or two instances of that family of particular movement activities that have fairly defined structures and which go under the general heading of sport. It will be seen that contextual movement meanings are less concerned with the way in which sport is characterized in general terms—as an ethical brotherhood, as competition, as to do with physical prowess and chance and so on—than with its particular instances as related, but independent activities, be they golf, soccer or gymnastics. Each individual family member constitutes a form of life in its own right. In the rules it imposes, in the strategies and tactics it evolves, in the skills it develops, in the demands it puts upon the participant in terms of strength, speed and stamina, in the rituals, shibboleths and language it adopts, it takes on its own special and distinctive character. It is into this sort of context which, both in general terms and in particular details, a person gets initiated, and once initiated has to perform as an agent. Contextual meanings in movement then involves an induction into and a personalization of the general features and particular characteristics of *a* form of movement. As an agent in action within a particular form or context of movement he performs and as he does so some of his experiences that are reflected upon and made discrete become constituted as meaningful.

It should be appreciated that contextual movement meanings involve a large number of different factors each one of which affects and is affected by every other. No part that forms a part of the whole can be fully understood apart from the other parts. The whole notion of contextual movement in fact can only be satisfactorily grasped if it is regarded as a particular kind of situational milieu that is compounded of bodily, social, environmental, semiotic and psychological factors out of which personal meanings come. It will not be possible here to examine each of these in turn which a full treatment would demand. Rather in the interests of illustrative but partial exposition I shall look at contextual meaning in movement under the headings of (a) sports' skills as particular instances of contextual meanings, and (b) sports as rule-based social realities.

Each will be discussed in turn.

Sports' Skills as Particular Instances of Contextual Meanings. * First, some preliminary observations. Just as in language one looks not for the meaning of a word but for its use in a particular context of conversation or 'form of life' so in the sphere of sport one can look not for the meaning of a skill *per se* (what I have called primordial movement) but for its function in the context of an individual game or activity. Here the similarity between language and skills in sport ends for, although in language the *same* word can be used in a variety of contexts, sports' skills cannot because they are *specific*. (N.B. As a form of non-verbal language, as will be shown later when dealing with movement as communication, movement has, of course, many more parallels with vocalic language to offer. Perhaps the best analogy with vocalic language is to say that a sport's skill is like a technical word and meaningful only to those who use it in a specialized context.) Sports' skills become what they are, unlike the

---

* For a general discussion of the relation between context and meaning see chapter 3 of Hill, T. E., *The Concept of Meaning* (Allen & Unwin, 1974).

vast majority of words, because they have been acquired to efficiently fulfil specific tasks in particular contexts. It is in these contexts that they find their contextual meanings. The 'leg glance' for example, only has meaning in cricket; just as a 'top spin lob', a 'flip flop', a 'Western roll' or a 'christie' only have meaning in the sports of tennis, gymnastics, athletics, and skiing respectively. Even where a movement appears to be common to two or more sports, e.g. the forehand drive in tennis and squash, they are in fact not the same; they vary both objectively and experientially in certain particularities that make them different. If one were employed in the context of the other, error, if not disaster, would ensue as many will testify. Contextual meaning then, as it relates to sports' skills, means not only recognizing that certain specific techniques need to be acquired, but also being able to employ them appropriately in the activities to which they apply.

In terms of the performing agent, it means that although I may be in 'possession' of certain skills I must in addition be able to utilize them within the structure of the game. I must in other words be able to actualize what I possess in terms of their concrete relevance.

As a cricketer, for example, it means that I need not only a technical knowledge of *how* to play a cover drive and have a theoretical grasp of *when* to play it but also *actually be able* to play it appropriately in the situation of an ongoing game. It is the ability to actually be able to perform a skill appropriately in the light of all the interdependent variables that make up the situation—the state of the match, the positions of the fielders, the weather, the condition of the pitch and so on—that gives me a real grasp of what contextual meaning in cricket entails. What is true of cricket in this respect is no less true to one degree or another of all other sports that are in part characterized by the different skills that each of them employs.

Contextual meaning *in* movement to pin it down to the employment of *a* skill in *a* game for a moment, necessitates that I do successfully what I perceive needs to be done in the situation as it presents itself to me as a performing agent. If I attempt to do what I perceive needs to be done but am unsuccessful then meaning for me in terms of that project is never fulfilled. It was started but never completed in the way that I intended. The action was envisaged, entered into, but never fully actualized. My ongoing action was never constituted into an act in that I accomplished what I set out to do. Unless I achieve what I set out to do, or decide upon doing as the action unfolds, then full meaning in the contextual sense of action is not possible. The project as envisaged or ongoingly changed to is never realized. Since the meaning of an action cannot be fully constituted until it is over—in other words as an act, it follows that an unfulfilled action can never be fully meaningful. This has important implications for movement as action, especially perhaps in the skilled contextual sense, for it recognizes that full meaning is constituted only in successful practice. Theoretical understanding, without the ability to appositely perform, is insufficient.

Sports as Rule-bound Social Realities. A sport is contextually meaningful to me as an agent and performer in that I have to envisage and attempt to fulfil my ongoing projects within the framework of its rules and at the same time take account of its norms, practices, principles and standards. In these and other aspects a sport is a 'common ground' which I share with others. To me as a participant in its affairs, it is a distinct form of life and a reality. Although it is possible for me to view a sport objectively as an institutionalized social situation with its own distinctive value-orientations and interests, which impinge upon such diverse elements in society as international understanding, race relations, entertainment, status, social mobility, clothing design and advertising and so on, I, as an agent and performer, am concerned only with its own distinct intrinsic workings. As an activity which offers me a mode of existence it takes its place with others in my everyday life.

Let us consider the sport of soccer as an example of contextual meaning in movement. As a soccer noviciate I find that I have entered a competitive team situation, the purpose of which is to score more goals than the other side by kicking the ball past their goalkeeper into the net. I learn that in each team there are eleven players and that they have certain positions which involve the putting into effect of certain differentiable functions. Furthermore I discover that play is subject to certain rules which, if I am not to be penalized, have to be instantiated in the actions I make. In terms of the actualization of my projects within the situation of the game I come to realize that some actions I make are permitted by rule; others are not. Some forms of conduct exemplify the 'spirit' of the rules whilst others are corrupting though remain within their framework. Having mastered such basic skills over a period of time as trapping, dribbling and passing I learn what it means to be 'offside', 'to lay off the ball', 'to maintain possession' and so on in terms of the play in which I am engaged.

Eventually, on looking back upon the process of my initiation, I come to realize that although what meanings I have developed are personal they are also 'soccer-bound' and social. They are soccer-bound in that they have been accrued *in situ* as a player of *this* game and no other game. What I have accomplished and performed as a maker of my own actions I have done within the confines and legal constraints of *this* game. As a player I realize I have entered into an unwritten contract to abide by the rules of the game in order to play it at all. I realize the rules are necessary to engage in that activity so that a specific state of affairs can be brought about which prevent it from becoming something else, even maybe a 'free-for-all'. The moves that I make in the contextual rule-bound sense are meaningful to me in that they provide a frame of reference by and through which they are sanctioned and made possible. In the same way that a player of chess has to find a contextually meaningful move within the rules of *that* game so I as a soccer player have to find my actions contextually meaningful within the rule structure of *this* game. Furthermore, implicit within my action making is an element of self-appraisal. On reflection I see my action as contextually 'good', 'bad', or 'indifferent' in terms of the circumstances, including rules, that led, or potentially led, to the scoring of a goal. In other words I enter into a form of self-evaluation whereby I in effect ask myself: 'Was my action both constructively envisaged and effectively actualized given the rules that help make the activity what it is?'

Soccer, like other forms of institutionalised sport, is rule-bound in the sense that its rules are a necessary condition for the game to exist as a social reality. To play soccer and find it contextually meaningful as Suits suggests is 'to engage in an activity directed toward bringing about a specific state of affairs, using only means permitted by specific rules, where the means permitted by the rules are more limited in scope than they would be in the absence of the rules, and where the sole reason for accepting such limitation is to make possible such activity'.[15]

It will be seen in addition that the strategies and tactics, which are a part of the game and to which I contribute as a team member, also have to be planned in accordance with the rules. When such strategies and tactics are actualized or put into effect I see my own *'sub-projects'* in these as parts of *'collaborative projects'* and find them meaningful in terms firstly of whether or not my own sub-projects were fulfilled and secondly, whether or not the collaborative projects were fulfilled.

It was said earlier that the meanings I develop are not only 'soccer-bound' in the sense that the actions I make are rule-governed but also social. What exactly does the word 'social' entail? First that the rules I have absorbed and made my own are not just 'there' and applicable to me. They are also applicable to others, who have also agreed to abide by them. In addition, however, it means that they have been developed and subject to change with the passing years and are a part of an ongoing tradition. They are in a sense artificial but human constructs. They are 'handed down' yet subject to further modification. In a sense they enshrine and publicly describe the structure, character and purpose of the game. To an extent the meanings that I have personalized as 'mine' have also been personalized by others. The 'common ground' we have as players, however, does not provide us with identical personal meanings. It simply ensures that in terms of contextual meaning there is a considerable degree of correspondence between what I mean and what they mean. In this sense the personal contextual meanings that I accrue as a player are not only 'soccer-bound' but also social. The social aspects of the meaningfulness of a sport which I have personalized are reflected partly in its inheritance as a social phenomenon, and partly in the HERE and NOW structure of its rules as they are presently given and to which I as a player have to make reference as I plan and carry out my actions. A sport, like any other form of social life, both generates its own meanings and in so doing provides a dynamic contextual background into which others in turn are initiated and who, over a period of time, develop their own personal meanings from those which were originally taken as 'given'. To me, the participant performer, this is a process which occurs naturally, for as an agent in the game I plan and actualize my projects in accordance with the rules as they exist. They are for me the reality with which I am confronted. In the contextual rule-bound sense, meaningful movements for me are those actions that I recognize and am free and able to make within the framework of rules that help make that activity what it is. As a player I have chosen to enter their ambience and advisedly or tacitly agree to comply with the way in which they are made to operate.

In conclusion and in general terms it can be said that contextual meanings in movement arise out of the distinctive structuring of particular activities be they sport in the form of soccer or dance in the form of ballet. They are concerned with the specific set of factors, skills and rules especially, that characterize them and which when taken together as a 'patterned situation' form special types of action frameworks out of which meanings are personalized and made 'mine'.*

---

* It is of interest that in commenting about sporting events and activities from the symbolic interaction perspective, Yates comments that they are only meaningful 'to those who have been socialised into commonly understood sets of meanings, which have been learnt over a period of time through a negotiation of meaning and through

3   Existential Meanings

Existential meanings in movement refer to those meanings that 'stand out in', relate to and are a part of a person's individual existence as a result of his involvement in movement situations within the world. Existential movement meanings are unique; they are irreplaceable and non-interchangeable. As an existent they are distinctly and peculiarly 'mine'. They stress the dynamic quality of human existence and emphasise its ecstatic, authentic and transcendent possibilities.

In elaborating upon existential meanings in movement I shall as before look to sport to provide me with illustrative material. In doing so, however, it should be emphasized that such meanings are not in any way confined to sport any more indeed than existential meanings are limited to movement.

Three themes will be pursued. These are:

(i)   The existent as agent;
(ii) Sport as a quest for authentic existence;
(iii) Dimensions of existential meaning in sport.

The Existent as Agent. From the existentialist point of view man is what he does. In actional movement or sport man *is* as he performs. The project upon which he is engaged involves the whole of him in his total unity. Movement, thought and passion are brought indissolubly together. In actional movement man is more than his observable deeds and the roles he plays. He exists as an agent and as such, unlike in some forms of work, he is not devoid of mystery, dignity and personhood that makes him human.

Paradoxically in doing what he does man not only *is* but at the same time *becomes* what he is not. Man in actional movement both *expresses himself* and concurrently *makes himself.*

He expresses himself in that he has freely chosen to do what he is doing regardless of the manner, style or execution of it, yet as the action unfolds he also makes himself different in and through the choices and decisions he makes. Actual movement then not only implies a freedom for the realization of personal intentions but also a freedom to make himself into something different from what he was before as a result of so doing. This freedom for the bringing about of change can be irrational or rational; good or bad. It is precisely because freedom implies freedom to choose that the exis-

---

an internalisation of formal rules and codes of conduct'. See Yates J., 'Sport as Symbolic Interaction' in *Scottish Journal of Physical Education*, May 1974, p. 19.

tential claim that there is no humanity without freedom is made. It is in choosing that man differentiates himself from others in the world. 'In choosing I am', says Jaspers.[16] In this respect actions in sport are in principle no different from actions in other walks of life. They differ only in that they always involve the use of the body.

Decision making in actional movement is a decision *against* as well as a decision *for* something. To decide for one possibility is *ipso facto* to renounce every other possibility that was open. To decide one thing rather than another as the action unfolds is to thrust forward with a new commitment and run the risk of cutting oneself off from the other possibilities that were previously open. The either/or factor in decision making in action can be critical. In activities and events like skiing, tobogganing and motor racing, for example, the ability to decide in a split-second way can literally be the difference between life and death.

Over a period of time it is from a process of choosing and deciding that the self emerges. Macquarrie in commenting upon this writes: 'A self is not given ready-made at the beginning. What is given is a field of possibility, and as the existent projects himself into this possibility rather than that one, he begins to determine who he shall be.'[17] In committing oneself to *a* sport one commits oneself to courses of action that are necessarily limited. The runner must run, the thrower must throw, the swimmer must swim. Yet to the agent the full content of the commitment is not grasped at the outset. It is only as the action unfolds and one becomes embroiled in it that one discovers there is no easy going back. What is more the action is real—the tackle involves me having to make it. There is no shirking or deferring of responsibility. It is I, the agent, who has to decide and do. In terms of commitment and resolution the actions I make *in* sport have to be dealt with; they are uncompromisingly present and demand decision. There is no time for armchair deliberation. In engaging myself in actions that are concrete and actual I both discover who I am and what I may wish to be.

To *be* in sport—as in most other dimensions of life—is basically to be alone. It is I who suffers the rigours of training; the pain of effort; the joy of success; the humiliation of failure. To *be* with others, however, is also possible. There is no contradiction here. Both can happen in sport as will be shown later. The self as agent, even though he may be in the company of others, is alone. This is especially the case in matters of choice and decision for it is I and no one else that has to choose and decide what it is that I should do. Were it otherwise I should no longer be an existent and an agent. I can be informed, advised, cajoled, prevailed upon and persuaded but ultimately choice and decision are mine. Without the freedom to choose and decide there can be no true agency. Boxers who receive instructions; football players who play to order; athletes who respond to someone else's signals and are no longer agents but functionaries who have abrogated the agency of self. Choice and decision is not theirs but someone else's. Agency means to be autonomous and the one cannot exist without the other.

Sport as a Quest for Authentic Existence. In an age of mass media and 'other-directedness' many find it difficult to know who they are and what they want to be. Heidegger[18] in referring to the 'they' was talking of the faceless anonymous power that pervasively eats away at individuality and identity. The 'they' of which he speaks denies true existence in that it takes away choice and disburdens the individual of his responsibility. Macmurray[19] writing with something of the same concern speaks of the cultural crisis of the present as being 'a crisis of the personal'. To live life inauthentically is to de-personalize one's existence by giving way to the 'collective'. This does not mean that one cannot exist fully in the presence of others—indeed 'to be with others' is necessary to exist fully, for it is only in the presence of others that one can find one's own self. It means rather that one should not be under the influence and control of others to the extent that one is no longer autonomous and capable of being an agent. A true community, as a 'good' team is, allows for such tensions to be reconciled. Nonetheless, in general terms, an existence is authentic only if the existent is able to take possession of himself and live in accordance with his choices and decisions. Conversely an existence is authentic to the extent that the self is not its own agent.

Sport is authentic to the extent that it is a medium in and through which man can both find himself and make himself. This is perhaps more so in the modern industrial world than ever before. Jaspers[20] saw sport as a means of combating the de-humanizing influence of the 'mass-order'. 'Contemporary human beings,' he says, 'wish to express themselves in one way or another, and sport becomes a philosophy. They rise in revolt against being cabined, cribbed, confined; and they seek relief in sport . . . it contains the aforementioned soaring element . . . as a defiance to the petrified present. The human body is demanding in its own rights in an epoch when the apparatus is pitilessly annihilating one human being after another.' He adds: 'We see him when engaged in sport as a man who . . . stands erect to cast his spear.' Nobody, least of all Jaspers, thinks that through sport alone can man win freedom—least of all permanently. Nevertheless there are times in sport when one is free. The self as agent is its own master and is free to go out from its socialized structuring in quest of authentic existence.

The self as agent both chooses to exist in sport and once having chosen has to face up to what sport involves. Sport is not an escape from reality but a confrontation with it. The man in sport depends not upon artificial aids and gadgetry but upon himself. He is thrown back upon his own vital powers and wins or fails by these alone. 'Naked of all pretence, he must use himself as he is, and he must demonstrate his ability to use himself fully, under circumstances which permit him to function in the wholeness of his being as a man.'[21] When engaged in sporting projects man re-affirms his presence in the world by doing and becoming.

The spectator may *look upon* the actual but it is the performing agent who exists *in* the actual. In 'peak moments' man transcends himself by extending the barriers of his own experience. In such moments the person both exists and finds his essence. They satisfy him and so he returns to them. One competes in order to self-actualize and find out who one is. In actional movement the self finds unity and once found 'being' is attained. It may last for but a moment but in that moment meaning is constituted and never to be forgotten. Herzog[22] captures something of this transcending power of sport. In writing of a particular mountain climb he says:

> In overstepping our limitations, in touching the extreme boundaries of man's world, we have come to know something of its true splendour. In my worst moments of anguish I seemed to discover the deep significance of existence which till then I had been unaware.

In sport man finds meaning in deep and special ways. To gather up oneself into a concentrated act of will is 'to be rescued from the scattering and dissolution of the self in the trivial concerns of the crowd'.[23] Action in sport demands effort in a full, wholehearted and unified way. In this there is great appeal. It provides opportunity to give of one's all and in giving it the truth about oneself is discovered. For the person in search of self and authenticity sport is a possible answer. It offers a form of freedom in which meanings and values stem from the choices and decisions that are made and lived out in real and committed terms. Once found these meanings and values become motivations for participating in the continuing quest for authenticity.

Dimensions of Existential Meaning in Sport. Arising out of the general comments to do with the existent as agent and his quest for authentic existence in sport comes the question 'How is it that an individual existent derives meanings which "stand out" for him as a result of engaging in particular sporting activities?' There are, of course, psychological explanations to do with constitutional typology, personality traits, interest and motivation: and sociological explanations to do with culture, sub-culture, class, opportunity, facility provision and so on, all of which are of interest but are of no real help when it comes to the metaphysical question of man's being. What we are dealing with here is not the 'objective look' of the scientist but with the ontological reflection of the agent. The starting point here is not the reason or intellect but existence in its total range. It concerns not a differentiated segment of human knowledge and understanding but man's situation in its entirety. It is concerned not with intellectual separation but with experiential fusion. In sport special moments occur (see previous reference to 'peak experiences' on page 00) which disclose to the existent as agent something significant about himself in relation to the activity upon which he is or was engaged. On occasions he may actually lose his self as he is taken up with the project as it unfolds. On other occasions he seems to enter into a mystical affinity with the object be it a breaking wave or with a 'right' shot from a bow. The point then is that existential meanings which are often impregnated with ontological undertones are simply disclosed to the existent as agent. How they come is not known. It is a mystery. He may predispose himself towards having them but nothing can be guaranteed. They emerge as unheralded unveilings about himself and his situation in the world. They do not always fit neatly into previously worked out systems of enquiry. When an existent resorts to language as a way of revealing what he has experienced it is a language that evokes rather than a language that describes. What has been disclosed can only be hinted at or partially picked up by another but can never be fully shared.

Existential meanings that occur in sport, as in other walks of life, arise from the existent's particular position in the world, and all that this implies in the way of his individual biography, and are experienced by him as distinctly 'mine'. They can be relatively inconsequential like 'Oh! that's a pleasant sensation' or deeply significant as when a person might exclaim 'This is the greatest moment of my life'.

In order to show some of the range and complexity of existential meanings that can arise in sport there follows a series of quotations. They are drawn from a variety of sources and are arranged under what I discern to be recurring themes. They are not always tidily categorized for one type of meaning in the existent's experience sometimes tends to merge with and run into another. It should be emphasized that the quotes assembled here are by no means exclusive or exhaustive. They are illustrative only and are arranged in two sections. The *numbered quotes* are those that attempt to look into sport from what is known of it in a relatively detached way. The *lettered quotes* on the other hand arise from a direct and personal involvement with a particular activity and are in no way put forward as generalizations or universal 'truths' about sport. Rather they should be regarded as varied and idiosyncratic instances of the existential situation.*

The quotes should be looked at in the light of what has previously been said to do with agency and authenticity. The themes are in the following order:

  (i) Freedom, autonomy and aloneness;
 (ii) Self mastery and self-fulfilment;
(iii) Challenge, excitement and power;†
 (iv) Achievement and perfection;
  (v) Unity with self and nature.

Quotations Demonstrating Range and Complexity of Existential Meanings

1 Freedom, Autonomy and Aloneness

  (i) 'One basic reason why man emerges in sport is the sense of freedom which he finds there.'
      Coutts, C. A., 'Freedom in Sport', *Quest*, X, May 1968, pp. 68–71.

 (ii) (Mountaineering) 'You take complete responsibility for your own life. You choose and are responsible.'
      Alvanez, A., 'I Like to Risk my Life', *Saturday Evening Post*, 240, 9 September 1967, pp. 10–12.

(iii) 'Sport turns man to himself by making existence a personal matter and causing him to "face up" to each crisis as it unfolds.'
      Slusher, H. S., *Man, Sport and Existence* (Kimpton, 1967), p. 119.

* Several other quotes that are of general interest but not immediately related to the sports' experience are also included since they offer possibility for further illumination.
 † The B.B.C. film *Beyond the Boundaries*, especially in relation to man's need for challenge and conquest, is of interest.

(iv) 'Freedom in sport is a necessity, not because of the ability to achieve desired ends, in terms of victory or defeat, but because of the *for-itself* autonomy.'
Slusher, H. S., *Man, Sport and Existence* (Kimpton, 1967), p. 187.

(v) 'The surfer (qua surfer) *is* what he makes himself *to be*. He alone is counted responsible. And this is the way it should be; for it is man who has the freedom, and thus the responsibility for his actions.'
Slusher, H. S., *Man, Sport and Existence* (Kimpton, 1967), p. 179.

(vi) 'He (the surfer) is alone; he is by himself and free *from* the world. He determines his own identity. If *he* has the ability, *now* he can demonstrate it.... The action is a constant reminder of his own truth. Failure cannot be blamed on a sudden gust of wind or a strong current. This is a part of the sport. In fact it is the sport. These forces make up the *whole* and comprise the *nature of the act*. This is what man asked for and this is what he is free to determine.'
Slusher, H. S., *Man, Sport and Existence* (Kimpton, 1967), pp. 178–9.

(vii) 'Parachuting enables man to be very much alone. In fact it's a very private thing to do.'
'The Joys of Falling Through Space', *Saturday Evening Post*, 239, 8 June 1966, pp. 82–5.

(a) (Parachuting) 'You feel free when you jump. And when that red canopy opens, it's like the hand of God has caught you up. You look down on the world, and you think how nice it would be to stay up there.'
Furrell, D., 'The Psychology of Parachuting' from Slovenko, R. and Knight, J. A. (Eds.), *Motivations in Play, Games and Sports* (Charles Thomas, 1967), p. 663.

(b) (Parachuting) 'It's a funny thing, but you just don't know the thrill, the real thrill of soaring—you never become light-heartedly alive with joy—until you are up there alone.'
Gannon, R., 'Half Mile Up Without an Engine', *Popular Science*, 192, April 1968, pp. 98–101.

2 Self Mastery and Self Fulfilment

(i) 'Not merely by keeping his body fit, by soaring upward in vital courage, and by being careful "to play the game", can he overcome the danger of losing his self.'
Jaspers, K., *Man in the Modern Age*, (Doubleday Anchor, 1957), p. 70.

(ii) 'A mastery over himself which it is the aim of every athlete to achieve.'
Bannister, R., 'The Meaning of Athletic Performance', from *International Research in Sport and Physical Education* (C. Thomas, 1964), pp. 64–73.

(iii) 'The sportsman is consciously or unconsciously seeking the deep satisfaction, the sense of personal dignity which comes when the body and mind are fully co-ordinated and they have achieved mastery over themselves.'
Bannister, R., 'The Meaning of Athletic Performance', from *International Research in Sport and Physical Education* (C. Thomas, 1964), pp. 64–73.

(iv) (Surfer) 'As he rides the wave he is aware of a sense of freedom which comes from a mastery over his body.'
Turner, G., 'Surfs Up', (unpublished paper, University of Southern California, 1966).

(v) 'Football gives people in it the potential for self-fulfilment, which is the only thing you can ask from life. A man in football has a sense of purpose . . . it teaches him a lot about himself.'
Dunphy, E., interview with Chris Lightbown, *Sunday Times*, August, 1973.

(vi) 'Mountaineering is more a quest for self-fulfilment than a victory over others or over nature.... The aim is to transcend a previous self....'
Houston, C. S., 'Mountaineering', from Slavenko, R., and Knight, J. A. (Eds), *Motivations in Play, Games and Sports* (C. Thomas, 1967), pp. 626–36.

(a) 'In overstepping our limitations, in touching the extreme boundaries of man's world, we have come to know something of its true splendour. In my worst moments of anguish, I seemed to discover the deep significance of existence of which till then I had been unaware. I saw that it was better to

be true than to be strong. The marks of the ordeal are on my body. I was saved and had won my freedom. This freedom which I shall never lose, has given me the assurance and serenity of a man who has fulfilled himself.'
Herzog, M., *Annapurna* (Dutton, 1952), p. 12.

(b) (High Jumper) 'I'm fulfilling what I want out of life.'
Campbell, C., interview with Chris Lightbown, *Sunday Times*, August, 1973.

3 Challenge and Excitement and Power

(i) 'Sport ... attracts young men because it allows them to extend, and thereby test themselves.'
Weiss, P., *Sport: A Philosophic Enquiry* (Southern Illinois University Press, 1969), p. 30.

(ii) 'Challenge (in sport) is a concept which transcends competition. It is a personal response to one's environment, a willingness to test oneself within various contexts and media.'
Progen, J., 'Man, Nature and Sport', from Gerber, H. (Ed.), *Sport and the Body* (Lea and Febinger, 1972), p. 198.

(iii) 'The secret of the greatest fruitfulness and the greatest enjoyment of life is to live dangerously...'
Nietzsche, F., *The Joyful Wisdom* (T. N. Foulis, London, 1910), p. 97.

(iv) '... men surrender to the intoxication of many kinds of dance, from the common but insidious giddiness of the waltz to the many, mad, tremendous and convulsive movements of dances. They derive the same kind of pleasure from the intoxication stimulated by high speed on skis, motor cycles, or in driving sports cars.'
Callois, R., *Man, Play and Games* (Free Press, 1969), pp. 23–5.

(v) 'The will to power can manifest itself only against obstacles; it therefore goes in search of what resists it.'
Nietzsche, F., *The Will to Power* (T. N. Foulis, London, 1915), p. 130.

(vi) 'Where will one find more freedom and excitement than when gliding swiftly down the hillsides, through woods, your

cheeks brushed by the sharp cold air and frosted pine branches—with eye, brain and muscles alert and prepared to meet every unknown obstacle and danger which the next instant may throw in one's path?'
Nansen, Fridthjof, *The First Crossing of Greenland* (Longman, 1890), p. 35.

(a) (Mount Everest) 'There was the challenge, and we would lay aside all else to take it up.'
Hunt, J., *The Ascent of Everest* (Hodder and Stoughton, 1953), p. 231.

(b) 'At no point did we feel we were fighting the mountain; the battle was only with ourselves.'
Alvarez, A., 'I Like to Risk my Life', *Saturday Evening Post*, 240, pp. 10–12.

(c) 'The pleasure (of climbing) is in doing something difficult, something that extends your concentration and effort and resourcefulness without ever losing control.'
Alvarez, A., 'I Like to Risk my Life', *Saturday Evening Post*, 240, pp. 10–12.

(d) 'I sought (through surfing) a meaning for life and found it when I ventured helplessly among the towering waves of Makaha. I was no match for their awesome power, but, with courage and the confidence that comes from overcoming one's fear and ineptitude, I got a brief glimpse of glory.'
Quinn, C. H., 'The Readers Take Over', *Sports Illustrated*, Vol. 23, 1965, p. 85.

(e) (Parachuting) 'The physical sensations of the jump occur as sudden contrasts. From noise, vibration, immobility and confinement, the jump brings rapid motion and suddenly, as the canopy opens suspension in what seems for the moment an absolute quiet in endless time and space. The subjective release of tension with a surge of exhilaration ...'
From Farrell, D., 'The Psychology of Parachuting', from Slavenko, R., and Knight, J. A., *Motivations in Play, Games and Sport* (C. Thomas, 1967), p. 663.

(f) 'Surfing's a feeling, man: you can't tell somebody about it.'
Cleary, W., *Surfing: All the Young Wave Hunters* (New American Library, 1967).

(g) (Skiing) 'It cannot be explained satisfactorily to anyone who never has stood on a mountain top commanding a view of a

hundred miles of winter, felt the wind whip through his clothes, quaked at the thought of the plunge ahead and then shackled himself to a pair of hickory boards and let fly down the hill.'
Swenson, E., 'Let Fly Downhill', *Harper's*, January 1948, pp. 19–27

(h) (Baseball) 'It was the third game that I had pitched that day. I did not think I could last through another game, but suddenly I was overcome by a power that rendered me capable to pitch forever. I lost the immediate awareness of my team around me. It was just me, alone, on the mound grasping at a round weightless orb. I became extremely sensitive to the motions of my body. The minute muscles in my fingers were waiting for the signal to release their power and force; I could feel my whole body moving through the air, transcending all barriers; I could feel the initial thrust as all of my body force was extended with the pitched ball.'
Houts, J., 'Feeling and Perception in the Sport Experience', *Journal of Health, Physical Education and Recreation*, Vol. 41, October, 1970, p. 72.

(i) '... skiing draws us into a tense and moving play about ourselves and our lives. It would be a poor play indeed—and it would certainly not be about our lives—if it ever lost its most dramatic and spell-binding quality, the quality of danger—real, genuine, leg-breaking danger.'
Welter, G. H., 'The Secret Life of a Man on Skis', *Harper's*, January 1954, pp. 49–51.

(j) (Gymnast) 'You start to feel the tremendous friction caused by the unbelievable speed at which you travel round the bar. Your hands are aching, the bar tears and rips at them. You must hold on. They burn now; your hands are trying to shed an unwanted annoyance. But you must hold on.... The ceiling trades places with the floor, then floor with the ceiling. And then abruptly and seemingly miraculously, you find yourself standing on your own feet. You feel like you have transgressed into one exciting world and back again. You feel wonderful. You cannot name what that feeling is, but it does not matter. As long as it is there you keep returning to that world.'
McDonnell, P., 'The Bar and the Body', *Modern Gymnast*, IX, March, 1967, p. 6.

4 Achievement and Perfection

(i) '... And this in the hazardous sports, in mountain climbing, in the hunting of big game, and in the tremendous adventures of war, risks and excitement and sense of power surge up together, setting free unsuspected energies, and bringing vividly to consciousness memorable fresh revelations of the possibilities of achievement.'
Cannon, W. B., *Bodily Changes in Pain, Hunger, Fear and Rage* (Harper Row, 1963), p. 239.

(ii) 'Unlike other beings we men have the ability to apprehend the excellent. We desire to achieve it. We want to share in it.'
Weiss, P., *Sport: a Philosophic Enquiry* (Southern Illinois University Press, 1969), p. 3.

(iii) 'An athlete carries out to completion one of the types of effort everyone occasionally makes to be or to become an excellent man.'
Weiss, P., *Sport: a Philosophic Enquiry* (Southern Illinois University Press, 1969), p. 13.

(iv) 'It is a great achievement to make oneself ready and willing to discover the limits beyond which men cannot go in a rule governed bodily adventure.'
Weiss, P., *Sport: a Philosophic Enquiry* (Southern Illinois University Press, 1969), p. 84.

(v) 'When he enters into a contest or a game he (the athlete) already knows fairly well what he can and what he cannot do. He is therefore free to learn in the contest or game how he meets various tests, what it is that perfection demands, and what man can bodily do and be.'
Weiss, P., *Sport: a Philosophic Enquiry* (Southern Illinois University Press, 1969), pp. 141–2.

(vi) 'Sport has remained an attraction to thousands and millions because it exemplifies man's search for perfection ... it allows glimpses of what man is, but also of what he could be.'
Neal, P., *Sport and Identity* (Dorrance and Co., 1972), p. 21.

(a) (Archery) 'After right shots the breath glides effortlessly to its end, whereupon air is unhurriedly breathed in again. The heart continues to beat evenly and quietly, and with concentration undisturbed one can go on to the next shot. But

inwardly, for the archer himself, right shots have the effect of making him feel the day has just begun. He feels in a mood for all right doing, and, what is even more important, for all not doing. Delectable indeed is this state.'
From Herrigel, Eugen, *Zen in the Art of Archery*, translated by Hull, F. R. L. (Pantheon Books, 1953).

(b) 'Basketball enabled me to discover the true feelings that accompany the pursuit of perfection. I now can appreciate what a musician experiences as he strives for the perfect blending of notes, or a writer for the perfect arrangement of words. ...'
Ralbavsky, M., 'At Kenyon, John Rinka Scores, Thinks', *The Ashville Times*, 7 February, 1970, p. 9.

(c) 'The surfer communicates with the power under his board. He controls it as a part of his action, even though the wave has the power to "wipe" him out forever. There is a relationship between the daring and the power. One flows into the other, and as a result one *exists* in the truth of the forces around, about and *within*. One perfects one's potential beyond the boundaries of fear. One finds *value* in being alive ... and in *seeking* perfection.'
Neal, P., *Sport and Identity* (Dorrance, 1972), p. 55.

(d) 'Once I have to stop playing football I cannot think what else in life can give me the same sense of satisfaction and achievement.'
George Best, from Gaskin, G. and Masterton, D. W., 'The Work of Art in Sport', *Journal of the Philosophy of Sport*, Vol. 1, September 1974, p. 53.

5   Unity with Self and Nature

(i) 'What exists is opened to him in happenings, and what happens affects him as what is. Nothing is present for him except this one being, but implicates the whole world.'
Buber, M., *I and Thou* (Charles Scribner, 1958), p. 32.

(ii) 'The existent cherishes his existence because of its inherent value in comprehension of the world as a unity.'
Slusher, H. S., *Man, Sport and Existence* (Kimpton, 1967), p. 179.

(iii) 'There is (in sports) but one other cycle from apartness to oneness, including the reaching or the complete oneness with the elements in nature. In the transition from subject to object there is a complete elimination of schism, and an existential experience of oneness.'
Wenkart, S., 'The Meaning of Contemporary Sports for Contemporary Man', in Slavenko, R., and Knight, J. A. (Eds), *Motivations in Play, Games and Sports*, (C. Thomas, 1967), p. 398.

(iv) 'The skin diver becomes a part of the sea, the skier a part of the mountain, and the hunter a part of the woods.'
Slusher, H., *Man, Sport and Existence* (Kimpton, 1967), p. 36.

(a) 'I have a great longing for the great simple primeval things, such as the sea, to me no less of a mother than the Earth. It seems to me that we all look at Nature too much, and live *with her** too little. I discern great sanity in the Greek attitude. They never chattered about sunsets, or discussed whether the shadows on the grass were mauve or not. But they saw that the sea was for the swimmer, and the sand was for the feet of the runner. They loved the trees for the shadow they cast, and the forest for the silence at noon.'
Wilde, Oscar, 'De Profundis' in *Selected Essays and Poems*, (Penguin, 1954), p. 207.

(b) '... every time I fall at skiing, or every time I poke cautiously down a hill I feel an urge to get back up and *do* something that will make the hill work for me, with me, to bring about the ecstasy of oneness with nature ... the mogul, the slope, the snow, the skis, the body and the awareness of my body in motion. When such a state of being is achieved I feel like yipping and yelling down the entire slope.'
Anderson, B., quoted in Harris, D., *Involvement in Sport* (Lea and Febiger, 1973), p. 181.

(c) (Surfer) 'I sought harmony and found it when I joined together with a curling wave.'
Quinn, C. H., 'The Readers Take Over', *Sports Illustrated*, Vol. 23, 1965, p. 82.

(d) (Surfer) 'You must try to blend into the wave, you match the wave's movements, you become a part of it.'

* My italicization.

Ottum, R., 'The Charger Sinks the Dancer', *Sports Illustrated*, Vol. 25, 10 October, 1966, p. 27.

(e) (Pentathloner) 'I flow down the mountain. In time with the moment. In pace with the universe. Watching from inside and out. Unity and all.'
Jones, R. F., 'The World's First Peace Pentathlon', *Sports Illustrated*, Vol. 3, 11 May 1970, p. 52.

3. Movement as Social Interaction and Communication

General Introduction

Before proceeding to the main content of this section it would be helpful to clarify the meaning of two important terms which are central to its understanding—social interaction and communication.

This is an important and necessary preliminary because in many writings even of the most academic kind the meaning of the two terms is left confused, so much so that on occasions one is left with the impression that one is the other.

Social Interaction

Social interaction (hereinafter referred to as interaction) is a broader term than communication. In general it refers to the give and take between individuals in social situations.

> We do not merely react to other people with whom we meet, talk and have dealings: we ourselves constitute patterns for others. What we respond to in their words and deeds at a given moment is partially determined by how we have affected people previously. Interaction among persons is an ongoing process of reciprocal influence.[1]

The process of reciprocal influence which is dependent upon co-presence, has two interdependent aspects—the outer or behavioural acts and the inner or psychological impressions. The behavioural materials are 'the glances, gestures, positionings and verbal statements that people continuously feed into the situation, whether intended or not'.[2] The psychological impressions, on the other hand are dependent upon a host of variables but mainly upon perception, whether accurate or inaccurate. The special character of the psychology of interaction is that 'the participants stand on common ground and they turn "toward one another", that their acts interpenetrate and therefore regulate each other'.[3] The reciprocity of influence can involve amongst other things ideas, thoughts, feelings and motives and these can be as much generated by touch, winks and nods and the like as by grammatically structured acts of speech.

The outcome of 'face to face' interaction is that people are likely to be more or less attentive to what the other says, more or less attracted by the other's appearance, more or less interested in what the other does. Interaction, in other words, is a generic term applicable to varied interpersonal situations in which a reciprocal influencing takes place which may be conscious or unconscious and which can lead to positive or negative changes of attitude. The notion of interaction embraces such instances as the dyadic confrontation of boxers or chess players set upon some particular purpose to such small group, less structured chance encounters, as meeting new people in a pub.

Communication

The term communication has been used in many different ways. In a broad sense it includes, according to Shannon and Weaver, 'all of the procedures by which *one mind* may affect another. This, of course, involves not only written and oral speech, but also music, the pictorial arts, the theatre, the ballet, and in fact all human behaviour'.[4] The narrow sense of communication is brought out by Ross when he says it is a 'process involving the sorting, selecting, and sending of symbols in such a way as to help *a listener** perceive and recreate in his own mind the meaning contained in the mind of the communicator'.[5]

For our present purpose neither definition will do. The first is too embracing and lacks meaningful content. The second is limited to that form of communication known as speech.

Communication as I propose using the term is a sub-category of interaction. It is that sub-category of social interaction that involves the transmission of meaning through the use of symbols. By meaning I mean more than information giving: it involves the affective as well as the cognitive aspect of man's nature. For communication to take place in a reasonably reliable way there has to be intention on the part of the *encoder* (or sender) and understanding on the part of the *decoder* (or receiver). This necessitates the mutual employment of a *code* (or a system of shared meanings).† It will be seen then that

---

* My italicization.
† The terms encoder, code and decoder will be used (ugly though they are) rather

communication is concerned with accuracy and involves more than the random picking up of cues or signs from which inferences are then drawn.

A Note on Non-Verbal Communication

The phrase non-verbal communication (NVC) is a somewhat vague and unsatisfactory term for it clouds over and obfuscates the very two terms I have just attempted to clarify and separate.

It is usually applied to a wide range of phenomena which cover 'everything from facial expression and gesture to fashion and status symbol, from dance and drama to music and mime, from the flow of affect to the flow of traffic, from the territoriality of animals to the protocol of diplomats, from extrasensory perception to analog computers, and from the rhetoric of violence to the rhetoric of topless dancers'.[6]

One survey of the area to which the label has been given, which indicates something of its unsatisfactoriness, identifies no less than eighteen divisions: (a) animal and insect; (b) culture; (c) environment; (d) gestural, facial expression, bodily movement, and kinesics; (e) human behaviour; (f) interaction patterns; (g) learning; (h) machine; (i) media; (j) mental processes; (k) music; (l) paralinguistics; (m) personal grooming and apparel; (n) physiological; (o) pictures; (p) space; (q) tactile and cutaneous; and (r) time.[7]

It will be seen then that non-verbal communication is too blanket and amorphous a term to be equated with either social interaction or communication in the way they have been outlined; or even indeed, as a utility term that could be used to cover both processes.

Confusion about NVC exists at three levels. These are:

(i) What the boundary line is between the verbal and non-verbal;

(ii) What constitutes communication as opposed to non-communication;

(iii) What happens if anything when people are in a state of non-communication?

Attention has been drawn to the difficulties implicit in the term because some workers in the field of movement have mistakenly regarded it as if it were a 'silent language', with all that this implies,

---

than other terms that could have been used as (i) they emphasize the active involvement of the participants, and (ii) they draw attention to the fact that there is reference to a shared symbolic system.

It will be noted that the term code as used here is not to be thought of in a restricted or narrow way, though it can be, but rather in terms of a 'form of life'.

or they have interpreted it as a term which glosses over some necessary distinctions that have to be made such as the one between cues which are unintentionally 'given off' and signs which are intentionally 'given'.

All in all, because of the difficulties and confusions, the term 'non-verbal communication' will be avoided.

Movement Communication, Meaning and Expression

To restate what has been said, movement as communication can be regarded as a form of human interaction in which the encoder (or sender) intentionally sets out to transmit a message to a decoder (or receiver) by means of a mutually shared and understood code. It should be emphasized that intention is a central and constituent part of the action. In communication intention is most usefully characterized by the giving of reasons in answer to the question 'Why?'

Communication can take place at various levels ranging from *intra-personal*, which may be regarded as a form of 'inner dialogue' to what is known as *mass-media* whereby news is transmitted to large numbers of people by impersonal means. The level of communication with which I shall be principally concerned, however, is that of *inter-personal* communication, particularly that form which takes place between two people. In addition some reference will be made to *small-group* communication or that communication which occurs when a few people meet on a face-to-face basis. A small group for our purposes will range from three up to as many as thirty or so and will therefore be applicable to most forms of dance and games.

It should be mentioned in passing that communication can operate as a *one-way process* or a *two-way process*. Figures 1 and 2 illustrate what this entails.

It will be appreciated that before inter-personal communication takes place the encoder may engage in some form of intra-communication (i.e. with himself) in order to select, organize and shape what he wants to code so that it will be interpreted accurately by the decoder.

Providing the code itself is sufficiently versatile, communication encoding and decoding will proceed in a reliable manner. Barriers to communication, however, can be set up if (a) either encoder or decoder have limited knowledge of the code, or (b) there are too many distractions, unstated assumptions, limitations of capacity and

FIGURE 1 *One way system of inter-personal communication*

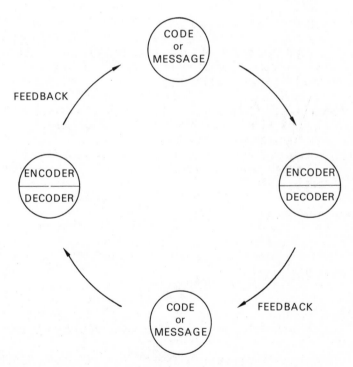

FIGURE 2 *Two way system of inter-personal communication with feedback possibilities*

so on. Just as in speech, for example, bad encoding might arise from not knowing or not selecting the most appropriate words to say what is meant, so in movement communication body language can be mismanaged.* Until languages are thoroughly learnt mistakes by both sender and receiver are bound to occur. This is made plain when one tries to communicate in a foreign language or when one listens to or observes young children. Poor encoding or decoding can, and sometimes does, occur in speech communication and the same holds true for movement communication. From what was said earlier and from what has just been said two things emerge. Firstly, to engage competently in movement communication the encoder must have *an adequate movement vocabulary* from which to make appropriate selections so that what is done can be interpreted accurately by the decoder and so be understood. Secondly, that although *intention* is a necessary feature of movement communication it is by no means sufficient. Knowledge of the code together with skill in using it are essential. From the decoder's point of view it is always helpful to know what the encoder's intention is, for this at least provides a frame of reference to the decoder, by which he can interpret and make judgements about what was meant, even if the intention is badly expressed. To make judgements without knowing the agent's intentions can lead not only to misunderstandings by the decoder but also to lost opportunities in the development of inter-subjective experience, as will be shown later.

The process of communication involves more than the encoding and decoding of messages at a cognitive level, central and important though this is. In addition it involves (especially when considered at an inter-personal level, and whether intended or not), the introjection of what are sometimes conveniently referred to as sources, message and receiver variables. *Source variables* are best explained as those qualities and characteristics that the encoder has or seems to have to the perceiving decoder in the way of status, expertise, trustworthiness, motive, identification, and dynamism. Apart from these trait and character variables there are others such as race, religion, appearance, dress, and physical condition, which if perceived as pertinent, can affect the credibility of the message no matter how accurately encoded and decoded.[8] *Message variables*

---

* It should perhaps be made clear that I am using the term 'body language' in a code-sense and not as is sometimes used by popular writers in a sign-sense, i.e. signs made from which inferences are then drawn. See, for example, Julius Fast's *Body Language* (Souvenir Press, 1970). A more serious book in this vein written from a psycho-analytic point of view is one by Alexander Lowen called *The Language of the Body* (Collier-Macmillan, 1971).

refer not so much to what is being communicated but to how it is being communicated. The way in which a message is structured and ordered in relation to the person receiving it, and in some instances the manner or style in which it is delivered is often no less important in terms of receiver responsiveness than the nature and content of the message itself. If this is true of speech, as it seems to be,[9] it is no less true of movement communication where bodily presence, together with technique and style, are constituent and inseparable parts of the message.

The third group of factors that can affect the communicative process and which are called *receiver variables* are concerned with the personality make-up of the encoder himself. Having decoded a message, the receiver, it has been found,[10] is likely to accept or reject it according to whether his self-esteem is low rather than high; whether he has high rather than low regard for authority figures; whether his cognitive needs are great rather than small, and whether he is in a state of mental equilibrium or neurotic anxiety. The personality structure of the receiver and the sort of condition he happens to be in at a particular time all play their part in whether or not he is predisposed to accept and maybe respond to a message or simply reject and disregard it altogether.

Such source, message and receiver variables, especially in interpersonal and small-group movement situations, can be and often are highly significant. The effective transmission of messages is as much dependent upon whom they are sent to and how they are sent as upon their content—as teachers, dancers and actors know full well. The process of movement communication in common with other forms of live inter-personal communication is in no way analogous to a computerized input–output information type transmission system. Human communication, especially on a face-to-face basis, is full of hidden and subtle complexities. Meaning and the interpretation of what is meant go far beyond what has so far been touched upon, but for the moment it would be best to speak of movement communication as a form of instrumental body language which is concerned with the intentional transmission of messages.

Conceptual Framework for Human Movement Communication
Before going on to say something about the nature of movement communication as a form of non-verbal instrumental body language, it would be helpful to spend a short while on clarifying the overlapping phases that are involved. The terms I propose using in doing this are 'encounter', 'exchange', 'influence', and 'feedback'.

Encounter refers to the medium by and through which two or more individuals come to be linked in a face-to-face situation. Encounter is a preliminary but necessary phase for successful communication. It serves the purpose of allowing the interactants to take in what the situation involves and appreciate how intentions are going to be best furthered by the medium through which they are relating. Encounters frequently come about as a result of having common interests, shared frames of reference and mutual expectations. Thus when politician meets politician, banker meets banker, actor meets actor, or athlete meets athlete there is little difficulty in proceeding to the next phase in communication; that of exchange.

Exchange is concerned with the flow of shared meaning. This in practice involves not only the common acceptance of a code by which information is encoded and decoded accurately. It involves also the interpretation and meaning that the message contains beyond its mere informational content. For example, when the message 'Churchill is dead', was relayed across the world it was factually understood by all, but the meaning given to it by individuals was strikingly different according to whether the recipients regarded him as friend or foe, with admiration or contempt, and so on. It will be seen that for two people to engage in a process of bringing about shared meanings is a very much more complete form of communication than the relatively simple process of bringing about shared information. In communication the meaning attached to a word, a gesture or movement sequence invariably involves a good deal more than the information derived from agreement about its use in context, important though this is.

Influence in communication refers to the degree to which a person changes his attitude or movement or both as a result of communication having taken place. To express it in another way: influence is the amount of impact one person has on another as a result of exchange. This is not always easy to determine and frequently defies techniques of measurement altogether but in theory it represents the differential between what the situation was before and what it is after the process of exchange. It will be understood that action or intentional movement is made up of both 'mental' and 'bodily' phenomena and that these are frequently bound up with the predisposition of a person to respond to a person, object or situation in a given manner. In this case the degree of influence can be looked for against a background of what is known about a person's change in predisposition as a result of exchange.

Feedback draws attention to the fact that human communication is conducted on a two-way basis of exchange and comprises both negative and positive elements. Negative feedback refers to those responses of the receiver which indicate to the sender either that he has not fully understood the content of the message or that he does not accept it in some way. Positive feedback on the other hand refers to those responses of the receiver to the sender that indicate that information and meaning have been successfully transmitted, though, as has been suggested, the extent to which this is so can never be completely known.

Movement and Meaning

It has been suggested that movement communication, in common with linguistic and other forms of communication, involves more than the one-way transmission of information. It involves in addition the intentional two-way exchange of shared meanings. Since the notion of 'shared meaning' is fundamental not only to communication of all varieties but to the subject of inter-subjective understanding, I propose making a short excursion in looking at what it entails in relation to three terms which are commonly used in connection with it. This will serve two main purposes. Firstly, it will provide a more complete idea of how thinking, perceiving and knowing are all a part of the communication process. Secondly, it will clarify the use of terms so that when they are used in other contexts they can be employed with greater discrimination.

The term 'meaning' in relation to movement communication can be used in many different ways. These, however, can be broken down into three principal categories:

(i) *Meaning as an index or symptom of some occurrence.* An example here is 'Jim's facial twitch means that he is nervous'. Meaning in this sense really equals that which is inferred by an observer on the basis of his experience in general, and perhaps of his experience of Jim in particular.

(ii) *Meaning as 'intent' or 'purpose' of a deliberate action.* An act such as shooting at goal can be said to be meaningful from the player's or agent's point of view when the act is performed with intention, but also in the context of the game it is construed by others, as well as by himself, as meaningful, in the sense that the act is seen as contributing to the overall purpose of winning. Moves in a soccer game are not unlike the moves of a chess-player: both involve intentional acts, the full meaning of which can only be understood in terms of the purpose, context and rules in which they take place. Meaning is both *community-given* in the sense that certain acts are commonly construed as being done with purpose because of the shared and public nature of the context in which they occur;* and *person-centred*, in the sense that only he, the agent, knows what an act means to him in particular in the light of his intention to perform it.

(iii) *Meaning as whatever is referred to, signified, or expressed by movements of the body (postures and gestures and so on).* This third category of meaning is concerned with the symbolic nature of some forms of movement. The most clear-cut illustration of this comes from 'body language' as a form of communication. In deaf and dumb language, for example, the hands, through a pre-arranged and agreed coding system, allow those who know the system and can use it to hold a non-verbal conversation. When movements are used in this way, with intention and understanding, to refer, signify or express something they can be said to be *symbolically endowed*. To put the matter another way: the meaning of a symbol is whatever the symbol is intended or understood to refer to, signify or express.

As far as movement communication is a form of body language it would be true to say that its meaning is a function, not a property, of movement. In the same way that words have different meanings in different contexts so too do movements. As Wilson says, 'It is our agreement about its use, and not the sign itself which enables us to communicate.'[11] Furthermore since movement communication, unlike speech, is always visually presented it is possible to perceive how and to what extent the 'literal' interpretation of the adopted code is modified and affected by the effort and expressive qualities that, consciously or unconsciously, become a part of what is transmitted. The sign for love can be given and received in terms of body language but for it to be understood in keeping with the sender's intent it must be expressed appropriately so that not only the code but the feeling associated with the idea can be communicated. As far as the recipient is concerned the sign of love comes to be symbolic only if it stands for, or represents much more than the formal properties it exhibits. As Ogden and Richards observe our interpretation of a sign is largely a matter of 'our psychological reaction

* See section on 'Sports as rule-bound social realities', pp. 35–7.

to it, as determined by our past experience in similar situations, and by our present experience'.[12]

From what has so far been said it can be concluded that movement as a language system not only helps the sender of a message to think and formulate what it is he wants to express but allows the recipient to perceive what he is looking at with comprehension. To put the matter another way: movement as communication is meaningful only in so far as it is able to convey what was intended by the sender in şuch a manner that it can be understood by the receiver. Clearly if a high degree of correspondence is to be achieved between what was intended by the sender and what is grasped by the receiver, especially in relation to such complex states as feelings and moods, then both the expressive powers of the former and the interpretive abilities of the latter, must stem from a 'common ground' into which each has been initiated.

Inferential Interaction, Code Communication and Expression
From what has so far been said it should be clear that not all behaviours are actions, nor all actions communication. This is worth emphasizing for not all research workers and writers in the field of communication recognize the distinctions that exist between those movements that are done unintentionally, those that are done intentionally, and those that are done intentionally within a system of shared meanings. For movement to communicate in such a manner that it can properly be called a language, it must entail (a) intention on the part of the encoder; (b) the employment of a publicly shared code; and (c) the understanding of that code by the decoder.

As was noted earlier, movement falls short of communication when observers of signs 'given off' without intention, take the statement 'I take x to be a sign of y' as being equivalent of the statement 'He communicates y via x.' Signs 'given off' are not the same as symbols *intentionally given* via a code and those academics who apply the term communication to both phenomena are not only being illogical but inconsistent and confusing.* To make the inference that 'the behaviour x is a sign that y is angry' is of a quite different order from being able to say 'y was able to communicate via x that he is angry'.

Difficulties about this important distinction sometimes arise from the fact that movements are said to be expressive. The phrase

---

* Many social scientists in particular fail to satisfactorily differentiate, when they differentiate at all, between communication as explicated here and that much vaguer conglomerate of interactive processes called somewhat misleadingly 'non-verbal communication'.

'movements are expressive' can be and often is interpreted in one of two main ways. In the *inferential sense* the phrase 'movements are expressive' is taken to mean that everything a person does can be taken as a basis for inferring about his state, thoughts, feelings, personality or cultural patterns. The fact that what is inferred can sometimes be very far from what is the case or what was intended in no way seems to deter some research workers from using the term communication. In the *communicative sense* the phrase 'movements are expressive' is taken to mean the application of a socially shared system of symbols for the encoding of experience by the sender and its decoding by the receiver(s). The correlation between what is sent and what is received need not be perfect but the fact that the transaction is based upon a shared symbolic system should ensure a high degree of accuracy. Movement in this communicative or language sense of the phrase 'movements are expressive' demands (a) that individual movement be specified, (b) that each individual movement be observably different from each other unit, and (c) that the meaning attributed to each unit be clear in the context in which it is used.

In this second or communicative sense of the phrase 'movements are expressive' it will be seen that relatively few movement systems exist. Indeed if the strictest canons are adopted it is only in such well-developed activities such as mime, classical ballet and deaf and dumb language (where a shared code is available) that communication in any sophisticated sense of that term takes place. Games such as charades, which make use of improvised gestures, are entered into with intent but the absence of a shared vocabulary does not permit the receiver to pick up reliably what the sender is attempting to convey. Again basic signalling systems such as those used by the army, although useful to a point, can hardly be said to constitute a language by means of which a two-way flow of shared meanings takes place. The application of the phrase 'shared meanings' is employed in too limited a sense.

All in all, movement as a non-verbal form of communication, compared with vocalic language, has restricted value. Its resources are not nearly as rich nor its codes anywhere near as developed as speech. As a source from which inferences can be drawn, however, bodily movement is almost limitless in its offering. These signs whether 'given' or 'given off', whether liked or disliked by the observer and whether or not understood by him provide, whether he knows it or not, much of the life-world out of which he learns about and reacts to other people. It is to movement as a source and means of inter-personal perception that we shall now turn.

Movement Interaction and the Phenomenology of Inter-Personal Perception

Communication has been characterized as a symbolically shared system of meanings (code) by which a sender (encoder) can be understood by a receiver (decoder). It has also been suggested that it is best to regard movement communication as a speech substitute by means of which ideas, thoughts, wants, feelings and so on can be expressed by intentional bodily actions. It is in this sense that the phrase 'body language' is best employed. The phenomena with which the term 'non-verbal communication' sometimes purports to deal and which concerns not only the cognitive drawing of inferences from overt physical signs but the affective and volitional aspects of 'people-in-relation' will be put under the general heading of interaction.

In brief, this section will be concerned with those aspects of interaction which are uncoded ways by which one person gets to know another. To this whole area to do with inter-personal relationships and understanding the term inter-personal perception will be applied. The French phrase *la connaissance d'autrui* is perhaps even more representative of what is involved here. Needless to say inter-personal perception involves co-presence and interpenetration in the thinking and feeling as well as the perceiving areas of living.

It is important to realize that inter-personal perception is concerned with what actually happens between two or more people at a particular time and not with whether this is confirmed or denied by others. Inter-personal perception is concerned with the *is* or actuality of the matter for the interacting persons, and not with accuracy or verification as it is seen to be through the eyes of 'others', or as it may be seen by one or both of the participants later. Perceiving is a *now* process and what happens between two people at a given moment is not likely to be the same as that which occurs between them later. Inter-personal perception must be seen as a *series* of nows which are subject to modification in the light of what happened during the course of past nows and by what has been thought about, reflected on, maybe at the behest of others, *between* nows.

Like communication, inter-personal perception can be intentional and therefore conscious, or unlike communication, unintentional and relatively speaking unconscious.

Similarly *inferences* made about other people can be rational or irrational according to the degree to which they are made against an objective framework of reference. The doctor, the teacher, the psychiatrist, for example, might attribute meaning to a symptom, an achievement or a form of behaviour within the context of a situation about which they have knowledge. When inferential judgements or opinions are made by acknowledged 'experts' they can be said to be informed, though of course they are still liable to be inaccurate.

It should be made clear that the form of inter-personal perception with which I propose to deal is not of this 'external' inferential rational kind, informed (or misinformed) though it may be. Rather, attention will be focused upon inter-personal perception as it occurs in the ordinary everyday world. In other words I shall be predominantly concerned with the phenomenology of inter-personal relations.

Something of what is involved here in relation to the body and the surrounding environment is caught by Merleau-Ponty when he writes:

> As soon as my glance falls on a living body about to act, the objects which surround him obtain a new significance: they are not only what I myself can do with them, they are also what the other can do with them. Around the perceived body a whirl forms itself which attracts and, as it were, sucks in my world. And in so far as that is the case, my world is not any more exclusively my own, it is not only present to me, it is also present to X, to this other behaviour which begins to appear in him. Already the other is not only a simple fragment of the world but the place of a certain elaboration and of a certain 'view' of the world.[13]

In the passage from which the above is a quotation, two general but related points about how one person can perceive his position in relation to another emerge and are of importance. The first is that only persons, not objects, can be dynamically involved in a relationship: only they can be actively threatening or comforting. The second is that as one person perceives another he is able to influence and yet at the same time be influenced by the other's intentions, sentiments, attributes, emotions and so on.

Inter-personal perception should be seen as a two-way process, a process of reciprocal influence whereby, so to speak, the perceiver not only perceives but reacts to being perceived. In this respect the eyes among all the sensory mechanisms that play their part, especially in the early stages of interaction, are normally the most important. Simmel writes:

> The mutual glance between persons, in distinction from the simple sight or observation of the other, signifies a wholly new and unique union

between them. . . . By the glance which reveals the other, one discloses himself. By the same act in which the observer seeks to know the observed, he surrenders himself to be understood by the observer. The eye cannot take unless at the same time it gives.[14]

Knowledge 'about' Inter-personal Perception

Inter-personal perception or 'person perception' as it is sometimes called, has received a good deal of attention from social scientists, and before proceeding to the phenomenology of relationships as they relate to movement activities it is proposed to look at some of the findings that have emerged in this area in order that what follows can be better appreciated.

The study of inter-personal perception starts from the supposition that to know another person involves more than a knowledge of his 'external features'—his height, weight and appearance and so on. It involves, too, those aspects of a person which, rightly or wrongly, are called 'inner' or 'private'. Research workers in the field of inter-personal perception, of course, recognize this. Asch, for example, writes: 'To take our place with others we must perceive each other's existence and reach a measure of comprehension of one another's needs, emotions and thoughts.'[15]

Enough work has now been done to enable us to recognize that the area is extremely complex and that what is being examined is a whole series of notions ranging from abilities, purposes and traits to intentions, attitudes, emotions and ideas. Observations about other people are frequently made in relation to their *actions* and whether they are friendly, boastful, arrogant, fearful, hesitant or aggressive and so on. It has been discovered too, that in making judgements about others the perceiver must be on guard about falling prone to such phenomena as the 'halo effect' or the 'leniency effect'.

It would, of course, be possible to provide a survey of the field in which these and other findings could be enumerated. This temptation, however, will be avoided, interesting though some of them are, since a rationalistic and objective approach is only of interest in so far as it provides a help and a better understanding of what is to follow.

Of the two main directions of research into inter-personal perception—that to do with the *process of perceiving* and that to do with its *veridicality* – we shall only briefly be concerned with the former.

The Process of Perceiving. The process of perception is conducted within a framework of three elements—the situation, the subject and the perceiver.

The *situation* is the context of which the person to be judged is a part. The person rarely sees a person *per se* but a person in a particular setting who may or may not be doing something. The situation not only takes in setting and environment but factors such as role and status. The person as teacher in the classroom is not seen in the same light as the person as father playing the piano. The perception of another as a stereotype is a danger if a person is always perceived in the same role category and comes to be regarded merely as a functionary of that role. The situation (or number of situations) in which a person is seen to be embedded is an important element in the perceptual process for it provides a frame of reference within which the perceiver views the other and makes judgements about him in relation to the other's overall predicament.

The *subject* is the person apart from any particular situation, who can be 'known'. The subject, regardless of where he is can be perceived as comprising a mixture of 'static' and 'dynamic' characteristics. It should be stressed that both terms are only relatively permanent. Thus a person as subject can come to be seen as dishonest, a poor games player and a troublemaker (static); or, as a person who is not listening, angry and being objectionable (dynamic). In terms of the body and movement the person would be viewed 'statically' when being seen as ugly, tall or strong and 'dynamically' when being seen as slow, a walker with a limp or gesturally expressive.

The third element which is a part of the inter-perceptive process is the *perceiver*, who in interpreting what he sees becomes a judge. Whether he intends to or not the perceiver selects and attends to some particular aspects about the situation and the person rather than others. Because of this, what the person actually perceives is likely to be peculiar to him and therefore in part 'subjective'.

What complicates the perceiver's perceiving is that especially in situations of dyadic interplay he is conscious of himself being perceived. The process of perception, it has been found, is affected by the fact that observer and observed are simultaneously being observed and observing.* In inter-personal perception the perceiver is always a part of the ongoing dynamic and he never knows to what extent he himself is creating the states, responses and general

---

* Tagiuri, for example, observes: 'Their reciprocal feedback processes modify their self-presentation and, in turn, their reciprocal perceptions, in a continuous recycling but varying process during which each person uses the variations in himself and the other as a means of validating his hypotheses about the other.' See Tagiuri, R., 'Person Perception' in *Handbook of Social Psychology* (Addison-Wesley, 1969), p. 426.

conditions which he purports to be examining. If this is so in ordinary life, it is even more so in most experimental situations.

One important variable that the perceiver commonly attends to in getting to know another are his *intentions*.* The way in which one person is seen depends very much upon whether it is thought what was done was done intentionally or otherwise. There is a tendency to see the performers of actions as being responsible for them:[16] this being so, people are perceived to be stupid, selfish, cruel, considerate or kind according to whether or not it is thought what was done was intended.

On the question of what sort of person constitutes a 'good judge' of others Allport,[17] basing his comments on all sorts of evidence, concluded that he would possess such characteristics as breadth of personal experience, intelligence, cognitive complexity, self-insight, social skill and adjustment, detachment, aesthetic attitude and intra-receptiveness.

Summary and Conclusions. It would be fair to say that for empirically based research workers the process of inter-personal perception has proved decidedly difficult. Tagiuri, a leading exponent in the field, recognizes this when he writes:

> The subtlety and delicacy of the process of coming to know other persons has never been underestimated but empirical, naturalistic and theoretical evidence now available suggests that it is even more complex than ever dreamt of.[18]

As a final comment it seems necessary to point out that whenever scientific methods are adopted, especially in such areas as inter-personal perception, there are always two dangers present that are liable to hinder the very understanding that is the experimenter's quest. The first is the 'adoption of models' whereby the investigator replaces what actually happens by a *possible* explanation of what is the case. The second is that the 'subject' is seen as an 'object' rather than as a person with whom one is in relation. Whenever this occurs the validity of the situation is nullified. Needless to say this is most difficult to avoid in an experimental setting.

The Life World
Underlying the second-order world of hypothetical constructs, theories and models there is the everyday life-world in which you and I live and participate. The life-world is simply the world of daily

---

* This is apparently especially so when a subject's action is directed towards a beholder. See Heider, F., *The Psychology of Interpersonal Relations* (Wiley, New York, 1958).

life and comprises 'the whole sphere of everyday experiences, orientations and actions through which individuals pursue their interests and affairs by manipulating objects, dealing with people, conceiving plans, and carrying them out'.[19] It refers to that real world which the normal awake adult takes for granted as a matter of common sense.

In dealing with the life-world I take up a mental stance or *'natural attitude'* by which I assume that other people exist and that just as I can get to know something of their *'lived experiences'* so too can they get to know something of mine. Similarly, just as I assume that to some extent my life is inter-subjective I assume, too, that objects in the outer world are in the main the same for me as they are for my fellow men. In the life-world knowledge for me is what I think is the case; and what I know *in toto* is my *'stock of knowledge'* which is not necessarily coherent, consistent or clear. Essentially life-world knowledge relates to practical matters and frequently contains recipes for all kinds of conduct and activities. It is basically a *'store of experience'* from which pragmatic answers to pragmatic questions are given.

In so far as the *'natural attitude'* in the life-world relates to inter-personal perception it can be said that the following propositions are taken as so:

(a) that other people exist corporeally;
(b) that these 'bodies' are endowed with consciousness which is essentially similar to my own;
(c) that I can enter into interrelations and reciprocal actions with my fellow men;
(d) that the things in the outer world are there and that they constitute a part of the human situation both for me and others;
(e) that because there are common referrents I can make myself understood to my fellows just as they can make themselves understood to me;
(f) that the frame of reference for me and my fellow men is largely that world which is historically, socially and culturally pre-given.*

The *'social reality'* of the life-world recognizes that there is a pre-givenness of the other. It acknowledges too that relationships are formed and that understandings do develop. *'The other'* is seen to have an intentional consciousness and therefore able to act and react with me. In its entirety the life-world comprises our natural and social environment which sets the limits of *my* and *our* recip-

* For an elaboration of these points see Schutz, Alfred and Luckman, Thomas, *The Structures of the Life World* (Heinemann, 1974).

rocal action. 'Our bodily movements—kinaesthetic, locomotive, operative—gear, so to speak, into the world, modifying or changing its objects and their mutual relationships.'[21]

Meaning in the life-world derives from that which is sensorily perceivable and which is interpreted by me as having some sort of significance. It is subjective in the sense that it is I who ascribe the meaning rather than it being ascribed to me by an 'objective' observer. It is to this world of direct acquaintance through the senses that William James[21] gave the name 'paramount reality'.

The Phenomenology of Inter-Personal Perception
That I experience my body as peculiarly my own is unquestioned. It is a part of the 'natural attitude' of living in the life-world. The lived-body is not that body of mine which is objectively known in terms of scientific datum as it may be to the doctor or dentist. It is *my* body which *I* experience in *'lived acts'* and which I am able to apprehend as being peculiarly and uniquely my own. To me my body is a mode of orientation rather than a conceptual abstraction. My body is not only self-referential but allows me to perceive and get to know others.

It is to an exploration of how this comes about that attention will now be given.

What has so far been argued is that the body and its capacity to move and express is an important interactive influence. Its power is sometimes no less real than that of speech and is on occasions more so. With regard to making judgements about others the behaviours and actions of the body provide 'hard data' from which it is possible to know something about people in general. They also make it possible to 'infer' about individuals in particular with varying degrees of accuracy. The task now is to look at the process of coming to know others not as objects from which signs intentionally or unintentionally emanate but as people with whom we are in relation. As far as the perceiver is concerned it involves making a deliberate, imaginative and sensitive attempt to enter into the situation *in* which the other person or agent is engaged. This, if it can be accomplished, does not lead to a loss of selfhood or identity on the part of the perceiver but to an entering into the 'internal frame of reference' of the other with the idea of understanding him better. Movement situations, formal and informal, structured and unstructured, provide many opportunities for such inter-subjective insights to take place. Before looking at these, however, it is desirable to make some preliminary comments.

In the 'life-world', as has been suggested, it is taken for granted that my life and the lives of others is inter-subjective. I enter into relationships whereby I act upon others and they in turn act upon me. Further, our experience is that there is a common world 'out there' which is interiorized by us in a substantially similar way. One important feature of the 'natural attitude' is that the other person can be partially seen in terms of the actions he performs. 'By the mere continuous visual perception of the other's body and its movements, a system of apprehensions, of well ordered indications of his psychological life and his experiences is constituted.'[22]

It will be appreciated that in an action situation there is opportunity to share not only the other's *objective space* (i.e. that which is quantifiable and measurable) and *objective time* (which is also quantifiable and measurable) but something of his *subjective sense of space and time* as well.* Space and time in this subjective sense are to do with how they are humanly experienced and immanently perceived in the actions that a person performs. Although such experiences and perceptions are autonomous in the sense that they are a person's own, they can to an extent be shared. This can be brought about by the perceiver in different ways and to different levels of involvement. If a person moves, for example, I can by 'muscular mimicry' follow him and occupy approximately the same space as he occupied whether it be in terms of sideways bends, vertical jumps or forward and downward rolls. Similarly I can move fast or slowly, jerkily or rhythmically to keep more or less in time with him. Just to blindly imitate in this fashion and follow him, however, in roughly the same spatio–temporal parallelisms would take me only so far in my understanding of him as a person even though I have perceived his body and observed its capacity to perform certain movements.

To advance my understanding of him further it is necessary for me to know something about the *intentional* nature of those 'behaviours' and what *'meaning-context'* they have for him. In other words I must move from the position of following and perceiving to one whereby I make a deliberate attempt to see them not just as physical events but as consciously lived experiences. As Schutz puts it: 'My intentioned gaze is directed right through my perceptions of his bodily movements to his lived experiences lying behind them and signified by them.'[23]

Lest it should be thought that what I come to know of the other amounts to no more than the making of inferences (in the

* If not exactly then nearly so. I cannot occupy the same space as the other person occupies it at the same time but by moving I can adopt similar orientations that give closely comparable if not identical perspectives.

behavioural or rationalistic sense), it should be said that this is not the case. In entering into an 'intentional relationship' with another I do not remain detached from the person or the situation within which he acts. Rather I attempt to see things as he does in the light of our common stock of knowledge which arises from the fact that I have done what he has done and to some extent experienced and perceived factors like space and time in the same way as he has. The basis of my understanding of another is in no way inferential in the usual sense of that term. Neither is it empathetic in the way that word is sometimes used. That is to say I do not have direct access to the mind of the other person in that I can enter into his very *'stream of consciousness'*. Nor for that matter do I, in perceiving his actions and reading into them situational meanings, ever lose a sense of my own identity. Inter-personal perception, as the term is being used here, involves neither inference nor empathy in the way these terms are commonly used. Rather it refers to a mutual process by which one person can to some extent enter into *a common situation* and in so doing attend to the intentions, the acts and the meanings attached to them by the other.

Although I can sympathetically 'attend to' the actions of another person it should be recognized that I can only begin to grasp the lived experience he has in terms of *my own* lived experiences *of* them. It is phenomenologically impossible ever to be what the other person is. What can be comprehended is always only an approximation of what is the case. I alone am the centre of my consciousness just as he alone is the centre of his. Each of us has a different biography, despite our sharing many referents and situations in the life-world, in consequence of which I can never fully enter into his stream of consciousness any more than he can enter mine.

Nevertheless, even if I can never understand another person completely by inter-personal perception I can by 'attending to him' bring about what is sometimes called an *I–thou relationship* whereby I set out to see him as a person whose intentional acts I see occurring other than, yet simultaneous with, my own. By sharing situations, whether they be closely tied like riding in unison on a tandem, or more loosely related, like playing cricket on the village green, a relationship is forged whereby our respective meanings are drawn from the same context. It is from this bond of *'common contexts'* that inter-subjective understandings can emerge. By closely attending to *your* acts in the light of *our* common contexts our two streams of consciousness can run simultaneously and in parallel. This does not mean, however, that our two sets of experiences are identical. My lived experience of you bears still the mark of my own subjective HERE and NOW and not the mark of yours. Nevertheless although we each retain our own individual states of consciousness each does approximate to the other and on occasions may even overlap as if they were one. When this occurs it can be said our relationship is one of *communion*. It is when, for a while, I am in 'touch' with your stream of consciousness that I am able to inter-subjectively perceive and understand you as fully as I am able.

'I–Thou' and 'We' Relationships. Before proceeding to see how inter-personal perception and understanding can arise from the common contexts of interactive movement situations two further preliminary comments are necessary. The first is to do with the I–thou and we–relationship. The second with the two stances the perceiver can adopt.

The basis of an *I–thou relationship* lies in my ability to perceive you as a particular fellow person who, like me, has consciousness. It refers to those situations of which it can be said you and I are co-present and face-to-face. In such situations each of us is bound by a community of space and a community of time. Being in such proximity I can perceive you in your corporeality and by attending to your acts learn something of what you are. Implicit in the I–thou relationship is the moral point that I see you as an autonomous being and not as an 'object' or an 'it'. The I–thou relationship represents an idealized attitude of mind whereby I intentionally relate to you as another person. It is concerned with understanding and not judgement. In an I–thou relationship there is a sense in which you and I 'grow old together'.

The I–thou orientation can be one-sided or reciprocal according to whether I am the only one 'attending', or whether in mutual awareness of the other's presence, each of us is 'attending'. When each is aware of the other and attending to him in what can be called an I–thou reciprocity a *'we–relationship'* can be said to exist. As with the I–thou relationship the we–relationship can vary in width and depth according to the variety and intimacy of our contact. For example in three 'common context' situations one would not expect to find as many opportunities for inter-personal perception as in thirty. Similarly, one would not expect to find the same degree of intimacy or involvement in and with the other when playing table-tennis as when making love.*

It should be made clear that the we–relationship, like the I–thou relationship, is spatial as well as temporal. It embraces the other as a

* For an interesting analysis of inter-subjective relations between persons see Owens, T. T., *Phenomenology and Intersubjectivity* (Martinus Nijhoff, 1970).

consciously embodied presence. I am able to grasp what is going on in his 'mind' by my perception of his movements and the extent to which we share common meaning-contexts. It is only when a similar *amount of importance* is attached to those common meanings that arise out of participating in common situations that a more complete form of we–relationship comes into existence. In the purest form of we–relationship, however, it is not only a question of a sympathetic sharing of *common situations* and *common subjective meanings* but a full immersion of both persons in a *common enterprise*. So involved might they both be for a while that they cease to be aware of their relationship. They simply exist as a *unitary we-ness*. It is in such 'peak moments' of we–relatedness that my originally necessary intentional awareness of the other ceases to exist.

Double-sculling is an example that can sometimes induce a sense of unitary we-ness. Here the two oarsmen are locked in a space and time relationship. They move together over the water, their bodies are in patterned unison driving with the legs and pulling with the arms. The rate and rhythm of the blades is set by one and picked up by the other so that at times their actions are in perfect accord. They swing, punch and sway together. When the harmony is sweet and for a while sustained the attention to bringing about unison dissolves into a pure involved we-ness. The stream of consciousness of the one is overlapped and becomes almost synonymous with the other. A state of communion exists. The two are close to becoming one. It is a state in which the one experiences the other *as if* he and the other were together as a single being, having the same intentions, concerns and exhilarations, while yet remaining 'him' and 'me' within the encompassing unity. In reflecting upon what happened 'the pair' might each agree with the other that the subjective meanings taken from the experience and the importance attached to them were substantially the same.

Subjective meanings, it should be made clear, by which we are sometimes able to enter into and understand the other, although personal, can be shared. It is not uncommon to find, however, that *what* is shared is difficult to verbally express. It is because a person is often able to perceive and understand more than he can explicitly state that the 'scientist' has such great problems with regard to validation in the sphere of inter-personal perception. His 'interpretation' therefore must always be received with considerable circumspection.

The Two Stances of the Perceiver. In 'attending to' another a perceiver can adopt one of two major stances. The first is what will be called the *spectator–perceiver stance.* The second is what will be called the *participant–perceiver stance.* *

The stance of the *spectator–perceiver* is basically that of a sympathetic observer. His predisposition to the other is not a 'look' of impartiality and detachment such as an objective scientist might adopt so much as a 'gaze' of intentional relationship. Even so, not being a participant he remains outside of or is peripheral to the action. He is separate from the immediacy of the subject's intentions and purposes. Being only a spectator the 'I–thou' orientation is one-sided, the many-faceted mutual mirroring characteristic of a genuine face-to-face relationship is absent. The subject, of course, may be aware or unaware of the spectator–perceiver to varying degrees and be influenced accordingly. As far as the perceiver is concerned, however, he is in no way mediate to the action he is witnessing and can therefore focus upon and perceptually relate to the actor or actors that are engaged in it.

The spectator–perceiver who seeks to understand the other, because he is not a part of the action but essentially removed from it, is left, no matter how sympathetic he might be, with only three indirect forms of approach. First, he can 'search his memory' for similar acts of his own and attribute to 'the other' purpose and meaning to them as if they were his. The second approach, lacking comparable meaning contexts and assuming some knowledge of the other, is to deduce 'because of' and 'in-order-to' motives which would be in keeping with what the subject does normally; be he doctor, dentist or teacher. The third approach which assumes no knowledge of the other is to infer intention from the other's actions by asking whether such and such a motive would lead to being done what is being witnessed.

Sometimes, of course, the spectator as an ex-participant in the activity he is perceiving has special knowledge about it and is able to enter into what is going on almost as if he were there. The processes alluded to above are not therefore gone through in any self-conscious anthropological way but are naturally drawn upon as he imaginatively enters the action. The ex-boxer, for example, will perhaps become involved with one of the contestants as he weaves, ducks, feints and jabs, almost identifying himself with the searing blows that are taken and delivered. The spectator–perceiver's grasp of the situation in everyday life is often of this kind. It arises not so much through the ability to formally analyse as upon a knowledge and experience of the action combined with the use of the imagina-

---

* For further comments on the two stances see pages 126–129.

tion. When this occurs it helps bridge between what can otherwise be a 'polarized' gap between the viewpoints of the spectator and a fellow participant.

The spectator–perceiver's observation of *groups* is, of course, more complex because of the more complicated nature of the situation and the relationships of the individual subjects involved. It does not differ in principle, however, and I therefore do not propose to say more about it here.

The *participant–perceiver*'s stance, by contrast, is normally different from that of the spectator. As has been suggested the participant is involved *in* and is *a part of* the situation. Both perceiver and subject form a co-presence and each shares with the other a community of space and time. When each intentionally relates to the other the basis of a we–relationship is formed. It is primarily this fact that marks off the participant–perceiver's stance from that of the spectator–perceiver. He not only is a constituent part of the action but enters into a form of direct reciprocity with 'the other' that is of a different kind from any of the three indirect approaches mentioned above. In a 'we–relationship', particularly of the pure variety, a kind of bond is set up which gives to each a privileged insight into the other for they act together, experience together and share the same meaning–contexts together. Occasionally too, they may touch upon and even overlap completely the other's stream of consciousness. It is when inter-personal perception is based upon such happenings as these that an understanding of the other is at its most true for it is based not upon deductions, inferences or imaginings but upon the lived experiences of a shared relationship.

The task now is to look at a few cases of interactive movement in order to illustrate how the participant–perceiver can come to understand if not fully know his fellows.

Movement and the Phenomenology of Interactional Relationships
It has been suggested that the process of inter-personal understanding is more in keeping with what is taken for granted in the everyday life-world than the hypothetical constructs and models that are put forward by way of exploration by the objective scientist. It has been suggested further that real understanding can only come about between persons when they are *in* relation. Interactive movement is capable of providing not only situational encounters but more important opportunities for the perceiver to share in the lived-experiences of the other. When the perceiver is able to bring about an 'I–thou' or 'we–relationship' he is not only able to observe the

actions of the other, but enter into and comprehend the intentions and motivations as well as something of the hopes, fears, thrills and concerns etc. that lie behind them. The degree to which he is able to do this and share in the situations, enterprises and meaning frameworks of the other is the degree to which he can inter-subjectively understand the other. Sometimes as has been mentioned there can be 'peak moments' of involvement when the other's stream of consciousness is contemporaneous with the perceiver's own. When, as there sometimes is, a mutual loss of self-awareness and there remains only a state of 'we-ness', a pure relationship for a while exists.

What follows now in the light of the above comments are descriptive accounts and analyses of how interactive movement situations can assist inter-personal understanding. In looking at these it should be remembered, of course, that movement is not the only medium by which inter-personal understanding can be gained—music and art are others that function at a non-discursive level. What is being claimed, however, is that interactive movement forms provide distinct and direct face-to-face encounters in which the person is perceived as an *embodied totality*. In action the lived body is made manifest. In action man is his dynamic self; his mind and body are not separate but exist in a 'unity of consciousness'. In action the person both *becomes* what he is and *is* what he does. To be in relation with a person so engaged is to have access to privileged understanding.

Dyadic Relations. There are many forms of movement that demand a face-to-face relationship though not all, of course, result in an 'I–thou' or 'we–relationship' being brought about. What happens depends partially upon the situational context and partially upon the intentional predispositions of those in the relationship. To indicate something of the advantages a participant–perceiver has, as a result of being an intrinsic part of a common enterprise, let us take two cases: one co-operative, one competitive.

In the everyday life-world ballroom dancing is a situation in which two people of opposite sex come together with the idea of moving in collaborative partnership. When dancing they are literally face-to-face. At the outset each may regard the other as an 'it'—a sexual object, a 'body' with which to dance. The phantasy that each has of the other lies in what the other *may* be like. On first encountering one another there is no content to the relationship. 'The other' is present only in terms of *expectations* which may turn out to be false. When and as each begins to 'attend to' the other, however, perceptual details begin to be filled in. At each twist, turn and bodily syncopation each gets to know of what the other is capable. Their proximity permits not only conversation but an awareness of the 'lived body' of the other that comes through touch, the sharing of agreed action sequences and to an extent the subjective meanings that go with them. If they continue to dance together over a period of time they will in that context directly come to know and understand something of the other. The movement experience of the one is dependent upon and related to the skill and reciprocity of the other. When the two move and are mutually aware and conscious of the other's corporeality, feelings and intentions, a 'we–relationship' comes into existence. If *a* dance ever comes to be *their* dance, it is certain to be enriched by a contact that is polymorphously endowed with perceptive cues from a variety of sources: sight, touch, sound, smell and the sense of movement—each of them offering part understandings of the other.

In dyadic dancing a *pure* 'we–relationship' can sometimes develop whereby each partner ceases to 'attend to' the other; they do not mutually observe but find co-presence in one another; they simply *live through* and experience what they are doing jointly and in concert. They exist as a unity. In essence they are but one, 'two distincts, division none'.

To break off, stand back from, bracket and reflect upon what was experienced in a 'we–related' lived experience is to become clearer about it and therefore in some ways more understanding of it. *What* I understand arises from, and is inherently a part of, what *we* experienced. In such circumstances it is likely that our subjective experiences are substantially the same. As a result I am able retrospectively in some degree to understand her in the same way that she in some degree can understand me. I–thou and we–relationships not only arise in co-operative enterprises such as dancing but in competitive ones like tennis, fencing, golf and judo. To elaborate still more upon the inter-subjective nature of phenomenological dialogue, which can lead to inter-personal understanding, the case of squash will be taken.

Two players enter the court. They are strangers. What happens between them is for them to determine. They spin for service. The knock-up begins and each takes note of the other's strengths and limitations. At first I evaluate the 'it' qualities, the 'object' *you* possesses—the serve, the forehand, the ability to volley are all taken note of whilst preparing for the match to begin. Each of us takes stock of the other's potentialities. As more becomes known about the other an impersonal relationship gradually dissolves into a personal one. Each of us affirms the other's presence and each of us is affirmed in his own presence.

Play begins. Action is upon us. The reality is that each of us is directly engaged in a form of non-contact combat in which all intentions, decisions, judgements are acted upon immediately and concretely for better or worse. Shot is matched with shot; angle with angle, lob with lob, rally with rally. As the sweat begins to pour, breathing becomes difficult and the limbs take on a feeling of heaviness. I become aware of our mutual predicament. We are caught up in a sequence of 'heres' and 'nows'—running, serving, boasting, retrieving. One crisis is replaced by another. He is doing that; I must do this. Move is met with counter-move. The geometry of play is imposed by the spatial dimensions of the court and I must find and create space to do what I can. A chance! I volley into the nick. I'm pleased. It was a crucial point.

The match continues—moments of joy, moments of despair, moments of relief, moments of disappointment. All the time we are bodily and psychologically aware of one another. Each stratagem has to be answered. I am now involved in the play and caught up in the cut and thrust of the action. As competitor everything that I am is demanded of me and occasionally I am able to rise to heights that I have not scaled before. For this I'm thankful to my opponent. I see him now not as a bundle of potential qualities but as a person whose personality and expertise is reaching out to me from every corner of the court. I am both grateful for his presence yet fearful of it lest it should overpower and conquer me. His will must be resisted by my own. This aspect of play is no less important than the court craft that is appreciated from the balcony by occasional bouts of clapping. Down here though I must concentrate lest yet another chance slips by. Two wasted points. What a fool I've been! He serves out and I have a chance to think about what has happened. I deliberate upon what needs to be done. He looks tired. His return of my high lobs has not been good. I must serve, play through the ensuing rally and at the appropriate time hoist up my lob. It works. The match is over. I've won!

It will be appreciated that in a closely contested match encounter in which both players have been involved and given of their best a form of reciprocal bonding takes place. Each leaves a 'common ground' knowing and understanding a good deal more about the other than when they started. The inter-subjective nature of what they know and mutually experience is sometimes difficult to communicate. It is essentially something that is shared and lived through. Reflective description can only hint at a fraction of what actually went on within each and between each. Persons in sporting competitive dialogue find their meaning *within* the encounter, *within* the relationship, and thus have no real need to speak of it. The 'filled present' for them lies in participating.

Group Relations. In principle all that has been said of dyadic relations is equally applicable to small group relations. Differences, when they exist between paired relations and small group relations, lie not so much in kind as in the degree of complexity and intimacy involved. Even so it would enable us to pursue the present theme that much more thoroughly and fully if something further were said on the phenomenology of team and inter-team relationships.

Although we shall be thinking mainly in terms of sports teams it should be recognized that 'teams' are not peculiar to sports. They exist in a variety of everyday situations where people are working towards some common goal or purpose. In general then the word *team* refers to a group of people who are engaged upon a joint enterprise on a face-to-face basis. The team members are co-present and are able to interact and relate to one another. Small teams such as a board of directors, assembly plant operators, air-crews and repertory theatre players are like small communities who for considerable periods of time share a common life.*

A necessary feature of team life is that there shall be some degree of *co-operation* in order to fulfil the aims and purposes for which it was formed. Relations between members in co-operation can be personal or relatively impersonal. If relations are impersonal there is a tendency to see other members of the team merely as units or cogs in a wheel that turns uncaringly towards the achievement of a utilitarian, if common, end. In some work situations team members are no longer regarded as persons but as serviceable 'you's' each of which have particular roles or skills to contribute and are therefore 'useful'. Sports teams, professional or unprofessional, can and sometimes do co-operate in this functional way, but teams that do perform in this mechanical manner cannot be considered as real communities for a *team community* is unity of persons, who, in addition to getting things done, are able to intentionally relate to one another. In relating to one another they achieve not only co-operation but a feeling of fruitful fellowship.

Fellowship is often spoken of as a derivative of teamwork and there is some truth in this. More importantly though it arises from the attitudinal ethos that is generated by intentional relations

* For an interesting account of the inter-personal relations of an itinerant dance group see Cope, E., *Performances: Dynamics of a Dance Group* (Lepus, 1976).

between interacting team members. The 'team community' is not the automatic product of the efficient blending of talents or skills, important though these may be, but is the outcome of mutual respect and affection. The 'team community' rests upon the quality and nexus of dynamic and positive relations that are brought into being by the *intentional relations* of its members. It depends not upon success or failure in competition but upon a warm and intimate camaraderie. Fellowship in a team community cannot be defined in terms of group structure and function. It is neither a property of organization nor necessarily of purpose. Rather it is constituted in the conscious realization that each and every member perceives each and every other member as a person with whom he or she is in relation. The fact that a team is brought together in no way guarantees the fellowship that is characteristic of a team community. For this to occur team members must *be* in relation. Fellowship in a team then is a qualitative or special type of relationship that goes beyond the functional requirement of purposeful co-operation.

If the notion and 'lived experience' of fellowship is to do with intentional relations and mutual caring, the notion and lived experience of *togetherness* is to do with a sense of belonging and a desire to be with others. In the sharing of group endeavours the team becomes conscious of itself as an involved entity. It is not just a question of there being a collection of isolated individuals unified by a common interest and purpose. Rather it is a matter of *est coesse*—to be is to be with others. The feeling is not only that I exist more fully as an individual when in personal relation to others, but that in doing things together in terms of bodily action *we* exist together as a unitary group. In this latter sense togetherness is not unlike the 'we–relation' about which we spoke in connection with dyadic relations. Togetherness in a team at its most intimate and involved is a form of collective we-ness which arises initially by attending to others in the *process* of a shared enterprise but is at its most consummate when members lose for a while their reflective consciousness and enter into a co-existential form of communion. Togetherness as communion is not a common experience. It does occur, however, from time to time in sporting teams just as it must occasionally in orchestras and choirs. It is an aspect of authentic living. Something of what is undergone here is described by Salvan in connection with a rowing crew:

> It is intimately felt in the common rhythm of the rowers; each one of them feels within himself the same movement of transcendence toward a common goal, on the horizon of a common world, and feels it *with* the

other rowers. In this conception, however, being *for* others has been replaced by being *with* others. It reveals the co-existence of consciousness without explaining it.[24]

By way of summary it can be said that the notion of a *team as a community* involves more than members working towards a common purpose as co-operative functionaries. First, it involves *fellowship*, which is best described as a mutual and interacting ability in members to perceive one another not merely as useful in the striving towards a shared goal but as people who are interesting and valuable in themselves. It is felt amongst members as a kind of caring regard for one another. Presented as a rationalistic principle it is in sympathy with Kant's imperative that people should be treated as ends and never only as means. Second, it involves *togetherness* which is best described as a feeling of group 'we-ness' that ensues when one is engaged upon a co-operative enterprise of doing, thinking and feeling *with* others. In its more pure form it can immerse the individual consciousness to the extent that team-mates sense themselves as being in a state of *oneness* or *co-existential communion*. The notion and experience of togetherness gives some support to the associated but paradoxical view that a person is not fully constituted as a person except in a community of people. If this is so togetherness may well assist each member of the team community towards a greater sense of individual completeness.

Clearly a good deal more could be said *about* the team as a form of group life that is characteristic of various movement activities. For instance the social scientist could say a lot more about things like group structure and leadership qualities but these are not our present concern. In the terms of 'fellowship' and 'togetherness' an attempt has been made to describe something of the phenomenology of group relations. The question that remains is 'How do these team experiences give meaning and provide inter-personal understanding?'

Earlier it was said that the degree to which the perceiver was able to share in the situations, enterprises and meaning frameworks of the other is related to the degree to which he can inter-subjectively understand the other. To this observation, which holds true for all physical activity, will be added two others which are particularly apposite of team sports. The first is a general one. It is that a team engaged *in* sport is both formally and informally caught up in the notion of *sportsmanship*. What occurs is governed partially by an agreed set of rules and partially by an informal set of procedures with which they are conventionally associated. If the rules are to be more than a legal code a good deal depends upon the spirit of what lies behind them. The spirit of the rules or the informal element behind the legal code cannot be enforced by official action. It lies more in the intentional relations between players. If in competition the players are able to 'live out' the code in a spirit of fellowship so that it becomes a constituent and characteristic part of the action then the occasion can be said to be an authentically sporting one. It is when they do so in a community of shared understandings that the notion of brotherhood *in* and *through* sport takes on some credibility. To *be* a sportsman and to *be* in relation to another sportsman is to have understanding of him. Each knows with what sportsmanship is to do. This they have in common with *all* sportsmen whether they have met face to face or not.

Apart from sport providing a generalized *esprit de corps* to which all sportsmen to some extent are bound, it provides also a variety of specific situations which are in fact 'meeting places' for people who want to share in the same type of enterprise. These range from baseball to basketball, from hockey to handball, from soccer to sailing. Although some sports have many properties in common each of them has certain features about them that make them *distinctive situations*. Sports vary in such considerations as environment, equipment, skill and the degree to which factors like stamina, danger and chance enter. We are not so much concerned, however, with these 'objective' differentials as with the subjective understandings that arise from the experience of shared meanings. Let us take the situation of rugby. Here is a distinctive activity in which people are engaged in a common context. No matter where and on what occasion the game is played, the rules, the dimensions of the pitch, the ball, the number of players enjoined are objectively the same. These objective externals, however, are not all that the participants have in common. As a result of engaging *in* the sport and knowing from the inside they have, in addition, a shared but not an identical first-hand experience of what it is to play rugby. They have a privileged insight into what constitutes the 'lived experience' of the game. Participants in the game are sometimes in relation not only bodily but also in terms of human time and space. They co-exist as they run, pass, ruck and maul. Each team member's 'stream of consciousness' touches upon, reaches out to, and sometimes overlaps with one, some, and occasionally all of his team-mates. The sport experience is a direct confrontation with reality. Wet, cold, wind and rain; elation, fear and despair are no less a part of the 'lived experience' than the breathlessness and bruises, or the tackles, scrums, and line-out play. At the time all is fusion. The lived experience of the game lies in the action it generates. Much is undergone but not all will be recalled or described. For the participants rugby becomes that which is perceived and meaningfully rendered in the course of play. It is associated with what is individually and collectively gone through. The meanings that come from participating in the game of rugby will in varying degrees be shared. Rugby constitutes a particular form of joint enterprise. It provides a specific experiential frame of reference within which members of teams engage. In reflection something of the corporate nature of what is done becomes known and collectively understood. Rugby playing for players of rugby is a 'community world' which forms a part of their everyday 'stock of knowledge'. They constitute a fraternity, as do participants in other sports, that enables them to meet in relation with mutual understanding. That such mutual understanding exists even between such people who perhaps have not even met before is conveyed by the following quote from *The Fifth Down*, a book to do with American football.*

I was shopping in San Francisco with my wife. We were in the women's department and I was putting myself in for a bad half hour. I found a chair and sat down. Across the way I could see this guy looking at me, like he knew me from somewhere.
I never saw him before in my life but I decided to take a chance. I walked over to him and said,
'Where'd you play?'
'Oregon State,' he said.
'When?' I asked.
'Nineteen forty eight to forty nine,' he said.
'You must have played against SC in the Coliseum,' I said. (Davis had played for Southern Cal at that time)
'Hell, yes. Those were some mean games.'
We sat there for an hour and talked. I told him who I was ...
We didn't know each other when we walked in there but we were still as close as two guys can be. The point was we knew what the other guy was ... There was no worry about what we had to do to become friends. We knew what we could do. I've got guys I haven't seen in twenty years who I played ball with in college; I can go to them and ask pretty important questions, personal and private. I'd never ask them for things they couldn't do. I know what they can do. I know how far they'd go. That's pretty important, because I don't think there are people in many areas of life who can do that.[25]

* I am indebted to Seymour Kleinman of the Ohio State University for drawing my attention to this extract. See his article 'The Nature of a Self and its Relation to an "Other" in Sport', *Journal of the Philosophy of Sport*, Vol. 11, September 1975, pp. 45–50.

4. Perceiving and Knowing in Movement

It was said earlier that the person is best regarded as an embodied consciousness and that it is in ongoing action that the agent does not think and then do but think *as* he does. The task now is to show that in, by and through his movement actions he comes to know and understand something about himself in relation to the world in a special and particular way. Instead of starting as if knowledge were 'there', apart from the knower, let us look at knowing from the point of view of the existent.

The Existent as Knower

To the existentialist the existent is more than man the thinker. The statement *cogito, ergo sum* or *I think, therefore I am* is therefore an unacceptable premise upon which to build a whole system of knowledge. Not only does it introduce into the notion of personhood a dualism which is unacceptable but in addition it assumes that man is primarily a thinking subject. The existentialist contests this and says this is not so. The person, on the contrary, is not primarily a thinking subject. First of all he is an existent and the existence of a person is much broader than his ability to think. Hence, the existentialist would say: *I am, therefore I think*. The nub of the argument in turning the statement round is that reality is not something to be established by means of dialectic or epistemological theory but is the raw datum which comes to me and upon which I reflect. Speaking as an existent who has come to know, I am concerned not with abstract thinking but with my concrete multidimensional being in the world. In attempting to fulfil my projects in the world as an existent the 'I act' precedes the 'I think', and it is from this prior baseline that I begin to know and understand the world. It is not that 'I act' and 'I think' are opposed to one another. It is rather that the former incorporates the latter as has been shown in the discussion of the concept of action (pages 15–22). But further, it is because actional movement is frequently bound up with the ability to survive and cope with the day to day affairs of life that it must be regarded as a more fundamental mode of existence than one that is concerned only with reflective thinking.

As an existent I find my world is organized around the various environments or human activities in which I am involved and with which I am concerned. It is by engaging in these various environments in direct and practical ways that I come to know them. Just as there are environments for the various forms of movement whether they are called sky-diving, sub-aqua, potholing, or games. To engage in them is to get to know them in a direct and pragmatic way. What I come to know by doing precedes that which I may later come to know about them as theory. At all times in my knowing I accept without question the incarnateness of my existence and it is from the standpoint of my embodied state that I attend to the things and persons that make up the world and come to understand them better. My body is not something separate from me. I do not say that 'My body is thirsty' any more than I say 'It is my mind that knows'. It is I who am thirsty just as it is I who know.

Actional Movement as Practical Understanding
It has been upheld throughout what has so far been said that action is a full concrete activity of the self in which our different capacities are employed. The very notion of action denies a dualism which upholds a view that man is comprised of two separate entities called mind and body. It has been maintained that the person is a unitary whole. As an embodied existent he takes his place in the world and both acts upon it and interacts with it. It is the person in his entirety who experiences the actional projects he undertakes and it is the psychosomatic unity of the person who by interpreting the world comes to understand it.

By 'projecting' himself into the various possibilities that are open to him in this world the existent as agent builds up for himself an intelligible understanding of it. He learns, like a child, in a practical and pragmatic way. In the first instance to understand the world is to be able to cope with it; to know one's way about; to avoid dangers; to utilize and gain a sense of things; to contact and relate to other people. This practical understanding of the world precedes and is independent of a theoretically constructed one. It arises predominantly from the various actions in which the existent engages. As existents we come to know and understand as a result of what we do. To try to learn *about* the world from theory is not to know it in its actuality at all. To mistake the real world for a theoretically constructed one can lead to a belief in the existence of a supposed world—a reification of the world, rather than one that I occupy and experience directly. In terms of movement and skill the knowing and understanding I have lies in the thinking and doing of the activity or action itself rather than in propositions that can be formulated about it.

If it can be accepted that in the practical world thinking without action moves nothing this is not to say that theoretical knowledge is of no relevance to practical understanding. On the contrary when intelligently incorporated into what is being undertaken it can and frequently does advantageously affect the efficiency and grasp of what is being done. If on the other hand theoretical knowledge remains as so many hypothetical and speculative constructs, never tested and never utilized in the service of practical understanding, there is the chance that it will remain inert, separate from, and irrelevant to the world of action and praxis. Indeed it is perhaps true to say that the further one moves from practice to theory the greater is the likelihood that there will be a shift from the particular to the general, from the concrete to the abstract, from a knowledge based upon an active engagement in the world to a system of knowledge that is founded only upon ideas and the ability to think.

What needs to be made clear is that when actional movement is spoken of a form of practical understanding it in no way disregards the possibility of the incorporation of theoretical knowledge. The point rather is that no satisfactory grasp of practical understanding *in* movement is possible unless securely based upon the living experience of the action itself.

Moving as a Perceptual Form of Consciousness

Our initial standpoint in relation to knowing and understanding in movement is that of the existent as agent. It is only by engaging in actional movement that the existent as agent comes to know and understand what movement is in direct experiential terms. Without moving it is not possible to grasp fully what moving entails. Unless what is constituted derives from the living experience of the process any claims relating to knowing and understanding *in* movement must remain incomplete.

With regard to philosophical theories of sense perception it is a regrettable fact that they have always tended to be primary theories of vision as if vision were the model in terms of which all other modes of sense perception could, *mutatis mutandis*, be discussed and understood. This, however, is not the case. Kinaesthetic perception, as well as tactual perception for that matter, are markedly different and it is as well to recognize this if the basis of what is involved in knowing and understanding in movement is to be grasped.

The Sensory Basis of Perception

The bodily senses are modes of access to the world. They are a part of my unitary corporeal scheme. They interrelate to one another and affect one another. They are a part of my total organization by which I come to know and understand my self and the world in which I undertake my projects. What I perceive by means of my senses, however, is more than that which is merely 'sense given'. Although my senses sensitize me, it is only by my active participation in the act of perception as an individual existent that I become 'perceptually conscious of' something; be it to do with seeing, hearing, tasting, smelling, touching or moving. The senses then are inter-co-ordinated systems of the body by means of which I the perceiver become aware of objects, qualities or relations. While sensory contact is always present in perception what is perceived is always influenced by my unique position in space and time as an existent with a particular biography. Perception then is not a 'mental' phenomenon but an embodied process by means of which I come to know and understand myself and the world in which I am an existent. As Merleau-Ponty explains: 'Perception is a moment of the living dialect of a concrete subject; it participates in its total structure.'[1] If perception is an achievement in so far as it brings about a 'consciousness of' something, then it is an achievement brought about by the person as a unitary and embodied existent.

It should be noted, however, that for the agent engaged in action perception is by no means a straightforward one to one process. It is often extremely complex with figure-ground relationships changing all the time. Take the case of soccer, for example:

> For the player in action the football field is not an 'object', that is, the ideal term which can give rise to an indefinite multiplicity of perspectival views and remain equivalent under its apparent transformations. It is pervaded with lines of force (the 'yard lines'; those which demarcate the 'penalty area') and articulated in sectors (for example, the 'openings' between adversaries) which call for a certain mode of action and which initiate and guide the action as if the player were unaware of it. The field itself is not given to him, but present as the immanent term of his practical intentions; the player becomes one with it and feels the direction of the

'goal', for example, just as immediately as the vertical and the horizontal planes of his own body. It would not be sufficient to say that consciousness inhabits this milieu. At this moment consciousness is nothing other than the dialectic of milieu and action. Each maneuver undertaken by the player modifies the character of the field and establishes in it new lines of force in which the action in turn unfolds and is accomplished, again altering the phenomenal field.[2]

Kinaesthesis and Kinaesthetic Perception

Perhaps enough has been said to emphasize the point that when I get to know something as a result of what I do my senses work in conjoint harmony. In concentrating my attention on kinaesthesis and kinaesthetic perception then I do not want to give the impression that they are somehow independent and separate from the other senses. On the contrary the interplay of kinaesthesis with both touch and vision particularly is an intimate one and one about which some observations will be made later. The main point of this section, however, is to show that kinaesthetic perception, whilst being related to other forms of sensory perception, is at the same time uniquely different from them in that it offers a distinct mode of existence by which we become conscious of ourselves in relation to what we do in the world as a result of the actions we perform.

What then is kinaesthesis? Kinaesthesis is the sense by means of which we experience the sensation of moving. It arises from the stimulation of receptors in joints, muscles, tendons and for present purposes will be inclusive of the sensations which arise from the semi-circular canals of the inner ear.* Overall then kinaesthesis may be defined as 'the sense which enables us to determine the position of the segments of the body, their rate, extent, and direction of movement and the position of the entire body and the characteristics of total body motion'.[3]

As existents and agents we are not so much concerned with the scientific explanation of how kinaesthesis arises but with the way in which we experience it. To me as agent I experience it as a *moving feeling*—rather than a feeling of moving. It is unique and unlike the other senses in that its stimulation comes from *within* me as a result of the movements I make. What I become conscious of as I move is my own 'deeply sensible' animate organism not something that is *peripheral* to it such as when I sit and look at or touch my hand; or *outside* it altogether as when I look at or touch an object such as a

---

* Technically speaking, kinaesthesis is sometimes confined to the sensory feedback of the body's movements minus the feedback from the vestibular mechanisms.

tree, which is external to myself. To put the matter another way kinaesthesis provides me with the means whereby I can be conscious of the very motions I make when in action. Kinaesthetic perception occurs when through it not only am I aware of my own body in motion but in addition am able to make successful judgements with regard to such motion factors as space, weight, time and flow. Kinaesthetic perception enables me *to know what I am doing* without looking. It is a form of knowing without observation. This of course does not mean that other forms of sensory perception are not supportive in the knowing that is actional movement; it simply means that without kinaesthetic perception the full import of what it is to be a moving agent would not be possible.

What I know as a result of what I kinaesthetically perceive is concretized for me (but not shared by others as they watch) when what I do is experienced as a feeling of an identifiable pattern of motion. It is made particularly articulate in my consciousness when certain rhythms and movement patterns are repeated, refined in purposeful practice, and become established as skills. The 'stop volley' in tennis, the accurate 'pitch' in golf and the finely judged 'cross' in soccer are objectivized examples of kinaesthetic perception as a form of knowing. In such actions there is always a cognitive element at work. As I move I have to think what I am doing and make discriminatory judgements that issue forth in successful practice. Kinaesthetic perception (not just sensation) is not 'given': it is gradually 'acquired' in the light of experience in the overcoming and solution of particular tasks. It is the process by which I make discerning judgements that 'stand out' from the 'unorganized mass' of experiences in terms of the bodily motions that I feel when engaged in action. They are aptly described perhaps as personalized and felt kinetic melodies. They become, when established, a part of what I am and know.

Kinaesthesia, Action and the Self
It was said earlier that kinaesthesis is unique among the senses in that that to which I attend is *in* and *of* me rather than on the surface of or observable to me. To put the matter another way it can be said that the 'object' of my perception, so to speak, is *internal* rather than *external*. The importance of this is that what I know kinaesthetically is always *private*. That is to say there are no common referents as there are, for example, when we look at *that* tree or touch *this* apple. As percipients we can attempt to describe what we feel as we move but since the 'object' of our attention is inner-directed and self-referential, it can never be shared in the same way; for example, we

may listen to the same Haydn symphony even though what each of us may 'hear' is different.

From this it can be said that kinaesthesia as a mode of existence is unique in two respects. First, it is an important means by which I come to be acquainted with and know my own motions in terms of the discriminatory judgements I make when I perform my actions. Second, it is the means by which I am able to experience and become conscious of my self as a locus of feelings which occur only when I am moving. Taken together, kinaesthesia may be regarded as being to do with my awareness and efficiency as a mover and with my self as being dynamically embodied.

Since the kinaesthetic sense was 'discovered' less than one hundred years ago it is perhaps not surprising that philosophers, especially those brought up in the British tradition, have strikingly neglected it when dealing with matters to do with perception. Apart from the work done by some phenomenologists it is still even today largely ignored. Hampshire[4] in exploring the relationship between thought and action recognizes that something is gravely wrong with the way in which the problems of perception have been approached when he affirms that

> The deepest mistake in empiricist theories of perception, descending from Berkely and Hume, has been the representation of human beings as passive observers receiving impressions from 'outside' of the mind, where the 'outside' includes their own bodies.

Even Hampshire, however, whilst commenting that

> to act is to move at will my own body, that persisting physical thing, and thereby to bring about perceived movements of other physical things. I do not only perceive my body, I also control it; I not only perceive external objects, I also manipulate them.[5]

never quite gets as far as seeing that the attention I give to my kinaesthetic flow patterns as I perform my actions is itself a form of perception. He sees that the body is involved in the perception of other things, even his own body, but nowhere is he able to see and make the point that the conscious discriminations I am able to make kinaesthetically when actually moving is a sixth form of sensory perception; or that it is 'inner-directed' and therefore an important aspect of self. A prior condition in my awareness of self is not my contact with and manipulation of other 'objects' but the sense I have of my own body when in action. These feelings of self-validation can and do occur independently of those that arise from my manipulating and affecting changes in the positions of the things about me. It is likely that the young child develops a sense of self in and through the movement it makes long before it is able to reinforce it still further by the employment of other forms of sense perception.

Macmurray[6] points out that tactual perception is the only means of having direct and immediate awareness of the 'other' (i.e. things 'other' than one's self) by turning *outwards* to the world and by so doing gain a sense of self as opposed to non-self; so, conversely, kinaesthetic perception also reinforces a sense of self by making the agent aware of those feelings which occur whenever he attends to them in performing an action by turning *inwards*. When I get to know the feel of a skill, or get to know the rhythm of a dance, I get also to know that aspect of self which is perhaps best described as my self as a moving being. As moving being and agent I am both conscious of what I kinaesthetically perceive and of what I am doing in relation to the world. As a consciously embodied mover I always know more than I can tell.

Feeling, Thought and the Limitations of Language

It is perhaps because knowing in movement is largely dependent upon the *feeling* of motion that philosophy as rational reflection has either disregarded it or held it in considerable suspicion. Yet even Pascal acknowledged that the heart had its reasons and these 'reasons of the heart' were sometimes more important than those of the intellect. Man, however, as existent is a psychosomatic unity and feelings to him as agent are in no way either strange or embarrassing. They are accepted for what they are—a part of what it is to be a person who is participating in the world. Certainly when it comes to practical understanding in relation to our moving bodies the feelings of kinaesthetic perception is not only a distinct means by which I come to know myself but is able to offer guidance in coping with the tasks that I perform. As an embodied person in action it is in and through my kinaesthetic feelings that I live, move and have my being. 'Whatever being may be' says Ricoeur[7] 'feeling attests that we are a part of it'. If this is so it is not improper on occasions, as has already been intimated, when dealing with existential meanings in movement, to speak of kinaesthetic feelings as 'ontological' feelings.

Kinaesthetic perception is not just a feeling of undifferentiated motion; it lies more in the discriminatory motions I feel as I move. It is a form of thought that is dependent upon feeling. Actional movement can be partly described as thinking with feeling. Far from being antithetical in movement the two are not separate but form a single process. What I come to know in movement can be expressed as that which I thinkingly feel. The question arises—can what I know be adequately analysed and conveyed in terms of vocalic language? The answer seems to be that the one cannot be reduced to and made altogether intelligible in terms of the other, although of course to have access to concepts which are linguistically expressible provide some sort of common and ready-made framework against which it is possible to check out whether what I know coincides roughly with what others say they know. Language in other words is a medium rich in its possibilities for communication *about* knowing in movement, but this is in no way commensurate with or equivalent to the knowing I have as a thinking and feeling agent and performer. Phenomenologically speaking, whatever I attempt to say about my moving must be based upon my direct experience of it as a primary reality. Furthermore since I can describe only that which I can kinaesthetically perceive and that what I kinaesthetically perceive is *in* and *of* myself, as no other object of sensory perception is, *what* I know is peculiarly and personally mine. In other words what I know in terms of what I perceive kinaesthetically is subjective and private. Only because I can give such description of it by reference to some conceptual scheme is it made public. It should always be remembered, however, that the locus of truth in relation to knowing in movement lies not in the proposition but rather in its perceived reality. It arises from an involvement in the medium of movement itself. What I know as a mover arises always from what I am able to do and kinaesthetically comprehend. It is founded on the primacy of my kinaesthetic perceptions that result from my being engaged in a variety of specific if sometimes composite actions.

Conceptualizations of the Moving Experience

It has been maintained that when an agent kinaesthetically perceives the bodily motions he makes he perceives them in a way nobody else can. All forms of perception of course are private in a sense but privacy here refers to the fact that what I perceive kinaesthetically is indwelling in the motions I make. Unlike other forms of sensory perception—vision, touch and hearing, for example—there is no common 'object' to which reference can be made. There is therefore no way of checking, and maybe verifying, what I say I perceive by way of what others say they perceive since the datum to which I refer is a living event *within* me and is a part of me rather than a separate entity *outside* of me. It is *in* and *of* myself rather than that which is *other* than myself. It is this factor about kinaesthetic perception that makes it unique among the different forms of sensory perception. Epistemologically speaking, the only check I have against the possible falsity of what I perceive kinaesthetically is in the visual perception of the actions I make of myself. Not only is the 'feel' of a drop shot discriminatingly discerned as a result of my practising it and getting it 'right' but it can be checked up upon whenever there is doubt by putting it to the test. If what I kinaesthetically perceive with regard to the drop shot is matched by the successful performance of it then this is sufficient verification that what I 'felt' was correct. It can be said then that my kinaesthetic knowledge arises from and is confirmed by what I am able to do in terms of successful practice.

It will be appreciated that what I come to know through the process of kinaesthetic perception cannot be adequately expressed in terms of language. This having been said, however, it does not follow that no attempt should be made to give some sort of conceptual account of what perceiving and knowing in movement entails. What follows is an attempt to do just this.

Movistruct, Movicept and Movisymbol

The terms kinestruct, kinecept and kinesymbol have been used by Metheny and Ellfeldt[8] in an attempt to provide conceptual abstractions about what they determined to be 'three interrelated aspects of *every* movement experience'.[9] In presenting what they refer to as a general theory of human movement they draw upon Cassirer's[10] theory of symbolic transformation which, without going into detail, recognizes that man experiences his life through his senses and that it is through his sensory perceptions that abstract thought arises. It is in his symbolic abstractions of direct experience that man is provided with a basis of how he can comprehend himself and the world about him. Their work has been pioneering and important in an attempt to provide the field of movement with some concepts of its own. Regrettably, however, mainly perhaps because of the difficulties they enter into with regard to the relationship between the public and observable (by others) *kinestruct* and the private and non-observable *kinescept* and the relationship of each to the *kinesymbol*, certain difficulties ensue which have been partially pinpointed by Best.[11] I want to utilize a number of these thoughts and apply them to the concept of action so that here only one perspective will be dealt with—that of the agent. In order to do this I propose coining three new terms—*movistruct, movicept* and *movisymbol*. This is necessary first to avoid any confusion with those terms coined by Metheny and Ellfeldt and which are still in current use and, secondly, to emphasize the fact that these new terms refer only to the perspective of the agent. This was not the case with regard to the kinestruct. And, thirdly it will not necessarily commit us to the theoretical position out of which the terms used by Metheny and Ellfeldt grew.

Proceeding then on the basis that concepts without perceptions are empty and perceptions without concepts are blind let us look at three terms which could in the future encapsulate some of the things that have been discussed in relation to actional moving and its meaning for the agent, when looked at from the phenomenological viewpoint.

Movistruct. The movistruct is a general term which refers to an agent thinking about possible or actual patterns of movements which he may or may not perform. There are three main varieties—anticipatory, actual and retrospective. The *anticipatory* movistruct can be thought of as an envisaged pattern or sequence of movements, normally in relation to the fulfilment of a specific task, about which the agent thinks before acting. Here the agent visualizes movement sequences as a choreographer might before he tries them out.

The anticipatory movistruct can in principle include the following possibilities:

  (i) The movement pattern that the agent thinks he will be able to perform;
 (ii) The movement pattern which the agent ideally would like to be able to perform;
(iii) The movement pattern(s) that the agent definitely wants to avoid for one reason or another.

Since the movistruct remains a series of unexpressed thoughts it is *private*, though of course these thoughts can in principle be made *public* if the agent chooses to talk about them in such a way that other people can understand. An anticipatory movistruct can then *in principle* be shared though in practice it is virtually impossible to bring about if only because of the difficulties encountered in trying to describe the dynamic forms the body takes when in motion. This is why actions in dance, for example, tend to be 'presented' rather than described.

In the different possible anticipatory movistructs listed above it will be seen that they are all future-directed: they are therefore designated as *anticipatory*. An *actual movistruct*,* however, differs from them in that it relates to the way in which the agent pictures or cinematographically visualizes himself whilst he is actually in action. An *actual movistruct* then is one which is based upon the agent 'stepping outside himself' to observe the somatic pattern that he himself is creating through space as he performs, as if he were looking at himself in a mirror. What he movistructurally 'sees' is not necessarily what objective observers would attest to as being so. Nevertheless 'right' or 'wrong' it is the moving agent's movistruct. It is *actual* because even though it may be incorrect it is based upon how he pictures the reality of his action as it unfolds.

In the same way that a high jumper at different times can imagine various forms of *anticipatory movistructs* in the way he approaches the bar so he may be 'right' or 'wrong' about the way he sees his *actual movistruct* as he passes over the bar when performing. The movistruct then refers to those patterns of movement in relation to himself which are:

1 *Anticipatory* 'visualizations' of himself in action and
2 *Actual* 'visualizations' of himself in action even though they may be false.

It will be appreciated too that it is possible to talk about:

3 A *retrospective movistruct* as being applicable to a pattern of movement that is over, whether recently or sometime in the past, and which is 'witnessed' again so to speak as an act remembered.

It will be seen then that movement in the form of the movistruct is primarily 'visualized' rather than 'felt'. Clearly in the learning of physical skills the ability to create a movistruct as a visualized pattern of movement has much to commend it.

To movistructualize is to create a movistruct.

Movicept. A movicept is, or is based upon, the kinaesthetic perception of a movement pattern. Like the movistruct it can be experienced in one of three ways: it can be actual, retrospective or anticipatory. When *actual* it refers to those identifiable elements and discriminations that are kinaesthetically 'felt' as they are attended to and reflected upon by the agent whilst an action is ongoing.

The movicept in its secondary sense recognizes that an *actual* movicept can be 're-lived' by a subsequent process of recapitulation.

---

* All movistructs are actual in the sense that they occur. What actual means here, however, is that the agent envisages himself as the performer.

It is this possibility of re-constituting the 'immediacy' of a kinaesthetic flow pattern by recollecting it retrospectively that permits a distinction to be made between a movicept in its actual or primary sense and a movicept in its retrospective or secondary sense. It can thus be said of the movicept in its secondary sense that the agent can moviceptualize without having to move at all. It will be seen that when the kinaesthetic flow patterns of certain movements are repeated and attended to, they become progressively 'sedimented' in consciousness. The kinaesthetic flow patterns of established skilled movements, for example, are often able to be recalled without difficulty. When this occurs an agent can be said to be 'acquainted' with them.

Sometimes a retrospective movicept is able to be used in an *anticipatory* way by the agent when preparing to do something as a golfer might, for example, before making an actual swing. In this way the movicept, if well articulated and based upon successful practice, can be an aid in preparing to perform as well as acting as a check when actually performing.

All three forms of movicept are founded upon the ability of the agent to kinaesthetically perceive when engaged in movement actions.

To moviceptualize is to be able to attend to, identify and 'grasp' the kinaesthetic flow patterns of my own movements.

Rhythms, timings, spatial orientations and muscular tensions are all a part of this process.

Although the movicept is private in the sense that only the agent has (or possesses) what he kinaesthetically feels (or perceives or is aware of) it is also public (i.e. made shareable and communicable) in so far as it is physically expressed and/or linguistically described. Another way of putting this is to say that the criteria of identity lies in a) its expression and b) its description.

Another agent can be said to have the same type of movicept as mine if he performs a similar pattern of movement to the one I performed and describes the kinaesthetic flow patterns he experiences as being like the ones I experienced. When this occurs our movicepts can be said to be the same, i.e. it answers to the same description.

Movisymbol. A movisymbol is a term which refers to the import or significance a particular movement action has for the agent as a moving being. In the same way that not all movements are movistructed or moviceptualized, so not all movicepts are movisymbolized.

A movisymbol can symbolize either: (a) that aspect of myself that is my animate organism or (b) something about my existence in relation to the world.

As an example of the first form let us take the case of me as runner. I run not because it enables me to win against others, to beat records or to meet with others or for any other extrinsic reason. I run because I like to: the motivation is intrinsic to the action and experiential process of running. In running I recognize that there is something symbolic about what I am doing. It refers to the concrete experience of my own animate organism. In running, more than in any other action, I poignantly realize I am the bearer and activator of my own vital powers. It is this realization that makes it for me symbolic. The reality of my lived body in action is symbolized in the rhythm, effort, breathlessness and pain of running.

What, of course, running does for me, throwing, jumping or swimming may do for others. What action or actions are movisymbolic for me in other words are not necessarily movisymbolic for others, though clearly many forms of activity are shared and provide a common source for movisymbolism—athletics and cricket, for example. What is recognized by the agent as being movisymbolic is not observable by others. There is no objective criteria to which an observer can point and say *that* movement for *that* person is movisymbolic. The movisymbolic experience arises from the degree of importance or value put upon the process of action by the performer.

The movisymbolic experience in the case of me as runner arises from the degree of importance or value put upon the *process* of the action by me as performing agent. Others may witness my running and may even infer something of its lived body significance for me but only I as agent can know, until I chose to disclose to others what I know.

With regard to the second form of movisymbolism—that of symbolizing something about my existence in relation to the world—the emphasis is not so much upon the symbolization of that aspect of myself as an animate organism but upon a particular movement or action as a symbol of my existential presence in the world. Accordingly not all movement meanings are necessarily symbolic ones in the sense that they are regarded and recognized by *me* as particularly important even though they may be by others. Some are, however. Thus it can be said of this second form that all movisymbols have existential significance but not all movements or actions are necessarily symbolic in any public or generally agreed sense.

Movisymbols in this second sense most commonly but need not necessarily derive from being a participant in a particular 'form of life'. The movisymbol thus has connections with the social realities of engaging in a particular situation at a given time in a given place. An example that may serve to illustrate the movisymbol is the case of the high diver of Acapulco. Here the action of the dive in the context of the agent's socio-cultural situation and biography is what makes the movement probably for him movisymbolic—though only he as agent can know whether or not this is so. As with our first form of movisymbol observers may infer from what they are witnessing that an action is movisymbolic to the performer but they cannot for certain know. This is the agent's prerogative. The hole in one; the perfect cover drive; the successful ski run; the scoring of a winning try are all potential movisymbols.

The movisymbol as with the movicept can by an act of reflection be re-constituted into consciousness long after it has actually taken place. When this occurs it can be referred to as a recapitulated movisymbol. Movisymbols are frequently 'peak experiences' when they are in reality performed. Thus great feats which are constituted by the agent as symbolic are rarely forgotten. Take, for example, the description given by Houts of an occasion arising from baseball:

It was the third game that I had pitched that day. I did not think I could last through another game, but suddenly I was overcome by a power that rendered me capable to pitch forever. I lost the immediate awareness of my team around me. It was just me, alone, on the mound grasping at a round, weightless orb. I became extremely sensitive to the motions of my body. The minute muscles in my fingers were waiting for the signal to release their power and force: I could feel my whole body moving through the air, transcending all barriers; I could feel the initial thrust as all my body force was extended with the pitched ball.

But suddenly there came a moment of doubt. I felt that I was entangled in a silly, nonsense game with myself. After all, as soon as my acts were over, I would have to prove myself anew with each pitch, with each new play in the game. It was a never-ending entanglement, to prove with each move that I was my act. For a second fear gripped at me, pulling and pushing at the very core of my existence. What if I did not get another chance? What if this was it? The recognition of my own finitude had come about in my sport experience. The realization of death existed for me, in only a flash, and then it was gone. Why it had come, I do not know, but to feel so small, there on the mound, alone, in the midst of a tied ball game, was it the realization of the death of the game, or of me, through which the game existed?

My body continued to move and perform its function while my mind was caught in turmoil. The game did not seem to be going fast enough, yet I was lagging behind it.

Then I saw the ball reach its intended target. The pitch felt like a unique extension of my whole self, with the ball not to be touched by the 'object' standing at home plate. Vaguely, I heard the umpire call 'Strike!' It gave me a feeling as though I had made a safe but daring journey through unknown territories, breathing ultimate freedom at last. Freedom! I had transcended my environment. I was my act in sport and nothing more, nothing less. I felt my authentic being. I was aware! I was feeling sport! The honest effort and the complexity of my seemingly simple movements made my body, my mind, and my soul seem to reflect beauty and truth of a living, involved human being in sport.

Then the next pitch had to be thrown. I was trying hard to maintain my joy. All of a sudden the game was over. The opponents came into view. They were happy, screaming, throwing gloves into the air. The realization of the moment had come to me. I knew what I had done. The game was tied in the last inning; there were two outs, the bases were loaded. The count on the batter was three balls, two strikes. Yes, in my joy, in my transcendence of the situation, I had walked in the winning run. It was over. How absurd! Gone as quickly as it had come. I realized again how small I was among the complexities of life. The game was over and I had to continue to be me through the never ending responsibility of choices that shape my life. I knew that in some small way I left this peak experience a different person than when I entered the game. I was changed. Some small part of my being had become more total in its encounter with life.[12]

Whatever value or significance movisymbols have for the agent they can only be made intelligible to others in so far as they can be faithfully described and understood. This of course is often extremely difficult to do, though not impossible as the quote above suggests.

In explicating the above three terms it will be appreciated that although they are conceptually discrete they are often in practice functionally related. The movistruct encapsulates a spectrum of conscious possibilities that are open to the agent in relation to his bodily existence; the movicept recognizes that kinaesthetic perception is a distinctive aspect of self-experience; and the movicept acknowledges that an engagement in movement activities can result in significant forms of subjective meaning that could quite easily go undetected even by the shrewdest observer.

It may well be asked, of course, why it is necessary to give technical terms to the phenomena described when ordinary language is capable of doing the job. The answer here is the obvious one. If it were true that ordinary language could do the job as well there would indeed be no need for them. The fact, however, is that it does not, especially in any neat or shorthand way.* For those in the Movement community (dancers, sportsmen, coaches, lecturers and students of physical education, etc.) who want without difficulty to refer to the types of distinctions and discriminations that these terms allow, it is natural that a special vocabulary be established that permits them to communicate with ease and understanding. In this respect Movement is no different from any other field of enquiry. Language after all is not a static thing, but something that evolves in response to a need to identify and refer the pertinent phenomena in a more economic and/or illuminating way.

Movement: A Unique Amalgam of Knowledge Types

It has been suggested so far that knowing *in* movement is related to the kinaesthetic perceptions we have when moving. The task now is to examine to what extent movement as action fits in with other formulations of what it is to know something. This is desirable for several reasons. First, it will point up some of the things that have only been implied. Second, it will allow additional dimensions of what it is to know in movement to be raised. Third it will serve the purpose of making it clear that knowing in movement is a unique synthesis of acknowledged types of knowledge. This last point is important for unless knowing in movement can be shown to have some sort of epistemic claim it is in some circles not likely to be considered 'good' and therefore have value attached to it. This as will be shown later is particularly important in relation to education.

What then is it to know something? The verb 'to know' Ayer[13] makes clear is used in a variety of ways.

> We can speak of knowing, [he says,] in the sense of being familiar with a person or a place, of knowing something in the sense of having had experience of it, as when someone says he has known hunger or fear, of knowing in the sense of being able to recognise or distinguish, as when we claim to know an honest man when we see one or to know butter from margarine. I may be said to know my Dickens, if I have read, remembered, and can perhaps also quote his writings, to know a subject such as trigonometry, if I have mastered it, to know how to swim or drive a car, to know how to behave myself.

* It is of interest to note that Wittgenstein himself commented that in our descriptions of sensations ordinary language is 'slightly cumbrous and misleading'. See *The Blue and Brown Books* (Blackwell, 1975), p. 52.

In other words 'know' has many uses and it is as well to remember that it is not confined to the form which is concerned with upholding a claim that something or other is the case.

Philosophically speaking it is not unusual to speak of knowledge in relation to the world, ourselves and others. In this section, however, it is mainly movement in connection with ourselves with which we shall be concerned. Knowledge here is perhaps best referred to as being self-knowledge. It is not attained by attending to something which is external to oneself but by immersing oneself in the process of actional doing. Things and others are frequently present as we move which clearly have to be taken into account, but predominantly, if not exclusively, knowing *in* movement is concerned with the intelligent performance of one's animate organism in actional motion. What I as agent come to know is experienced as peculiarly mine. It has its own phenomenological structure. The general position in this respect is in keeping with other forms of experience. To quote Stace:[13]

> I cannot experience anything except *my own* experience. I can see my red but I cannot see yours. I can feel a pain in my leg. But I can never feel the pain in your leg. I can feel my emotion but not yours. Even if your anger infects me, so that I feel it in sympathy with you, it is yet, in so far as I feel it, *my* anger, not yours. I can never be you, nor you me. I cannot see through your eyes, nor you through mine.[14]

Knowing *in* movement then, in contradistinction to knowledge that can be gained *about* movement, arises through a direct participation in its many forms. It is founded on the experiential process of actually moving. It is in no sense to be equated with knowledge that might be discovered through an academic study *of* moving or with the conceptual abstractions which may arise *from* it.

In order to examine and clarify what is being contended here I propose looking at movement in relation to three related but distinguishable types of knowledge. Before going on to do this, however, I want to make it clear that underlying all of them, and in keeping with the unity of the person thesis, there are certain unspecifiable embodied processes which Polanyi[15] refers to as 'the tacit dimension'. In other words only a person in his full 'embodiedness' can be said to know something and not one aspect of him, as if it is divorced from body, called mind. One other point is worth making and that is that knowledge exists only in so far as somebody, not necessarily myself, has possession of it.

Movement in Relation to Types of Knowledge
Reference will be made to three types of knowledge:

   (i) Knowing that;
  (ii) Knowing how;
 (iii) Knowing by acquaintance.*

Each will be looked at in turn before saying something further about their being founded in what has been called

 (iv) Knowing by tacit inference or tacit knowing.*

1   *Knowing That.* 'Knowing that', sometimes referred to as theoretical or propositional knowledge, is concerned with what can be said *about* something. This is normally done in the form of a statement such as 'metals when heated expand'. Propositional statements or 'knowing that something is the case' are information giving and assert the existence of some state of affairs.[16] Nonetheless 'knowing that' statements carry with them a claim to truth even though they may not in fact be true. When a person claims to know that something is the case he is asserting that it can be justifiably believed. If I say something is true, that is make a proposition that something is true, and furthermore I can give *evidence* in support of what I say, then according to Scheffler[17] this can be considered a *strong case* of 'knowing that'. If, on the other hand, I say something is true, and I believe it to be true but have no evidence to support that what I say is true, then this may be considered a *weak case* of 'knowing that'.

Propositional knowledge in relation to movement as a field of study and research is, of course, important. Well-proven statements like 'the functional efficiency of an organ or system improves with use and regresses with disuse', or 'to every action there is an equal and opposite reaction' are factually informative and theoretically sound. When such propositions are understood against the disciplinary backgrounds from which they come they are able to usefully add something to our knowledge *about* movement as a subject or rational enquiry. In connection with the relationship of 'knowing that' statements to rational understanding Hamlyn has this to say:

No one could be said to have come to understand a subject, to have learned it, without some appreciation of general principles, some idea of

* Although some philosophers would question whether 'knowing by acquaintance' and 'tacit knowing' can be called knowledge at all, they are terms, which although discredited by some, occupy a place in the literature and are useful labels for recognizing certain aspects of perception and learning as will be shown.

what it is all about. But knowing and understanding general principles is not just a matter of being able to recite the relevant general propositions—he must be capable of cashing such general principles in terms which mean something to *him*, if understanding is to follow. There is in the growth of understanding of any subject an intimate connection between principles and the application of instances.[18]

In view of what follows, what needs to be emphasized here, if misunderstanding is to be avoided later, is that propositional or 'knowing that' knowledge is characterized by claims:

(i) That arise from particular *theoretical* perspectives or modes of enquiry each of which have their own 'objective' truth tests;

(ii) That they are stated in terms of written or vocalic language and because of this they are limited to what that form of language can meaningfully state.

The question then before us is can what I have called perceiving and knowing 'in' movement be rendered adequately in terms of 'knowing that'? Clearly, partially in view of what has already been said it cannot. It remains now for me to explicate the position still further.

2   *Knowing How*. In his 'Concept of Mind' Ryle's[19] purpose is to discredit once and for all Cartesian dualism and with it the 'intellectualistic legend' which assimilates the praxis of 'knowing how' to do something to the theoria of 'knowing that'. According to this legend to do something always involves two things: 'namely, to consider certain appropriate propositions, or prescriptions and to put into practice what these propositions or prescriptions enjoin. It is to do a bit of theory and then do a bit of practice'.[20] Ryle not only contests that this is always so but points out its absurdity. He not only maintains that 'there are many classes of performances in which intelligence is displayed ... the rules or criteria of which are unformulated,'[21] but points out that 'if, for any operation to be intelligently executed, a prior theoretical operation had first to be performed and performed intelligently, it would be a logical impossibility for anyone ever to break the circle'.[22] This last point seems logical for as Pears[23] amongst others recognizes, practice nearly always comes first and it is only later that people theorize about practice. Finally, Ryle maintains that 'even where efficient practice is the deliberate application of considered prescriptions, the intelligence involved in putting the prescriptions into practice is not

identical with that involved in intellectually grasping the prescriptions.[24]

In place of the 'intellectualist legend' Ryle suggests that

> What distinguishes sensible from silly operations is not their parentage but their procedure, and that this holds no less for intellectual than for practical performances.[25]

He continues

> 'Intelligent' cannot be defined in terms of 'intellectual' or 'knowing how' in terms of 'knowing that'; 'thinking what I am doing' does not connote 'both thinking what to do and doing it'. When I do something intelligently, i.e. thinking what I am doing, I am doing one thing and not two. My performance has a special procedure or manner, not special antecedents.[26]

In describing what is entailed by this special manner or procedure Ryle observes

> To be intelligent is not merely to satisfy criteria, but to apply them; to regulate one's actions and not merely to be well-regulated. A person's performance is described as careful or skilful, if in his operations he is ready to detect and correct lapses, to repeat and improve upon successes, to profit from the examples of others and so forth. He applies criteria in performing critically, that is, in trying to get things right.
>
> This point is commonly expressed in the vernacular by saying that an action exhibits intelligence, if, and only if, the agent is thinking what he is doing while he is doing it, and thinking what he is doing in such a manner that he would not do the action so well if he were not thinking what he was doing.[27]

Ryle's notion of 'knowing how' has been quoted at some length because it remains the most complete account with what 'knowing how' is essentially to do. It is especially important to what has been said about perceiving and knowing *in* movement in that it demonstrates that 'knowing how' cannot be reduced to 'knowing that'. Any complete characterization of 'knowing how' in relation to movement would include and put emphasis upon the following points:

(i) That it is *performative*;

(ii) That it involves *intelligent critical action* i.e. that the agent is thinking what he is doing *while* he is doing it;

(iii) That it involves *standards*. Knowing how always involves knowing how to do something and this involves trying to get that something 'right';*

(iv) That whilst performing the *judgements that are made do not necessarily arise out of previously formulated criteria*. Rather it recognizes an unpropoundable ability to respond to circumstances in a discriminate way and it is this ability that must 'precede the ability to codify the responses, if only because the use of distinct symbols to codify them is itself an example, indeed a sophisticated example, of discriminating response'.[28]

From what has been said it will be seen that whereas 'knowing that' or propositional knowledge is essentially concerned with the making of correct statements about a state of affairs, 'knowing how' which is practical, or what Hampshire[29] has called 'non-propositional' knowledge, is of a performative kind which in no way depends upon previously thought out theoretical constructs of what is thought to be the case. Knowing how in movement is centrally related to the question of *being able to* do something e.g. being able to swim. Now it may be objected that it is possible for a person to 'know how' to swim in the sense of his knowing the principles of flotation and being able to describe and maybe go through the movements of the breaststroke on the edge of the pool, but is actually unable to swim in the water. This is a question of knowing how 'in theory' but being unable to in practice. Such 'an-unable-to' form of 'know how' is not an authentic form of 'know how' at all since there is an absence of praxis or actually being able to swim in the water. As Curtis[30] points out ' "knowing how" in the sense of being able to do it and knowing how to do it in the sense of being able to say how it is done are often very different affairs'. He adds: 'This is particularly noticeable where the activity concerned is "mainly physical".'

In the case of a person who is normally able to swim but who is *prevented from* doing so because of injury or lack of facilities, for example, there is no real difficulty in attributing to him 'know how' for even though in *absolute* terms he is *at present* unable to perform he nevertheless *has been able to*, and given a change of circumstances will be able to again. He knows what it is like and has had the experience of what being able to entails. Looked at then from the

---

* Pears, D. (Reference 23, p. 32) expresses this point in the following terms: 'The first requirement for knowing how to do a thing is that the actual performance should be correct'.

point of view of reflective consciousness based on actual experience, 'knowing how' includes either that a person *is able* or *has been able* to perform to some minimal standard.

It is of course true that some performers are able to give some sort of account of what they are able to do and it is upheld by some* that unless this is done in addition to 'being able to' do something then the term 'knowing how' is not properly applicable. There is some merit in this view for it maintains that unless the person can say what he is able to do it cannot be said that he knows how to do it. This, however, is to attempt to make one type of knowing as a necessary feature of another. Now although it can be agreed that the giving of an account is perhaps a useful and desirable adjunct or complement to 'knowing how' to do something it is by no means a necessary feature of it. It is not necessary because what is known *in* movement (in contradistinction to knowing *about* movement), lies not in being able to give an account of it but in the intelligent and successful performance of the action itself.

Attributions of knowing how are frequently accorded to those who possess physical *skills* like playing tennis or pole-vaulting. Such skills may be regarded as *contextual abilities* by virtue of which the person is able to demonstrate that he knows how to do what is required of him. He does this without necessarily being able to give an account of what he does. For the agent the action which he knows is the performance and not some truth or proposition *about* the performance. Even where elements of 'knowing that' enter into a performance, as they are bound to in sports and games and, as it were, made a part of the action, there is conceptually speaking no reduction of 'knowing that' into terms of 'knowing how'† or vice versa.‡ The fact that both types of knowing are sometimes intimately and inextricably a part of what is involved in certain complicated activities such as cricket, for example, where the bowler punctuates his deliveries by critically appraising what he should next do in relation to such changing factors as the state of the pitch, the weather, the light and the wind as well as the skill of the batsman and the position of the fielders about him, by no means implies that the one type of knowing is reducible to the other. It means rather,

---

* See, for example, D. G. Brown's article 'Knowing How and Knowing That, What' in Wood, O. P. and Pitcher, G., *Ryle* (Macmillan, 1971) pp. 213–66.

† See Swann, J. Hartland, who argues that *all* cases of 'knowing that' can ultimately be reduced to cases of 'knowing how'. 'The Logical Status of "Knowing That"' in *Analysis* XVI April 1956, pp. 111–15.

‡ See Powell, B., *Knowledge of Actions* (Allen and Unwin, 1967), pp. 19–30.

according to the nature of the activity, that there is a close reciprocal relationship between them.

Kwant seems to recognize this when he writes

Of course the player has had some kind of theoretical training, but he 'knows' more and better with his legs, with his hands, and with his entire body than he knows in theory. If he has to teach another player how to pass a ball, how to tackle, he prefers to demonstrate rather than give a theoretical explanation. He adjusts the entire posture of his body to the approaching ball, without knowing in theory how this came about.[31]

Knowing how in the application of skills such as in the playing of games is a form of direct, spontaneous and non-discursive knowing. It is non-discursive in that what is known is intelligently expressed as a series of performances.

If the *mastered skill*, i.e. one that can be performed at will with judgement and reliability, is a paradigm case of 'knowing how' it must be recognized that not all instances of knowing how are cases of mastery or perfection. Below what standards then must a performance not fall if it is to remain a case of knowing how? There is no easy answer to this question but it clearly relates to the notion of success. Even the scratch golfer is not perfect and a complete master of his skills but few people would maintain on account of this that he does not 'know how' or is 'unable to' play the game. If then knowing how doesn't demand faultless perfection what are its general characteristics? *Relevant judgement* in what needs to be done in a given situation would seem to be one; and a minimal *proficiency* in being able to do what is required reliably is another. Both may be covered, perhaps by the word *competency*. There are stages of know how or relative degrees of competency ranging from those who are of the calibre of genius to those who are able to exercise a demonstrable competency in terms of relevant judgement and reliability. Thus 'know how' can be referred to along such a continuum as 'brilliant', 'mediocre' or 'poor'. By such descriptions it is possible to relate the notion of know how to the notion of *standard*. The performer as agent gets to know what his standards are by the success he has in relation to the task and in relation to those who engage in the same activities.

In principle 'knowing how' to do something does not necessarily involve *practice*. A child, for example, may find when he falls into the river that, rather like a dog, he simply knows how to swim. Normally, however, 'know how' in relation to movement abilities is improved by practice. Indeed in the acquiring of most skills practice is an indispensable prelude to being able to perform them. It is almost inconceivable that anybody would be able to do a dive with two and a half somersaults and a half twist off a five metre board without practice. Certainly it is highly improbable. In most cases it is safe to say practice goes hand in hand with the development of know-how. In practice the agent is purposefully thinking what he is doing as he is doing it with the object of improving his previous performances. In other words he is performing critically and trying to increase his competency. When practising he is being vigilant and intelligently critical of what he does. Always he is being attentive to how his performance can be made better. The notion of *purposeful practice* is to be contrasted with mindless drills and routines which tend to be automatic and with habits which tend to diminish the conscious attention to a performance which 'knowing how' demands.

In view of what has been said it will be seen that, if perceiving and knowing *in* movement is to do with critically thinking whilst performing to some standard without *necessarily* calling upon previously thought out propositions relating to them, 'knowing how' will occupy a place of central importance in life, for it is concerned with the actual practice of physical activities and not with what can sometimes be said *about* how those activities are done. To put the matter another way I have upheld the view that 'knowing how' in its *primary sense* is to do with being able to do something intelligently regardless of whether or not an account can be given of what is done. If in addition to being able to do something intelligently it is thought that an account of what is done is a desirable if not a constituent part of what 'knowing how' is, then this can be regarded as a case of 'knowing how' in a *secondary sense*. To me, however, this seems both unnecessary and confusing for it mixes up what are essentially two logically different modes of knowing.

3   *Knowing by Acquaintance*. In his *The Problems of Philosophy*[32] Russell distinguishes first between 'knowledge that' and 'knowledge of'. Then within the latter he differentiates between knowledge by acquaintance and knowledge by description. 'We have *acquaintance*' he says 'with anything of which we are directly aware, without the intermediary of any process of inference or any knowledge of truths.'[33] Acquaintance knowledge comes to me immediately, certainly and incorrigibly from sense data. If I look, for example, at a picture I see what is there before me. What I have is a direct knowledge of the picture. The colours that I see do not alter by the fact that they can be described with names; nor does the impact of

them alter if I can think of something to say *about* them in propositional form. It will be seen then that neither giving appropriate names to the colours I see, nor making propositional statements about the colours I see, makes me know the colour itself any better than I did before. The colour (e.g. red) I know perfectly and completely when I see it regardless of its name or what can be said about it. Acquaintance knowledge is something of which I have direct awareness.

It should not be thought, however, that acquaintance knowledge is confined to sense data that comes to us now in the present. As Russell explains there are a number of extensions of acquaintance knowledge that go beyond the immediate registration of sense data. These include memory and introspection. All in all acquaintance knowledge incorporates not only sense data registration and the particular thoughts and feelings it engenders but an ability to recall these things and be reflectively conscious of them.

In using the term *knowing by acquaintnace* in relation to movement I shall use it both in a 'strict' sense and a 'less strict' sense but both senses, it should be stressed, arise from and relate to actually being involved and participating in practical activity.

The *strict* sense of the term refers to

(i) the 'feelings' of which I am aware when I kinaesthetically perceive an action as a result of 'knowing how' to perform it.

The *less strict* sense refers to

(ii) the thoughts, feelings (other than kinaesthetic) impressions and desires etc., I have and am aware of as a result of participating in particular activities and of which I (or some other agent) can give some sort of descriptive account.*

Concerning the feelings I have when I 'know how' to perform something not a great deal more need be added to what has been said already. What is involved here has been more than adequately covered when dealing with moving as a perceptual mode of consciousness and what 'knowing how' entails should now be clear. However, there are a number of points that it is desirable to make in the interests of clarity. One is that knowing by acquaintance in movement activities is logically dependent on 'knowing how' to perform them. As was made clear earlier one cannot be said to know something by feeling, or in any other way, unless what one

---

* It will be seen that there is a difference between being familiar with a description of something of which we have had no direct acquaintance and the attempt by someone to give a description of something with which he is acquainted.

feels is correct. 'Knowing by acquaintance' in movement then is not concerned with feelings of motion in general but just with those particular feelings of motion that issue forth in successful practice. I can be said to be acquainted with tennis in the strict sense of the term only if I am able to kinaesthetically differentiate between the skills that make it up—the forehand, backhand, serve and volley and so on—and be able to successfully perform them. In 'knowing by acquaintance' in movement I know what I know as nobody else can because what I know is dependent upon those proprioceptive elements in my animate organism that are 'mine' and which I feelingly experience and meaningfully constitute as 'mine' as a result of attending to and reflecting upon the patterns of motion I make. If somebody asks of me what I 'know' by acquaintance in serving at tennis I am only able to reply those 'feelings' I have as a result of 'knowing how' to do it. I know in other words what it feels like to successfully serve. I might also demonstrate and say it is *this* that I feelingly know. Either way, however, nothing much will have been conveyed for it is only the agent who can feelingly know as a result of *his* being able to perform particular actions successfully.

'Knowing by acquaintance' in movement is a matter of both *degree* and *kind*. It varies in degree in that some movements are 'feelingly known' better than others. If I say that I am 'well' acquainted with the activity of pole-vaulting I would mean that I am able to go through the sequential series of kinaesthetic flow patterns that constitute that event as being feelingly meaningful to me. If, on the other hand, I say that I am only 'slightly' or 'vaguely' acquainted with the activity of pole-vaulting, I would mean that they are not nearly so well 'sedimented' in my consciousness and that I am able to live over only partially and 'thinly' some of the feelings involved.

Knowing by acquaintance in movement, it has been suggested, refers to an acquaintance with *particular* activities. When I say therefore that I am not acquainted with that *kind* of movement I mean that I have not personally tried to perform it and feelingly constitute it as being meaningful. It may be a reference to a particular gymnastic movement such as an overswing, an event in athletics or a choreographed dance sequence.

In general, the 'degree' and 'kind' of acquaintance knowledge in movement refers respectively to *depth*, or how well an activity is known: and to *width*, or how broad one's feeling experience is over a range of different movement forms. Of knowing by acquaintance in movement in the *strict* sense then it can be said:

  (i) That it is based upon a reflective grasp of recognizably different kinaesthetic flow patterns or 'feelings' which are constituted by me as meaningful;

 (ii) That because it is dependent upon 'knowing how', the feelings I have are entailed in successful performance;

(iii) That it is 'private' in the sense that the feelings I have are possessed only by me and are therefore peculiarly 'mine'.

It can be added:

  (i) That in common with 'knowing how' it is in no way reducible to 'knowing that';

 (ii) That, again in common with 'knowing how', it necessitates the *doing* of something. It can, therefore, like 'knowing how' be regarded as a form of 'practical knowledge';

(iii) That once 'known', i.e. firmly sedimented in consciousness, it is a form of knowing without observation. By it I am able to know what I am doing without having to look.

To contend that knowing by acquaintance is a distinct way of knowing in movement is not to say that it is unrelated to the other types of knowledge. On the contrary as was suggested earlier *there is an intimate relationship between all of them.** Just as 'knowing how' and 'knowing by acquaintance' are contiguously related so both are augmented by their association with relevant aspects of 'knowing that'. In the same way as Reid[34] suggests that discernment and feeling in art can be 'enriched' by contact with 'knowing that' so too can 'knowing by acquaintance' in movement. To know, for example, *that* Petrouchka is a Russian ballet; *that* it was choreographed by Fokine; *that* it is considered by some as the perfect dance drama; *that* it revolves round the main characters of Petrouchka, who is striving to express himself in love and beauty; *that* the Dancer is a heartless coquette; *that* the Moor is strong, savage and terrified of the unknown; *that* it was first staged by Diaghilev in 1911 and so on, is almost taken-for-granted information to a dancer who is to perform in it with some understanding. The point then is that 'knowing that' is almost an inevitable accompaniment to many

---

* Attempts to discuss the relationship between kinds of knowing and movement as if it were concerned only with the clarification of the 'knowing how'/'knowing that' issue are as limiting as they are ultimately reductionist. See, for example, Aspin, D. N., '"Knowing How" and "Knowing That" and Physical Education' in *Journal of the Philosophy of Sport*, vol. iii, September 1976, pp. 97–117.

forms of movement performance. When this is so it gives perspective and increased understanding to what is being done. This, however, is in no way to say that 'feelingly knowing' in movement by our acquaintance with the very motions we make can in any way be reduced to propositional statements that are relevant to a performance in a given situation. The tennis server who knows *that* he has to get the ball into the box diagonally opposite his own for it to count, in no way invalidates the appropriate kinaesthetic feelings that he gets to know and by which he comes 'to know' as a result of getting his action 'right'.

I shall quote two passages in order to illustrate what it is to know an activity by acquaintance in the 'less strict' though in some ways fuller sense by a direct involvement with it as a participant. Although each is concerned with the body and its motions this is not the only thing that is conveyed. By extension each is 'enriched' by other thoughts, feelings and impressions that are associated with the activity in what might be called a personalized gestalt of meaning. The first quote is from a chapter (entitled *On being a Potter*) from Robertson's book, *Craft and Contemporary Culture*. She writes *Contemporary Culture*. She writes

> To be a potter means to take a lump of clay, plastic from its damp thousand-year-long journey to the potter's bench, and to work it to increase its essential plasticity.... A good clay, like a good wine, has a bouquet.

The clay, she says, can be worked by 'walking' it. The potter stamps

> Up and down, treading the soft, squelching mass underfoot till it grips the heels and almost seems threatening to engulf one. By this time one's body is becoming deeply aware of the clay, and other awarenesses are falling away. One seems to have gone down into something unformed, primeval, and almost given oneself to it.

Describing throwing and centring she observes

> Here laved in more water, the lump is centred between the hands but with the whole body. The weight is taken on the ball of the foot and one is conscious of the force of the solid earth, which is felt through the muscles of the calves, of the thighs, of the loins, of the shoulders, a force drawn up and directed downwards through the arms so that beneath enveloping hands the thrust of the earth is poised against the thrust of the centrifugal force of the wheel. To learn to use one's body thus a mediator without strain, to centre the lump of clay until it spins like silk beneath the fingers, that is the perfection of co-ordination, an exquisite sensation of wholeness.[35]

The second quotation concerns the sport of skiing.

Glancing quickly at the steel-blue sky overhead, I decided that the snow which had been forecast wouldn't ruin the ski race after all. The almost-nonexistent breeze barely moved the pines lining the race course below.

My interest in my surroundings gradually changed to a feeling of excited anticipation as I awaited the starting signal. The explosion from the starter startled me momentarily as I pushed myself forward on to the course with my poles. With these first movements downward came an icy sting of air blowing against my face and a sensation of unrestricted speed. My eyes tried to focus on the first gate which was fast approaching to my left. I forced myself to concentrate on my form and timing as I entered the gate:

'Plant pole, shift weight, edge downhill ski, lean into hill,' I repeated to myself as I co-ordinated my movements with my thoughts. Coming out of the gate, I gathered speed again and set my skis for the next gate. It came up faster than I had expected, and I lost control for a moment sensing the total helplessness of falling. Luckily I caught myself and regained my proper position of the moment before.

Gate after gate I mentally repeated my instructions as I co-ordinated movement with words, 'plant pole, shift weight, edge downhill ski not so much into the hill, *faster*'. On I went: first to the right, then to the left. I was oblivious to my surroundings and intent only upon a world of whiteness intermittently dotted with bamboo poles. Judges and spectators flashed by me in splashes of kaleidoscopic color. Ice-crusted pines were mere blurs of green as I shot through gate after gate.

Suddenly I saw the final gate and the finish line beyond. Momentary relief spread through me as I realized the race was almost over. Quickly, *through* I forced the pleasant thoughts from my mind as I dutifully repeated my silent instructions and fought to gain speed. Three more gates behind me, and I was nearly upon the poles which marked the final gate. Now, fighting madly for extra speed, I thrust my poles into the snow and shoved myself forward. As I pulled my poles back to my sides, I realized that the push had been a bit overdone and had cost me my balance. My next sensation was a horribly delightful feeling of tumbling over and over as I rolled down the hill. Mixed with my joy at such complete freedom of movement was the sickening realization that this fall had cost me the most important race of my life: the Winter Olympics.[36]

4 *Knowing by Tacit Inference*. Tacit knowing or knowing by tacit inference is important to the underlying theme of this book: firstly, because it emphasizes that knowledge is not that which is 'out there' but that which is known by a knower, in other words by an embodied existent or person; and secondly, because it recognizes that everything we come to know is *ipso facto* that we have a body. Tacit

knowledge in other words is body-dependent. To Polanyi 'all knowledge is either tacit or rooted in tacit knowledge'.[37] A *wholly* explicit
knowledge, or what 'scientific rationalism' sets out to achieve, is
unthinkable.

Polanyi argues that each person is a member of the human species
and as such is expected to have an indefinite range of undisclosed
properties that affect his whole existence including those parts of it
that are to do with knowing. Although, being of the same species,
men have much in common, each and every individual comes to
know his world personally. Reality can only be discerned by the
judgements that we as individuals make. To this extent all knowledge is personal knowledge.[38]

Knowledge, Polanyi says, 'is an activity which would be better
described as a process of knowing'[39] for what we come to know
depends upon the comprehensive entity of that which we are. An
indispensable aspect of that which we are is the body and this
organic aspect of ourselves is central to how we come to know and
understand. The way in which the body participates in the act of
perception, for example, is an indication of the way in which what is
'seen' is made sense of and endowed with meaning. This applies no
less to kinaesthetic perception than to other forms of perception and
gives credence to Polanyi's claim that perception can be generalized
'to include the bodily roots of all knowledge and thought.[40] It is in
keeping with what Merleau-Ponty[41] means when he speaks of 'The
Primacy of Perception'.

Of the body Polanyi writes

> Our body is the only assembly of things known almost exclusively by
> relying on our awareness of them for attending to something else. Parts of
> our body serve as tools for observing objects outside and for manipulat-
> ing them. Every time we make sense of the world, we rely on our tacit
> knowledge of impacts made by the world on our body and the complex
> responses of our body to these impacts. Such is the exceptional position
> of our body in the universe.[42]

The theory of tacit knowledge in common with phenomenology
makes the distinction between the dwelling in of our body (embodiment) and the view of the body as seen from the outside. It regards
this contrast as the difference between looking *at* the body and
attending *from* it at something else.

On this Polanyi comments:

> Dwelling in our body clearly enables us to attend *from* it to things outside,
> while an external observer will tend to look *at* things happening in the

body, seeing it as an object or as a machine. He will miss the meaning these events have for the person dwelling in the body and fail to share the experience the person has of his body. Again we have loss of meaning by alienation and another glimpse of the meaning of dualism.[43]

Our body is the ultimate instrument of all our external knowledge, whether intellectual or practical. When we learn to use a language or a tool for example, we make ourselves aware of these things as we are of our body; they become, as it were, extensions of our bodily equipment and indications of what it is to be intelligent. By *interiorizing* these things and *dwelling in them* they become meaningful and it is by the progressive extension of meaning that a person comes more and more to know. It is this indwelling of things in ourselves that allows us to feelingly participate in that which we understand rather than be removed and alienated from it. In the area of personal relationships especially this is the difference between seeing people as persons rather than as 'its' to be used. A key factor in tacit knowledge is that there is a logical relation that links life in our body to our knowledge of things outside of us.

A central tenet about tacit knowledge is that it recognizes *that we know more than we can tell*.[44] This is implicit in all three types of knowing that have been discussed. Because 'knowing that' is associated with the formulating and giving of statements, however, its dependence upon the tacit dimension gets overlooked, yet it too derives from those same powers that are fundamentally *innate* and indwelling in us. They are part and parcel of our embodiment. In essence the theory of tacit knowledge maintains that man is an organic and unitary whole and contends that the person comes to know and understand through a process of *internal integration* for which in the last resort no account can be given. It will be seen that even in science where objectivity is so upheld the ability to observe things 'correctly' is dependent upon our tacit powers to perceive them as so.

Although such processes as imitation or such procedures as training can assist the individual to come to know and understand, in the final analysis what occurs is an act of personal discovery. The unspecifiability of the process of integration in tacit knowledge is exemplified in the way a physical skill comes to be possessed. For Polanyi the performance of a skill is not only a way by which we come to know our body but a paradigmatic instance of tacit knowing. He writes

If I know how to ride a bicycle or how to swim, this does not mean that I can tell how I manage to keep my balance on a bicycle or keep afloat when swimming. I may not have the slightest idea of how I do this or even an entirely wrong or grossly imperfect idea of it, and yet go on cycling or swimming merrily. Nor can it be said that I know how to bicycle or swim and yet do *not* know how to coordinate the complex pattern of muscular acts by which I do my cycling or swimming. I both know how to carry out these performances as a whole and also know how to carry out the elementary acts which constitute them, though I cannot tell what these acts are.[45]

The claim Polanyi makes that all knowledge is tacit or rooted in tacit knowledge is a powerful one. By it he reasserts together with the phenomenologists that man is not dualistic but one in nature and within each person there are hidden powers which do not disappear because they remain unexplained. In movement particularly perhaps, perceiving and knowing rely heavily upon the inexplicable integrations that occur. In skilful performance what has been going on tacitly is both constituted as meaningful by the agent and made manifest to the observer. In discovering what we are able to do in a practical way we come to perceive and know more than that about which it is possible to be explicit.

Summary and Conclusion. By way of conclusion the following is a short summary of what has been established in the preceding sections.

Perceiving and knowing *in* movement is primarily a form of practical knowledge of which a person has direct acquaintance. It is related to 'knowing how', in that the person is or has been able to perform certain movements intelligently, critically and successfully with judgement. Knowing *in* movement is actional in that what is intended or envisaged is subject to modification in the light of actual, ongoing and changing circumstances. Much of what is known is tacit in that the mover knows more than he can tell.

Relevant instances of 'knowing that' something is the case can of course aid and guide perceiving and knowing in movement (e.g. bio-mechanical laws in the learning of specific skills) but perceiving and knowing *in* movement is not necessarily dependent upon 'knowing that' (except in the obvious sense of knowing the rules that govern certain activities) nor can perceiving and knowing in movement be reduced to what can be said *about* it in propositional form. Perceiving and knowing in movement in other words derives predominantly from an involvement in and with one's own animate organism.

When one speaks of perceiving and knowing *in* movement, what one is essentially referring to are those conscious acts of awareness and judgement that come from the agent successfully performing particular actions thinkingly and feelingly. All three facets of what it is to be a person—thinking, feeling and acting—are combined in unique measure to give the person, as an embodied consciousness, the experience of what it is to be a moving being. What I get to know as a result of my constituting my performative experiences as meaningful are personal in that they are in certain important respects peculiarly 'mine'. This remains so regardless of whether or not what I do is accurately interpreted by others or I am able to communicate something of what I perceive and know in expressive or descriptive form.

5. Movement as a Source of Aesthetic Experience

Originally the word aesthetic meant perception, especially, perhaps, as it relates to feelings. It is only since the time of Baumgarten (1714–62)[1] that aesthetics has come to be associated with a theoretical form of enquiry to do with the beautiful and at the same time take on overtones of a particular form of *recherché* sensibility. Needless to say in the present context I shall for the most part be concerned with it in something like its original sense—as perceptual experience; though later I shall use the term more in keeping with its later and derived sense when looking at sport and dance in relation to art, the beautiful and the sublime.

Aesthetic Perception as a Distinctive Mode of Consciousness

Aesthetic consciousness is of course not a preserve of artistic appreciation. It can arise from any situation whenever a certain *attitude* is adopted. Thus it is possible to perceive anything from an aesthetic point of view—mass-produced objects such as cars and washing machines; man-made objects such as cathedrals and pictures; and natural objects such as mountains and sunsets. In aesthetic situations, whatever they may be, our attitude is such that we attend to them for their own sake alone rather than for any function or purpose they may serve. The aesthetic attitude towards an object is characterized by its 'disinterestedness'. It is non-practical and non-utilitarian. In terms of movement this means that a particular movement sequence or skill can be enjoyed and done for its own intrinsic satisfaction quite apart from the purpose it may be serving, e.g. conducting an orchestra.

When a person in an aesthetic attitude perceives an object it can sometimes, but not necessarily, bring about an aesthetic experience. The aesthetic attitude puts one into a predisposing and receptive frame of mind towards the object of perception but cannot guarantee an aesthetic experience. In principle it is both possible to 'put' oneself in an aesthetic attitude in order to have an aesthetic experience and conversely 'find' oneself in an aesthetic attitude as a result of the kind of experience being undergone. In the latter case it may be said that the aesthetic attitude is not a condition of aesthetic experience but is constitutive of it.

Aesthetic perception, it is generally acknowledged, is not confined to the visual, though regrettably most discussions concerning it are conducted as if it were but applied to hearing, taste, touch and smell as well. It is an odd fact that the kinaesthetic sense, despite the root meaning being contained within the term (i.e. *kine*-aesthetic), is rarely if ever discussed in aesthetic literature as a form of perception that can provide aesthetic experience. Perhaps once again this is due to the fact that unlike the other forms of sense perception there is no external 'object' to which one can make reference. Since what is perceived is not publicly accessible, as it is with an 'art-object' for example, it cannot be discussed 'objectively'. This, however, as I shall try to show, does not mean that aesthetic experience which can come as a result of moving is less real, poignant or meaningful than the visual experience of a painting, or the auditory experience of a piece of music.

To understand better how kinaesthetic perception can bring on aesthetic experience that is constitutive of an aesthetic attitude it will be necessary to say something further about the nature of the kinaesthetic 'object'.

Kinaesthetic 'feelings' as Intentional Aesthetic Objects

The 'objects' of kinaesthetic perception are the feelings or kinaesthetic flow patterns the mover attends to as he is engaged in the process of moving. The 'practical' purpose of the project upon which he is engaged is temporarily suspended and instead he disinterestedly and sympathetically responds to the muscular rhythms that *he* is able to discriminate between but which are hidden from the public gaze. The cross-country runner, for example, even whilst competing may either by design or by chance enter into an attitude (this is a cultivated technique with some long distance runners) whereby he attends to and enters into, so to speak, the pleasurable and satisfying patterns of his own co-ordinated and kinaesthetically felt motions. Like musical rhythms to the ear they can be the source of a distinctive kind of aesthetic experience. When what is intrinsic to the experience of moving is intensively felt as pleasurable it can be described as a form of 'peak' experience. When it is reflected upon and constituted as 'mine' it can become significantly meaning-ful. As Bouet[2] makes clear one of the reasons people are motivated to engage in physical activity is because of the aesthetic experience derived from the actual process of moving. It is not without significance that Bannister has observed 'We run not because we think it is doing us good, but because we enjoy it and cannot help ourselves.'[3]

Phenomenologically speaking the kinaesthetic object (which can be conceived of as a movicept) can be *real* or *imaginary*. When *real* it refers to the kinaesthetic feelings I attend to when actually in the process of moving. When *imaginary* it refers to feelings that are not associated with a present ongoing lived-body action but which is nevertheless dependent in some way upon actual experiences of moving from the past. It can in other words be either a 'past remembrance' or accurate image of that which has been meaning-fully constituted in the past; e.g. the 'feeling' of running in a cross-country race; or a fictitious dreamlike event which is imagined rather as children imagine things such as running in the air or scoring the winning goal at a Cup Final but which are nevertheless rooted in their actual experience of running or shooting at goal. With regard to the kinaesthetic object then it is necessary to distinguish between attending to a set of kinaesthetic flow patterns or feelings whilst *actually* running and attending to them whilst *imagining* oneself to be running. It will be seen that the object of both my perception and my imagination are my kinaesthetic flow patterns,* and that either they can be remembered in the form of an 'image' or a kind of kinaesthetic photocopy of the actual; or as imaginatively lived out, rather as children do in their play, and which does not accord with the 'real' but which nevertheless is grounded in 'doing' and the reality of kinaesthetic experience. There are thus at least three ways of considering the kinaesthetic object:

(i) As perception of an ongoing and actual pattern of move-ment;

(ii) As a 'past remembrance' of an actual pattern of movement feeling, or image;

(iii) As an imaginative flow of movement feeling which though

---

* This is not, of course, to say that my kinaesthetic flow patterns are the only phenomena of which I am aware. Rather it suggests that whatever else I may be conscious of (e.g. the environment about me) the focus of my attention is directed towards my kinaesthetic flow patterns. In gestalt terms the relationship between my kinaesthetic flow patterns and other peripheral phenomena is one of 'figure' and 'ground'.

not tied to an actual occurrence is grounded in actual experience that has arisen sometime in the past.

It will be appreciated that kinaesthetic objects are almost infinite in number and with varying degrees of specificity, ranging from gross-body activities like hammer throwing to a fine movement like the trigger release in rifle shooting; from the butterfly stroke in swimming to the touch of the pianist in playing the slow movement of a sonata; from the axe swing of the lumberjack to the delicate sewing of the seamstress. They can be actually done or simply done imaginatively by calling upon recollected experiences. The pleasure that can derive from engaging in such activities is not confined to the kinaesthetic feelings to which one can attend but is related to how well or how skilfully the performer thinks he is performing them.

As has been suggested, kinaesthetic objects in common with other sensory objects can be experienced from the 'practical' or 'aesthetic' standpoint according to the nature of the attitude taken up. When our attitude towards the kinaesthetic object is 'practical' we experience the feelings we have only as a means towards mastering something, such as the acquisition of a skill, or of getting something accomplished such as the completion of a gymnastic sequence. The practical attitude is essentially one that is utilitarian in nature. The aesthetic attitude towards the kinaesthetic object on the other hand is one which is orientated towards the feeling of the movement as being of interest in its own right; other concerns are put temporarily out of account. When a kinaesthetic flow pattern is feelingly identified and satisfyingly experienced, it becomes an aesthetic object and valued for its own sake. When aesthetically experienced the kinaesthetic object then becomes to the mover *intrinsically valuable*. The value of the experience is *felt* in the very experience of the moving process. The aesthetic experience of moving in different ways and contexts not only extends and clarifies an aspect of consciousness but in the pleasure it gives provides its own inherent satisfaction.

Although the practical and aesthetic attitudes with regard to the kinaesthetic object have been juxtaposed as being different they, of course, can and sometimes do co-exist. In projects such as the cross-country run the mover can be orientated both practically and aesthetically. He is both competing against others yet is able at times to take an aesthetic interest in his own feelings of patterned motion. It is unlikely that both attitudes can co-exist simultaneously (though they may oscillate frequently) but within the framework of an actional project, especially if it is over an extended period of time, there is little doubt that both can and do exist. The sculler, for example, can be both conscious of his intent to win and yet during the race be caught up with the regular and pleasurable rhythms of his kinaesthetic feelings as he glides, stretches and pulls his oars through the water. The dancer in her solo may at one time be conscious of her technique as a means of doing what she intends, and at another of her kinaesthetic feelings as she enters into or takes up an aesthetic attitude towards them.

Movement Activities: Artistic and Aesthetic

It was Dewey who pointed out that the English language has no word which unambiguously includes what is signified by the two terms 'artistic' and 'aesthetic'.[4] He goes on to suggest that 'artistic' refers primarily to the act of production and 'aesthetic' to that of perception and engagement. It is in keeping with this interpretation of these two terms that I want to discuss the various kinds of movement activities. In doing this I hope to clear up a number of misconceptions that are implicit and sometimes explicit in the literature to do with movement, especially in connection with those forms called sport and dance.

I shall approach the problem under two main headings:

1   The 'artistic' in relation to ends and means;
2   The 'aesthetic': the standpoints of the performer and the spectator.

1   The Artistic in Relation to Ends and Means

In an attempt to cut through some of the confusions of the aesthetic in relation to movement activities Best has suggested a three-fold categorial division:[5]

(i)   Those activities such as tennis, cricket, golf, athletics in which *the end can be specified independently of the means of achieving it*. That is to say the specific point of the activity is logically distinct from the means.

(ii) Those activities such as Olympic gymnastics, diving, figure-skating and ski-jumping, in which the *purpose cannot be considered in isolation from the means of achievement*. In these aesthetic yet competitive activities there is a close relationship between function and form within each activity.

(iii) Those activities such as dance and mime which are said to be 'artistic' and in which talk of *a distinction between means and ends is logically misconceived*.

It will be seen that in the first category, where the end can be specified independently of the means of achieving it, it is possible to win or be successful regardless of aesthetic experience or artistic endeavour. If either or both enter such 'quantitative' yet competitive activities such as sprinting, high-jumping or shot-putting which are decided ultimately by the measurable and objective factors of time, height and distance, it is a contingent but unnecessary matter. Similarly in mountain climbing, if the end is to reach the top, the important thing lies in the achievement not in the *manner* that led to the achievement, be it graceful or clumsy.

In the second category—in which the purpose cannot be said to be considered apart from the manner of achieving it—ends and means are brought closer together, though never absolutely closed. In competitive/aesthetic activities such as ski-jumping and men's Olympic gymnastics points are awarded for both the successful completion of a task and for their artistic merit or the qualitative manner with which they are performed. Anthony makes this point clear:

> Most sports have the straightforward, uncomplicated objective of scoring goals or points; any aesthetic element is incidental to the main aim. In some sports, however, and gymnastics, diving, and skating have been mentioned, one major aim is aesthetic—to create a 'good' or 'artistic' movement. The gymnastic judge is given official guidance to look for 'grace', 'general beauty', 'elegance', 'rhythm and precision', 'harmony' and 'perfect artistic execution'. His diving counterpart must look for 'grace'. In skating, marks are awarded for technical merit and for 'artistic impression'; among the terms used in this latter section are: 'harmonious composition of the whole'; 'conformity with music'; and 'carriage'. On the trampoline a good performer must satisfy requirements such as 'continuity and flow', 'symmetrical placing of body segments' and 'aesthetic manner', according to the 'established standards of art'.[6]

Even in relatively unstructured situations such as figure-skating and women's Olympic mat exercises the situation is never free of the rules which govern them any more than the sonnet writer can disregard the form through which he has chosen to express himself. In these 'mixed' activities where the qualitative aspects or *manner* of the doing is sometimes no less important than *what* is done, the means to some extent becomes ends. In ski-jumping, for example, the winner is not necessarily he who jumps the greatest distance, for 'style' is an element of the competitive situation.

In the third category, where the purpose of the activity is to be 'artistic', an attempt to make a distinction between means and ends would be to misconceive the purpose of the activity. When, for example, mime or dance is done with the idea of presenting it as an art form, means and ends are no longer distinct or even blurred but congruent. *What* is done can in no way be separated from the *manner* in which it is done; purpose and quality of performance are not logically distinct and identifiable elements conjoined in an activity but inseparable and in accord with the nature of the enterprise. In a superficial sense, of course, there are still tasks to perform—the mime must communicate his story; the dancer must dance what has been choreographed. But in a more fundamental sense ends and means are one and the same and are directed towards an artistic and qualitative production which is the sole purpose of the activity. In other words the means and end of *art qua art* is art itself.

2   Aesthetic Experience: the Performer and the Spectator

In discussing the nature of the aesthetic in relation to movement it is necessary to distinguish between the aesthetic experience of the performer and the aesthetic experience of the spectator. Failure to do so can lead to not only ambiguity and confusion about what standpoint is being adopted but, what is worse, sometimes a blurring of the very issues and discriminations that are crucial to a better understanding of what the aesthetic can mean *in* and *through* movement.

Although of course there are points in common between the two standpoints I intend here to concentrate more in bringing out their differences. I shall proceed by presenting at each stage of the discussion in the light of what has gone before firstly, what the performer's standpoint is; and secondly, compare and contrast it to that of the spectator's standpoint. By so doing I hope to demonstrate that aesthetic experience belongs no less to the performer than to the spectator; and further, that the former cannot be adequately discussed in terms of the latter. Although this second point is recognized by some it has been given scant treatment in the literature. What follows therefore is an attempt to rectify this state of affairs.

Basic Considerations. Before looking specifically at what constitutes aesthetic experience for both performer and spectator let us look at the two standpoints as occupying two basically different psycho-physical orientational centres. Perhaps the first point to be emphasized is that the performer is a *participant* and takes his perspective from *inside* the activity upon which he is engaged. The spectator on the other hand looks upon the activity as a *witness* from the *outside*. Whilst the performer is in and of the action, the spectator is removed and physically apart from it. The performer too (as player, dancer, contestant, etc.), is *author* and *agent* of his own actions. He envisages, activates and attempts to fulfil his projects in terms of the actual situations with which he is confronted. Ultimately he alone is responsible for the moves he makes. He knows and feels in a situation of doing in a way that the spectator is unable. The performer alone has access to the 'inner theatre' of his own consciousness. Whatever intentions he has remain *private* until such time as he chooses to voice them. The spectator on the other hand no matter how hard he may try to psychologically project himself into the action remains basically an onlooker and 'reader' of it. At best he attempts to bring understanding to what he sees acted out before him by *interpreting* what he observes to be occurring in terms of what makes sense to him as spectator. By taking account of what is *publicly available* in the shape and form of 'the other's' movements in given contextual situations the spectator is able to make certain inferences about the performer's intentions. These can be right but they can also be wrong and to contend, as is sometimes done, that intentions can be 'discovered' by observing the movements of others is, as we have seen, in need of considerable qualification.

If it is difficult to 'read' through the performer's physical movements his intentions, then how much more difficult it is if, indeed, it is ever possible, to 'share' his kinaesthetic feelings. Since this latter point is of central concern in this section let us look at the matter further.

The performer in action as we have seen is able to attend to his own lived-body experiences and constitute them as meaningful. As performer I am able to experience my kinaesthetic flow patterns as I engage in action. As I do, so I feel. *What* I feel arises largely from my direct acquaintance of knowing-how to do things. *How* I feel arises from the attitude I adopt towards those feelings. It is important to realize then that the 'what' I attend to as performer are the differentiatable kinaesthetic perceptions I have. Whether or not these become objects of aesthetic perception depends upon the attitude I take up towards them. When my kinaesthetic perceptions do become objects of aesthetic perception they are enjoyed and found pleasurable for their own sake. In my reflective awareness of these kinaesthetic feelings as objects of aesthetic perception, they are constituted as mine and given meaning. Since the feelings I have and the meanings I give to them are mine and not publicly available, they are subjective in character. They are peculiar to me as performer and by no means necessarily congruent with those that may be imputed to me by an observer.

As performer it is from the reflected-upon HERES and NOWS of my lived-body movements that my aesthetic gratification derives. It stems from my attending to my animate organism in action. As performer only I can know what I feel; only I can know whether or not these feelings become constituted as aesthetically meaningful.

It is, of course, sometimes said that the spectator is able to empathize with the performer and is in some way able to share his experiences. This, however, is logically impossible. The performer is, as we have seen, the orientational centre of *his* physico-cultural world, and similarly the spectator is the orientational centre of *his*. The experiences of two embodied consciousnesses are not interchangeable, nor is one ever able to project himself completely into the other so that he becomes the other; the more so since their respective situations and perspectives are quite dissimilar. This, however, is not to deny that an imaginative and sensitive spectator can to some extent step into the shoes of the other and visualize himself as the performer. He may even be able to kinaesthetically remember what *his own* feelings were when performing similar actions and in a sense live them out afresh. All this is quite understandable and is what some people refer to as 'communication'. What it amounts to very often though is little more than a re-awakening of their own kinaesthetic feelings as past remembrances, and is in no way commensurate with a complete loss of identity whereby they actually imagine themselves to be the other. Even when two people are physically proximate and doing the same movement patterns at the same time (e.g. double sculling) and attending to one another, as was spoken of when discussing the 'we–feeling' phenomenon and could be said to be in a state of co-existence, the one could never be said *to be* the other. As was made clear then (page 75) this is never possible though at times considerable psychological overlap can take place. At best the spectator, removed as he is from the performer and his situation, can imaginatively attend to the performer's actions *as if* he were that person. This in some measure can bring insight and understanding and even evoke comparable lived-body experiences based upon past remembrances but they can never be more than close approximations. The spectator's identification with the performer's action can take him so far but never so far that he can claim that 'my' experiences are 'his' experiences. This is so not only of his kinaesthetic perceptions but perhaps even more so of these as aesthetic objects. The aesthetic perception of kinaesthetic feelings is not only subjective and private but sometimes idiosyncratic. The notion of movement behaviour as a criterion for the discernment of feeling in others in no way meets this point. Furthermore neither kinaesthetic perceptions nor attending to them as aesthetic objects is in any way to be equated with kinaesthetic sensations which by comparison are crude, nebulous, undifferentiated and lacking in cognitive content. All in all only the performer can kinaesthetically perceive what movements he makes and transport them into recognizable feelings of aesthetic pleasure. When a performer is aesthetically experiencing his own animate organism as mover he is at the same time *self*-actualizing. He is living his embodied existence here and now, not vicariously but in reality. He is experiencing what in one sense he *is*. He is the sovereign authority of how he feels. The movicepts and movisymbols that mark out his movement experience are not mere discursive intellections but formulations of subjective movement experience capable of providing aesthetic gratification.

Qualitative movement. In introducing the notion of qualitative movement (sometimes contrasted with instrumental or quantitative movement)* the question of value is raised and once more the two standpoints of the performer and spectator are thrown into relief. From the performer's standpoint qualitative movement is not only a matter of attending to the kinaesthetic feelings he has as he moves, it is also a matter of appraisal. If, when attending to the feelings that are immanent in the actions I make I constitute them as not only pleasurable and meaningful but qualitative as well then there are grounds for referring to them as beautiful. In attributing to them the word beautiful I am according them of special value. They are not only meaningful but 'good'. Beauty *in* movement is literally embodied. It arises from the feelings I have and the value I put upon them. Kinaesthetic feelings when constituted as aesthetic objects and held valuable are beautiful. For the performer then qualitatively experienced movement and beautiful movement are the same. What is qualitatively felt is that which is valued.

* See Sandle, D., 'Aesthetics and the psychology of qualitative movement' in Kane, J. E., 'Psychological Aspects of Physical Education and Sport' (Routledge and Kegan Paul, 1972), pp. 128–62.

Logically what is qualitatively 'felt' by the performer to be beautiful is in no way dependent or parasitic upon art or artistic presentation. There can be and frequently is a connection but it is not a necessary one. Beauty in movement can be felt in running through the silent forest no less than in dancing Prince Igor.

'Qualitative movement' for the spectator on the other hand is not so much 'felt' as 'seen'. It is visually perceived and because of its public nature can be shared by others as something to be witnessed and appraised in terms of commonly held criteria. For the spectator it is not kinaesthetic feelings that are the focus of attention as they are for the performer, but the configurational body patterns of the mover. It is the performer's body motions as visually presented that become the objects of aesthetic perception. These body motions can be looked upon 'objectively' often in concert with others and are open to appraisal in accordance with well-established aesthetic (i.e. artistic) criteria. Thus such formal properties as 'rhythm', 'symmetry' and 'harmony' can be invoked and referred to as providing perceptual guidance. In dance, for example, it is not unusual to look at *compositional form* in terms of 'balance', 'continuity', 'proportion', 'unity', 'repetition' and 'contrast'.[7] Similarly, *expressive quality* can be looked for in terms of 'pity', 'fear', 'anger', 'sadness' or 'strength', 'dynamism', 'weakness' or 'boldness'. When movements are perceived in these formal and affective ways they may or may not be appreciated as beautiful. They may induce some sort of aesthetic response but for them to be designated beautiful there must not only be an imaginative fusion of form and feeling but a recognition that in this unitary experience there is pleasure, meaning and value.

Even, however, where common aesthetic criteria is adopted, it would be wrong to assume that the same responses are made by different spectators. Just as in language there is a 'semantic differential' between people with regard to word meaning[8] so in movement there are expressive movements that are commonly witnessed but differently perceived in one way or another.

The point then is that although there may be conscious or unconscious employment of public aesthetic criteria the intuition of beauty as Berndtson recognizes 'carries with it in any occasion a savour of individuality'.[9] Whilst for the performer the beautiful lies largely in the articulation and embodiment of kinaesthetic feelings, the beautiful for the spectator lies more in the visual perception of fluid configurational patterns of the human body in motion. Strawson[10] makes clear there is not only a logical distinction between that which is assessed favourably and that which is enjoyed (though they normally go together e.g. that was a 'good' game), but between what he calls 'participant enjoyments' and 'spectator enjoyments'. Although both points are important, it is the latter one in this context that is particularly significant, for in recognizing that the enjoyments of the participant and spectator are essentially of two different kinds he implicitly recognizes that there are basically two routes to that which can be aesthetically experienced. This applies to movement no less than to any other medium. One route is through the performer's direct engagement in an activity; the other is through the spectator's observation of it.*

Aesthetic Meanings: 'Artistic' and 'Non-artistic'. From what has so far been said it should be clear that the performer is able to constitute the experience he has from *doing* as aesthetically meaningful just as the spectator is able to constitute what he *sees* somebody else doing as aesthetically meaningful. Clearly in both cases the matter of *context* is important. Yet, as has been suggested, because of the different standpoints they have, the context they each find themselves in is dissimilar. The concept of context then in so far as it relates to meaning is only useful in so far as it is used somewhat more circumspectly than simply associating it with a particular form of social life, important though this may be. As Poole observes: 'Meaning in a full sense can only emerge in a context which is an existent temporal (and spatial)† reality, and not merely a formal cultural convention.'[11] It must allow for and discriminate between what is often referred to as *objective meaning* and *subjective meaning*.‡ Failure to make such distinctions is not only confusing but naively reductionist.

What is true of meaning in general in this regard is perhaps especially true of aesthetic meaning in relation to movement. Although all aesthetic meanings, whether performer's or spectator's, are 'subjective' in the sense of their being individually constituted not all of them arise from what might be described as 'objective' or artistically conventionalized meaning contexts. In other words not all aesthetic meanings can be explained and interpreted in terms of pre-established and culturally generalized conceptions associated with 'artistic' activities. The aesthetic, as has

---

* For a useful discussion about the use of good in aesthetic judgements see Helen Knight's 'The Use of "Good" in Aesthetic Judgements' in Elton, W., *Aesthetics and Language* (Blackwell, 1970), pp. 147–60.

† My brackets.

‡ *Subjective meaning* is that meaning which a person ascribed to his own experiences and actions, *objective meaning* is the meaning imputed to the conduct of another person by an observer.

already been noted, is wider than those activities—music, drama, painting, poetry and so on—that normally go under the heading of art.

In order to differentiate what might be called artistic aesthetic meanings from those aesthetic meanings which are non-artistic I propose to say something more about each in an effort to bring clarification to what may loosely be described as the 'movement aesthetic'.

By *artistic aesthetic meanings* I refer to those aesthetic meanings that derive from the socially learned conceptualizations of art and beauty. They are in a phrase 'acculturated' aesthetic meanings. Although they are constituted by individuals they arise predominantly out of being initiated into a particular form of conventionalized social life. Thus a person perceives artistic contexts largely in accordance with the way others do. The fact that there is a publicly agreed set of shared concepts and modes of bodily expression people are able in some measure to understand and participate in this form of life. When looked at in this light it makes some sense to point to particular shared or 'objective' contexts and say of them that they provide criteria for the establishment of meaning. When this stance is adopted, which is the one most frequently taken up by the spectator for interpretive purposes, it sounds plausible to contend as Best[12] does that 'it is the context of the movement which is all-important' for the constitution of meaning. It suggests that if a movement is performed or seen in an artistic context such as that of a ballet, for example, it will somehow provide aesthetic meaning. This, however, by no means follows. The fact that a context is recognized to be artistic in no way ensures that it will be perceived aesthetically. This holds true for either performer or spectator. For this to occur the mode of perception must be aesthetic. The recognition of an artistic context in other words does not guarantee the bringing on of an aesthetic attitude though it may assist in its being brought about. Only to the extent that what is constituted as aesthetically meaningful by the performer is also that which is constituted as aesthetically meaningful to the spectator can artistic aesthetic meanings be the same for both. This however in no way suggests they can be shared in the sense of their entering into a single stream of consciousness even when there is a genuine desire to communicate. Thus, even with 'common ground' artistic meanings, for someone to say he can see what *the* aesthetic meaning is by its context, or that what he constitutes as aesthetically meaningful for himself is the same as that which has been constituted as aesthetically meaningful by someone else, especially when it is the spectator speaking of the performer, is nothing more than interpretive guesswork. The observer, as a result of being initiated into a culturally shared artistic form of life, may be predisposed by the recognition of artistic contexts to perceive aesthetically but this in no way gives him the right to say that what he perceives is the same as that which others perceive or that what he finds aesthetically meaningful is the same as that which others find aesthetically meaningful. Again if this, as a generality, is true of spectators, it is even more true when there is an attempt by the spectator to ascribe aesthetic meaning to the performer.

To grant that artistic aesthetic meanings that belong to individual existents, whether performer or spectator, have some 'common ground' that derives from a shared culture and which within limits provides a conventionalized framework for aesthetic perception, is a long way from the 'objectivist' view that wants to accord aesthetic meaning to a movement(s) if it is perceived within an agreed artistic context. In the last resort aesthetic meaning is always subjective meaning and for the observer to attribute aesthetic meaning to the performer based upon what he thinks is comprehensible purposeful behaviour and which takes place within an artistic context of socially constructed conceptual frameworks and expectations is not only simplistic but misleading.

Non-artistic aesthetic meanings in contrast to artistic ones are those which tend to arise from idiosyncratic perceptions rather than those which are conventionalized through shared social learnings. Although they are constituted within a culture they arise more from the individual's reaction to *his* own biographic contexts and situations than to those which are presented to him 'secondhand' through the process of acculturation. As a result they do not depend upon being initiated into an agreed and specialized set of conceptualizations, such as 'form' and 'expression' so much as an intuitive sense of what is pleasing and worthwhile. In comparison with artistic aesthetic meanings non-artistic ones are not constituted in response to normatively recognized artistic contexts but are in response to those experiences which are somehow more personally biographic, unconventional, irregular, *ouiré, exceptional and distinctive of* one's self. They are not common but uncommon; not inclusive but exclusive; not learned but discovered; not customary but distinctive; not phenomenally objective but phenomenally subjective; not framed but unframed.

Non-aesthetic meanings in movement of course can arise in workaday activities like sewing, sowing and scything no less than from ones which are regarded as being recreative like boating or bowling. When aesthetic moments flit by in regularly done routines they tend to remain unexpressed and therefore unshared. Occasionally, however, descriptions are given in sport and other activities which bring to the attention of others the possibilities that exist. Bannister, the first four minute miler, describes something of how aesthetic meaning for him was unexpectedly discovered:

> I was running now, and a fresh rhythm entered my body. No longer conscious of my movements I discovered a new unity with nature. I found a new source of power and beauty...[13]

It is worth noting here that the meaning constituted is 'unframed' in any artistic sense, and is unpredictable and free of scholastic intellections. Such meanings are the prerogative of the performer and are at their most pure when they simply arise from the action in an unpremeditative way. They may never be rendered adequately into linguistic terms but are nevertheless articulated and rendered poignantly conscious in a direct acquaintance way *in* the movements made.

Similarly when Arnold Palmer, the golfer, exclaims:

> What other people may find in poetry or art museums I find in the flight of a good drive—the white ball sailing up into that blue sky, growing smaller, then suddenly reaching its apex, curving, falling and finally dropping to the turf to roll some more, just the way I planned it.[14]

it is possible to appreciate more fully how such actions and the results of those actions can provide countless opportunities for non-artistic aesthetic meanings to be grasped.

Here aesthetic meaning does not so much stem of the process of moving as when kinaesthetic feelings are constituted as intentional aesthetic objects, but from what results from the completed action. Although the meaning constituted is not intrinsic to the action it is logically related to it. The one could not occur without the other. Although the spectator is often able to appreciate the outcome in relation to the social context in which it takes place only the performer is able to accommodate both action and outcome in the flow of experience and identify each with himself. When aesthetic meanings arising *in* the action are reinforced by those that result *from* the action the performer is able to encompass and assimilate the two varieties of aesthetic meaning within, so to speak, a single sweep of consciousness.

Some aesthetic meanings in relation to sport do not arise only from the constitution of feelings immanent *in the motions* that are made as is the case when kinaesthetic feelings become intentional aesthetic objects; nor *in the consequences or outcomes of actions* as in the flight of the golf drive cited above, but in the constitution of pleasures and gratifications that are *associated with* sporting activities or achievements. Take, for example, this supremely poignant moment described by Herzog on reaching the summit of Annapurna:

> We were on top of Annapurna!
> Our hearts overflowed with unspeakable happiness. If only the others could know!
> Our mission was accomplished. But at the same time we had accomplished something infinitely greater. How wonderful life would now become! What inconceivable experience it is to attain one's ideal and, at the very moment fulfil oneself. I was stunned to the very depths of my being. Never had I felt such happiness like this—so intense yet so pure![15]

Another description which incorporates a whole concatenation of feelings, thoughts and impressions that are associated with running is provided by Atkinson.

> He stood up. Without thinking, he leaped. Then, in a rush, he was off. Along the river's rough bank, jumping at obstacles, he ran as free as the blowing of the wind. There was no effort. No sense of being driven by his stick-thin legs or arms. He was suspended. The river's bank, the logs, grass-tussocks, trees, were running backward beneath him. It was unlike anything the boy had ever known. He could run like that for ever. Across continents, jungles, mountains, the ocean. When at last he threw himself down, panting into the earth dungy with the smell of animal and the sap of grass, he had felt no tiredness, was unaware of his thin chest's heaving. He only knew a happiness deeper and higher and wider than anything he could imagine.[16]

Relationship between Artistic and Non-Artistic Meanings. Although at first sight it may seem as if these two broad categories of aesthetic meaning are mutually exclusive this is not so. In experience they may merge, each to some extent entering the other. The intensity and quality of the experience is not necessarily reduced or enhanced by the presence or absence of the other although of course it can be.

Whereas artistic aesthetic meanings tend to arise from traditionally recognized artistic contexts to which publicly rooted concepts are consciously applied in an 'objective' way, non-artistic aesthetic meanings tend to arise in situations that are not generally recognized as artistic and therefore there is no deliberate attempt to apply concepts which are not obviously appropriate. Because of this the aesthetic meanings that are constituted, if they are expressed at all, are not nearly so dependent upon an educated and considered use of terms. When they are used they tend to be used in a more idiosyncratic, biographic and phenomenally subjective manner.

What then is suggested is that what may be described as the 'movement aesthetic', in common with the aesthetic in general, has in principle two main sources from which aesthetic meanings can be constituted. The first is found in those contexts or activities that are culturally recognized as 'artistic' i.e. fulfil the conditions of art, such as dance and mime. The second is found in that wider spectrum of life and living which, whilst in some cases recognized as containing some aesthetic elements, are normally regarded as being 'non-artistic' i.e. do not, or do not fully fulfil the conditions of art. This second or 'non-artistic' source, of course, includes not only those activities like gymnastics, skiing and diving but also a great many other 'ordinary' activities like mopping, shovelling and dusting that do not come under the rubric of sport at all.

Just, of course, as an artist in a generally recognized 'artistic context' can fail to gain aesthetic satisfaction whilst perhaps providing it for the spectator, so it is equally possible for a performer in a 'non artistic context' to gain aesthetic satisfaction whether or not what is witnessed by the spectator meets with the behavioural or conceptual criteria that is normally called 'aesthetic', but which I, following Dewey, have called 'artistic'. In the last resort those experiences which either performers or spectators constitute as aesthetically meaningful are products of their imaginative responses to situations that are 'looked for' or 'discovered'. They cannot be confined to or explicated in terms of certain types of given contexts or given types of expressive movement. Despite its being a recognized artistic enterprise and capable of being discussed in 'artistic' terms, Swan Lake at Covent Garden can result in being aesthetically meaningless for both dancers and audience. In the end aesthetic meaning is that which is constituted as such by the individual with or without the aid of conventional context or objective criteria.

Finally, it should be made clear that aesthetic meanings in movement, whether 'artistic' or 'non-artistic', are always subjective, occasionally 'peak' and sometimes existential in significance. When moments of transcendence occur they take on something of the nature of a mystical experience and have intensity, unity and ineffability.*

* See Dickman, Arthur F., 'Dehumanisation and the Mystic Experience', in Ornstein, Robert E., *The Nature of Human Consciousness* (Freeman, 1968), pp. 216–33.

Dance: A Paradigm Artistic Movement Form

With regard to what has been said of the perspectives of the performer and spectator, the notion of qualitative movement, and the nature of aesthetic meaning, I want now to discuss dance as an art form, especially as it relates to the dancer, and some aesthetic aspects of sport.

Not all forms of dance, of course, can be considered as art. Clearly many dances are directed towards ends which are not artistic. Such forms of dance whether they are categorized as being to do with fertility, initiation, war, religion, freedom, harvest or ecstasy are not our present concern. Here discussion will be confined to those forms in our Western culture which are normally conceived, presented and accepted as artistic enterprises. Most forms of theatre dance whether classical or modern would tend to fall into the ambience of art. As such they are to some extent 'framed and set apart'. Within this public and culturally shared context of mutual understandings and expectations the dancer as performer sets out to communicate artistically and the spectator to respond aesthetically to what is being presented. If the spectator is 'educated' or culturally immersed in this *haute* form of life he will tend to understand and maybe judge what he sees in terms of the concepts, techniques and standards with which he is acquainted. Thus knowing that a dance like The Three Cornered Hat is considered art, he is alerted immediately to adopt a particular attitude towards it, attunes himself to the context in which it is presented, and intentionally or unintentionally calls upon and becomes sensitized to those acculturated yet personalized ways of 'seeing' what he is looking at. Knowing then, that an activity is regarded as artistic not only affects our predisposition towards it, but calls into play a whole battery of publicly rooted concepts by means of which what we see or experience can within limits be shared. When the aesthetic perception of dance is seen in terms of art it almost inevitably arises from a common contextual background of culturally assimilated experiences and understandings.

Because of this it will be seen that dance is a paradigm instance of a physical activity from which both dancer and spectator can derive what I have called artistic aesthetic meaning. As such it tends to be 'objective' rather than 'idiosyncratic' in nature.

The Dancer as an Artistic Performer

Leaving aside the question of whether or not the dancer is an artist, since in most works of art he (or she) is following the choreographer's instructions, it can be argued that he is endeavouring to be artistic. As an art, dance 'calculates' its display of aesthetic qualities and it is the dancer who does his best to express them. What is done, difficult and technical though it may be, is intrinsic to the creation of an artistic performance. Any self-indulgence or over-statement is likely to result in distorting and weakening the very effect that is intended. The discipline of the dancer is imposed by the medium of the dance itself. Each dance develops its own unique form and structure and becomes an independent, free and separate entity at the centre of which is the embodied dancing person. What then is the artistic situation in which the dancer finds himself?

In common with other arts the dance has characteristics that distinguish it as being an art object. It deliberately sets out to evoke an aesthetic, as opposed to a utilitarian, response in the spectator. 'Its fundamental office' in the words of Phenix[17] 'is to create in the percipient a significant emotion, valuable in itself, and not merely to serve as an instrument of some other purpose.' Each dance is a unique composition, expressing its own immanent structure and as such is subject only to its own inherent demands. For both dancer and spectator each dance requires an imaginative response that is not governed or unduly influenced by what has been done or witnessed before.

The spectator should look for what the dance aesthetically entails in an open way rather than with a critical predisposition about what it ought to mean. Similarly in making judgements about a dance the spectator should be concerned with the intrinsic features it exhibits rather than with its extrinsic factors except in so far as they affect the presentation of the form.

The dance can and sometimes does stand in its own right. Usually, however, it is performed to the accompaniment of music. Certainly sound in one form or another is its chief auxiliary. Stage design, costume, and lighting are other features which can add to or detract from the dance as an artistic production. It is, however, in the dynamic elements of space, time and force that dance separates itself from the other arts for it is in the moving form of the dance that these elements are entailed, expressed and made manifest.

> What makes each dance uniquely significant is the dynamics of the form: hence the unique interplay of qualities inherent in movement as a percep-tual revelation of sheer force. . . . The dynamics of the form, are therefore created by the nature of the forces themselves, tensional qualities, and by the manner in which those forms spatialize and temporalize them-selves. . . . The qualitative inter-relationships created by movement as a revelation of sheer force create the expressive character of the dance.[18]

It is the dancer who both exemplifies and personalizes what it is to be artistically dynamic. She is both author and agent both of what is seen and felt to be dynamic.

It is in and through the qualitative movements of the embodied dancer that the world of dance as an art form differentiates itself from the everyday world of ordinary movement. The dancer as artist has not only immersed herself in conventionally shared concepts that are appropriate to art but has been trained in such important practical matters as the ability to select, abstract and expressively articulate thoughts, feelings and ideas in a kinetically symbolic manner. What is 'said' *in* dance is said in the idiom *of* dance. Technical problems to do with line, rhythm, and projection have been mastered in such a way that maximum attention is devoted to 'good' expressive form. A dancer who is an artist not only 'knows how' to do things but is thoroughly 'acquainted' in a direct and immediate way with the medium within the constraints of which he performs.

It is perhaps in the creation of illusion* that the dancer's artistry is put to the greatest test. Whether it concerns a leap that seems to hang in the air or the projection of a feeling that is symbolically objectified, the dancer is on his own. Whatever 'magic' the production manager has to aid the effect of the dance it is the dancer's 'virtual powers' that gives or does not give the illusion desired. In the last resort it is the dancer's bodily artifice that encapsulates or fails to encapsulate the passing moment in the way she artistically intends.

As a spectator I am not concerned with the dancer's conscious state or whether or not he was feeling what he symbolically expressed, be it joy or passion, but only with what I aesthetically perceive. If I discover later that what I 'saw' coincided with what the dancer intended, then communication in the strict sense of the term can be said to have taken place. In passing it is worth noting that two errors in the spectator are likely to destroy whatever aesthetic potential there is no matter what the dancer's artistry: one is the error of the ignorant; the other is the error of the learned. 'The first' writes Jessup[19] 'supposes that knowledge is superfluous, the second that knowledge is enough'. Neither position is tenable, of course, it the spectator is to be able to grasp satisfactorily what it is to have artistic aesthetic meaning. For this to occur the spectator as has

---

* According to Langer 'The primary illusion of dance is a virtual realm of Power—not actual, physically exerted power, but appearance of influence and agency created by virtual gesture.' See Langer, S. K., *Feeling and Form* (Routledge and Kegan Paul, 1967 edition), p. 175.

been suggested must be sufficiently initiated into the concepts that relate to knowledge and understanding in art and be capable of entering into a sympathetic and imaginative relationship with the art object and not look upon it simply as a form of intellectual enquiry.*

As an artist the dancer is involved in the creative process of making a dance. In order to communicate with the audience he may at first have to think of himself as an 'object' that is going to present for the audience's perception a somatic pattern of the movements envisaged (*movistructuring* within the confines of the set). Having passed through this mechanical/orientational phase he may then dance through, live out and kinaesthetically perceive what is required in the way of such factors as balance, harmony, style, rhythm and grace. In this 'form in the making' stage he is able to expand and clarify his consciousness in terms of the movements he makes (*moviceptualizing*). When the dancer gets it 'right' and feelingly knows through his kinaesthetic flow patterns that it is right and is constituted by him as being pleasurable and valuable then artistic aesthetic meaning for the artist as performer can be said to have come about. If, in addition, in the context of the dancer's artistic experience, it is existentially significant (*movisymbolic*) it can be regarded as a peak form of artistic aesthetic meaning.

In his reflected-upon lived-body, qualitatively felt artistic aesthetic experiences the dancer is able to find unity both with the dance and with himself in his instantiation of felt yet objectified form, he is literally beauty embodied—he both manifests beauty as form and at the same time feels as beautiful what he expressively manifests. As a moving centre of consciousness the dancer can be both objective about what he is doing and at the same time respond subjectively to what he is experiencing. He is able simultaneously to achieve fluidity of form and qualitatively feel it. For the dancer the achievement of form without the accompaniment of feeling is not aesthetically meaningful. It remains correct but empty, without affective content.

Artistic aesthetic meaning for the dancer does not rest wholly upon the experiential process of feeling expressive form in the kinaesthetic sense. It depends also in part upon whether or not the symbolic expression of an emotion is coincidental with the emotional state the dancer is in. If the emotion expressed is genuine and actually felt, artistic aesthetic meaning of a separate but con-

---

* See Elliot, R. K., 'The Critic and Lover of Art' in Mays, W. and Brown, S. C. (eds) *Linguistic Analysis and Phenomenology* (Macmillan, 1972).

tingently related kind is experienced. The authenticity of the emotion symbolically expressed is not always discernible by the spectator but the dancer usually is aware of whether or not it is real or counterfeit. In the symbolic expression of form then there is the possibility of two separate but related varieties of artistic aesthetic meaning. One is dependent upon kinaesthetic feeling intrinsic to it and to which the dancer can direct his attention; the other is actually experiencing the 'portrayed' emotion as it is objectified in expressive form. Strictly speaking the abstracted but not necessarily felt expression of emotion is *symbolic form*; the objectification of an emotion as it is being experienced and expressed is *embodied form*. In the latter case the emotion expressed is literally embodied in the person of the dancer.* It is an actual emotion lived out in an objectively artistic manner. To the dancer either of these two possibilities may be experienced as 'peak'. Only to the former, however, where there is a conscious and qualitatively felt kinaesthetic identification of form can the term movisymbol be applied.

Aesthetic meanings in dance are not necessarily limited to what might be described as its 'lived-out' artistically objective properties. They can be phenomenally subjective and arise not from artistically objectifying expressive form but from reacting idiosyncratically—perhaps unaccountably—to the dance experience. Thus when May Wigman gives the following description of Whirl Dance it is not an example of artistic aesthetic meaning that is being explicated so much as an instance of non-artistic aesthetic meaning that occurs in an artistic context.

> I felt as if I were witnessing an hour of birth. Now, from the whispering and murmuring, from shimmer and glimmer, the sound-turned-tone emerged in all its purity. In immaculate beauty it went its course, finding completion in unending rotation. Full, warm, and dark, it was the voice of the depth, playfully alive in all its shadings. With breath-taking urgency it grew to its full strength, bronze that sounded and sang, in whose embrace the beating of one's own blood seemed to determine the rhythm of its vibrating revolutions. The walls turned around, the ceiling turned around, and so did the floor. Which was sound, which space, which movement?[20]

* The term 'embodiment' in relation to the arts is useful but is sometimes used in an ambiguous way. It is not always clear as to whether it refers to the inherent features of an art object or to what the perceiver is able to significantly grasp on looking at an object. Here of course the term is used in its foundational sense of consciousness embodied in the dance as the dancer himself dances it. In this sense the art of dance is primordial.

Creating and Becoming in Dance

The dancer as artist both creates dance and in so doing is in a sense created by it. In composing and structuring a dance with the intention of communicating its 'content' the dancer may at first see his moving body as an 'object' to be presented as an observable reality. It is not long, however, before the dancer ceases to be the observer of his body as an instrument. As he thinkingly moves searching for novel and relevant ways of objectifying what he wants to express, he himself becomes involved by the task and affected by what he is struggling to create. In the creative process man both 'makes' and 'becomes'. The dancer is no exception. In attempting to present dance as a kinetic and objective visual pattern he consciously invests his body with form. In doing so he subjectively feels what he expresses and is himself transformed by it. By his powers of 'abstraction' and 'objectification' he transforms a series of movements into a dance and in dancing it he clarifies and articulates his own artistic consciousness. The expressive objectification of the dance is complemented by its 'impressive' effect upon the dancer. If for the spectator artistic aesthetic meaning lies predominantly in the physically objective context of the presented action, for the dancer it lies more in the lived-body biographical context of being engaged *in* the dance as agent. For both audience and dancer artistic aesthetic meaning ultimately derives not so much from a critical conceptual analysis of what is going on as from an openness to that which is given in experience. If for the audience artistic aesthetic meaning derives mostly from the *product* that is objectively witnessed, for the dancer it lies more in the *process* objectively undergone. For both what is achieved is important. It is a curious but interesting fact that for the dancer it is often in the trials and tribulations of practice and rehearsal that the most poignant moments of aesthetic satisfaction and enlightenment come.

The dancer as artist is no mere puppet. Even under the direction of the choreographer the dancer expresses her own being in motion. In dance there is the possibility to act, think, feel, relate to other people as well as to the world. In dance then is the chance to enter into and become the object that is created. When absorbed by the dance the dancer is able, rather as in play, to be taken up by what he is doing. Its peculiar spatial and temporal character and distinctive qualities of motion take on a life of their own. In dance the dancer is at one with his dancing. He both is and becomes his dancing. It involves both a departure from and a return to reality. In losing himself in the dance the dancer also finds himself. 'My dance' Fraleigh observes, 'carries me beyond myself as a projection of myself, a vision realised.'[21] In the created dance the dancer is both object and subject:

> I am my dance, my dance is me,
> I exist my dance as I exist my body[22]

In dance man feels free. He is free to choose, free to act. More than that he is free to become his capricious non-rational self. In dance there is existential possibility. The dancer as creative artist not only uses his imaginative and perceptual powers but in using them is liberated and fulfilled. The artist is driven by an inner compulsion to satisfy himself. For the dancer the dance is more than the sequential presentation of objective form. It is life itself. In dance the human spirit is made incarnate—Zarathustra and Zorba understood this well.* In the objectification of subjective states the dancer as artist *is* and experiences himself as the personification of expressive form. There is unity between what is felt and what is objectified: expression is form and form is expression. Only the dancer can aesthetically live through and take meaning from the perfect experience of matching the one with the other. It is on such moments of ecstatic accord that the existential significance of dance for the dancer depends.

> In my dance, I am more than I am and all that I am. I am free to create my world and myself[23]

In the harmonious blending of *motion* with *emotion* the dancer realizes himself as few others have the power to do. What is felt and meaningfully constituted although sometimes described in words is not reducible to words. Its meaning lies in its own mode of expression.

Aesthetic Aspects of Sport

Sport and Art

Human movement as a subject of art is almost as old as culture itself. One has only to look at the literature, sculpture and pottery of the past to find ample evidence of man's interest in sport and other physical pursuits as forms of expression. In the ancient civilizations of Egypt, Greece and Rome bodily form and bodily action are

---

* See Nietzsche's *Thus Spoke Zarathustra* (Penguin, 1969). Nikov Kazantzakis's *Zorba the Greek*, translated by Carl Wildman, (Faber and Faber, 1965).

themes that recur again and again. In Myron's *Discobolus* sculptural athleticism has perhaps never been surpassed.

In modern times both dance and sporting activities continue to be subjects of artistic inspiration. In paintings like *Tennis Players* by Braque; *The Wrestlers* by Villon; *Fencers* by Zitman, or in sculptures like *The Hammer Thrower* by Robinson and *Rugby Lineout* by Dunlop, quintessential moments of action are caught and render possible our contemplative gaze. It was only with the coming of film and television that the joys and tragedies of human sporting encounters were able to be recorded as they are enacted; and more important, that the sequential flow of the motion itself was able to be seen and replayed again at leisure. In Leni Riefenstahl's masterpiece of the 1936 Olympics, the film as an art form, was brought as close as it perhaps can be to depicting human motion as being a spectatorial source of aesthetic experience.

Just as the question of sporting action as a *subject* for Art has never been in doubt, so the question of sport *as* a form of art is. Sport, it is sometimes said, is concerned with the quest for victory whereas art is concerned with the creation of beauty. The implication is that since the end of sport is victory and not beauty it cannot count as art. But as has already been shown the issue is not as simple as that for an *inherent* element in some sport, ice figure-skating for example, is the creation of beauty. The question of whether some sports fulfil the conditions of art is an open one.*

Interesting and central though the relation of Art to Sport is in looking at movement as a source of aesthetic experience it will be seen that it is but a part of the story, for human movement is not commensurate with sport nor can the aesthetic be adequately discussed in terms of art. The task then here is not to debate whether and under what circumstances some sports can be considered art—this is a somewhat arbitrary and pointless exercise. Rather it is to look at sport and see in what ways it is, or can be, a source of aesthetic experience. If, as will be the case, reference is made to art discussion will by no means be confined to it.

The Nature of Sport
The concept of sport is greater than that which is held in common by its different instances. It defies simple definition and embraces many activities not all of which are characterized by the same features. Some sports are marked by their dependence on machines, others upon balls, others still upon forms of equipment without which it

* A useful article in connection with this is Ward, P. M., 'Sport and the Instructional Theory of Art', Journ. of Human Movement Studies, No. 3, 1977, pp. 73–81.

would be impossible to proceed. Sport is a collective term and today embraces a large number of disparate activities. It includes motor-racing, water polo and weight-lifting, no less than 'field games' such as rugby, cricket and hockey or 'field pastimes' such as hunting, shooting and fishing. So far as sporting activities can be identified at all they seem to be associated in varying degrees with such factors as whole-bodied exertion, competition, the employment of skill, uncertainty of outcome and some element of danger. Most sports too, are rule-bound, ritualistic and institutionalized. They are in a word miniature 'forms of life' that put a premium on physical prowess and frequently also on speed, strength and stamina. Although some sports are like others in a number of respects—tennis, squash, and racquets, for example—they each have their own distinctive ways of proceeding; their own strategies and tactics. If any one phrase can usefully be applied to the divers and yet related series of activities that go by the name of sport it is probably that of 'family resemblances'.*

If sport is held together at all by something 'common' it surely lies in the notion of sportsmanship. For many, *sportsmanship* is an inbuilt element of the concept of sport. Keating[24], for example, has written of sportsmanship as a moral category and associates it with such moral virtues as courage, courtesy and magnanimity. Certainly for some participants (especially those maybe who were educated in an English Public School ethos) to engage *in* sport entails *being* a sport. It invokes the injunction to act in a particular way. This means more than paying a deferential lip service to the legal code of 'fair play'. It involves the living out of a moral dynamic based upon the principles of equality and justice that becomes a constituent and characteristic part of the action. Clearly not all sporting encounters are so conducted. Sometimes the very opposite is true; that the cheat and the spoilsport prevail. When this occurs one dimension of the nature of sport gets damaged and 'bad faith' ensues. 'Good' sport, by contrast, is not destructive of mutual respect and goodwill: rather, it is enhanced. In the pursuit of contest and effort the true sportsman is thankful to his opponent for the giving of his best in a climate of shared understanding and brotherhood.

Too much emphasis upon analysing the features by which a sport can be identified can lead to a neglect not only of its moral but also of its psychological elements. Originally sport meant to find amuse-

---

* By this phrase Wittgenstein wanted to combat the traditional view that because different phenomena are called by the same name there is necessarily a quality or set of qualities which is common to them all. See Wittgenstein's *Philosophical Investigations* (O.U.P. 1953), p. 31e.

ment, diversion, fun or pleasure, particularly in games and play but with the coming of professionalism and commercialism it became a more serious business.* The nature of sport, however, cannot be adequately grasped if attention is confined to an examination of the observable features of its separate instances. The *raison d'être* of a sport lies not in its outward characteristics and procedures so much as in the needs, cravings and satisfactions of those who participate in it. Although those who engage in competitive sport agree to abide by the rules and try to win, it should not be thought that these 'definitional features' are in any way equivalent to or commensurate with the reasons and motivations, if they are known at all, as to *why* people take part. The logical characteristics of a sport in other words do not necessarily offer an *explanation* of why people want to participate in it. The fact that a person tries to win, for example, when playing a game in no way suggests that to *win* is his purpose, least of all his *chief* purpose, in playing it. For many the attempt to win is but a *procedural feature* of competing.

Some people take part in sport not *in order to win per se* but because in taking part they find value and satisfaction in its outcomes. This can take the form of such dimensions as social experience, excitement, catharsis or health and fitness or a combination of them. Some people, it is worth recording, take part predominantly because of the aesthetic experience it offers.† The point then is that although the attempt to win is a necessary procedural feature for engaging in sport this by no means is the same as saying that winning is *the* reason why people engage in it.‡

Although sport is not play it is doubtful if 'modern' sport would have come into existence let alone survived unless something of the spirit of play were encapsulated by it. Certainly when fun and spontaneity cease to be a part of sport it can become a dull and serious business. This is why it is the amateur rather than the professional who is the guardian of sport, for it is the amateur, the lover of what he does that keeps the nature of sport alive. The amateur participates because he takes pleasure in doing so, not because he sees it as a means of earning a livelihood.§

---

* See Huizinga, J. *Homo Ludens* (Paladin, 1970), Chapter 12.

† See, for example, Kenyon, G. S. 'A Conceptual Model for Characterising Physical Activity' in Loy, J. W. and Kenyon, G. S., *Sport, Culture and Society* (Macmillan, 1969), pp. 71–81.

‡ In his article 'Games, Winning and Education', C. Bailey makes this mistake.

§ See Cambridge Journal of Education, Vol. 5, No. 1, Lent term, 1975, pp. 40–50. It is not suggested, of course, that professionals don't enjoy what they do; rather that they are not in sport *solely* for the pleasure it affords.

Although play is not sport it is doubtful if the notion of 'good' sport can be grasped without reference to it. Somehow in the *attitude* to life that is characteristic of play there is an important message for sport. It is possible to identify the conceptual features of sport without reference to play yet without its spirit it remains for the participant deficient. Play then is a vital but gratuitous element in sport. Without it sport would not be all that it can be. Unless the spirit of play is present in sport from time to time much that is done in its name would be lack-lustre and empty of exuberance and joy.

Just as play can be a source of pleasure in sport so too can its aesthetic aspects.* These are not always and invariably present but like the spirit of play, come and go. The hammer thrower can sometimes *feel* the patterned motions of his skilled gyrations no less than the onlooker can admire the control, fluency, poise and balance of their execution. For athlete and spectator alike sport as a family of physical activities offers a whole spectrum of aesthetic possibilities. Although in principle it would be possible to consider from the aesthetic point of view each sport separately this will not be attempted. Instead only a few of the more central aspects of sport will be called upon to illustrate the thesis that sport is an important branch of human movement and is, together with dance, a potentially rich source of aesthetic experience for both performer and spectator.

The Aesthetic Perception of Sport
It is generally the case that *sport qua sport*, even though some of its instances have high 'artistic' content as a part of their purpose, is not recognized as art. Yet despite this there is little doubt that for some people sport is beautiful. In his Ode to Sport, for example, Coubertin exclaims

> O sport you are beauty! You are the architect of this house, the human body, which may become abject or sublime, according as to whether it is defiled by base passions or cherished with wholesome endeavour. There can be no beauty without poise and proportion and you are the incomparable master of both, for you create harmony, you fill movement with rhythm, you make strength gracious, and you lend power to supple things.[25]

Similarly, Maheu sees sport as a creator of beauty. 'In the action and rhythm which testify to mastery of space and time, sport becomes akin to the arts which create beauty.'[26] The rhythm and

---

* The two, of course, are not unrelated. See, for example, Marcuse, H., 'Eros and Civilisation' (Abacus, 1972), pp. 127–41.

timing of an athlete's movements, he maintains, 'are not to be differentiated from the finest ballet, the most splendid passage of prose or verse, the most glorious lines in architecture'. The beauty of sport he claims is immanent in the act which creates it: and unless filmed is inseparable from the fleeting moment. In this it differs from the 'frozen' arts of painting and literature.

Despite such panegyric comments about sport by its lovers, most writers on aesthetics maintain that whatever aesthetic content there is in sport, it is parasitic upon its main purpose which is to win. This may be true of some sport, especially field games perhaps, as Reid* points out, but it is not true of *all* sports. In ice figure-skating, for example, the participants' purpose cannot be considered in isolation from the means of achievement. The 'calculated' aesthetic display in *this* sport, in other words, is an inherent part of its purpose and not just an incidental and parasitic matter.

The same is true of gymnastics:

A perfect exercise with a maximum rating is one that is presented with *elegance, ease, precision* and in a *style* and *rhythm* well adapted to the nature of the *aesthetic* performance with no faults in execution. The faults in execution or style are penalized by a deduction in points or fraction of points according to the following directions:
Defects in elegance in general. An exercise, although executed without fault, but presented in a rhythm *too quick* or *too slow*, or with an *ill-proportioned* display of force, counts less than a perfect exercise as described ...[27]

Perhaps enough has been said to suggest that it is something of an unfounded generalization to assert, as some have done without qualification, that the artistic in sport is but a 'gratuitous by-product'.

If there are two statements concerning the relationship between sport and art, which are separate but connected and which need to be carefully examined, they are these: first, that competition *per se* debars an activity from being art; and second, that in sport victory always takes precedence over beauty. It is not my task or intention here to discuss either of them fully. It is nevertheless perhaps worth saying in passing that the first statement seems very dubious—art does not cease to be art when some competitors are adjudged to be better than others at such events as music, drama, and literary

* Reid, L. A., for example, writes that it would appear that 'the aesthetic enjoyment is parasitic upon the central games-purposes of the game'. See his article 'Sport, the Aesthetic and Art' in the British Journal of Educational Studies, Vol. 18, No. 3, 1970, p. 254.

festivals. The second statement is much more difficult. On the face of it it would appear that until an activity called sport is able to demonstrate that the means and end of its logical features are one and the same the statement must remain true.

Interesting though the relation between sport and art is my purpose here is not to debate whether *a* sport can ever be considered art. Rather it is to suggest that a sport can normally be looked upon in an artistic way. Regardless of whether or not a sport is art it can be viewed, given the right frame of mind, *as if* it were. This entails calling upon the concepts appropriate to art and applying them to a sport even when there is no special 'invitation' to do so by virtue of its having recognized artistic content that is inherent in its purpose. Thus the spectator need not look at what he is witnessing from the point of view of winning or losing, or at a game in terms of its rules, strategies or utilitarian outcomes. Instead he can if he so chooses view it in an artistic way. As Elliott observes

If we wish to show that sport has aesthetic values comparable with those of art, then I think the qualities to be stressed, in the context of opposition, are swiftness, grace, fluency, rhythm and perceived vitality—the qualities which in various combinations constitute beauty. In soccer, beauty appears typically in a fluent and rhythmic passing movement, provided that it also possesses a sense of urgency; and when a player breasts the ball to his feet and sweeps it away as if in a single fluent moment, provided that his pass does not go astray; and when the ball is centred across the goalmouth and a player makes a running leap to head the ball into the net, minimally deflecting it and not seeming to reduce its velocity. In all these cases there is not merely skill but perceived fluency and vitality, and all possess, in addition, an aesthetically satisfying geometrical form or pattern. In the last case, for example, we are conscious of the lines of movement of the ball and player, and their resultant, the line of the ball's movement into the net.[28]

The aesthetic perception of a sport, in common with play, requires that the percipient uses his imagination. Only by doing so will he be able to bring about a suspension of the ordinary and the practical. As with the play spirit in sport the aesthetic perception of such activities as cricket, skiing or swimming, even when sought after, cannot be guaranteed. When it comes, whether by design or fortuitous occurrence, it comes like a shaft of sunlight through a cloud-ridden sky. It has the power, no matter how brief its span, to transform the action and reveal what is witnessed as something beautiful. In the criss-cross patterning of a good three-quarter movement; in the rhythmic yet balanced power of a disciplined eight; in the mesmeric attraction of a shuttlecock as it is angled, smashed and delicately caressed back and forth over the net in an amazing series of configurational shapes and parabolic curves, there is a kind of dynamic and fluent beauty.

Not all forms of aesthetic experience to do with a sport derive from the aesthetic perception of its intrinsic features. Sometimes, as suggested earlier (page 135), it is just contingently related. Thus a mountaineer may find great pleasure in the conscious use of his senses by breathing in clean air, feeling the freshness of the wind on his cheeks, and in watching the growing shadows of surrounding peaks and trees as they are bathed in the red glow of an evening sunset. The skier may find satisfaction in putting his imprint upon a sloping stretch of unmarked snow. The noviciate ski jumper may, at take off, find himself to be in a state of voluptuous but never-to-be-forgotten panic. The potholer may stand in spellbound wonder at the entrance to a newly discovered and unspoilt cavern. On such occasions consciousness can be expanded and the quality of life transformed.

The Skilful. It does not follow that because a sporting action is skilful it is *necessarily* aesthetic. This holds true of all movement activities whether or not artistic expression is an inbuilt part of their purpose. Just as it should not be *presupposed* that because an activity is recognized to be 'artistic' in some way, that its skills are inevitably going to be perceived aesthetically so it should not be *presupposed* either that because a sport is 'non-artistic' its skills are not open to being aesthetically perceived. What cannot be *'presupposed'*, however, in no way suggests that skills, whether associated with 'artistic' or 'non artistic' activities, are unable to be aesthetically perceived. On the contrary they can be and often are. The rhythmical grace, majesty and control of Margaret Court's tennis serve is or can be no less aesthetically appreciated than the consummate ease and mastery of line with which John Curry in figure-skating does a double axle jump. The point then is that skills in sport, in common with skills in general, can be perceived aesthetically, independently and in isolation, if necessary, from the activity from which they come.

Stolnitz, in touching upon the matter of skills in relation to artistic values and aesthetic experiences, makes the following pertinent comment:

> Outside the arts, there is a large class of actions, appropriately described as skilful, which, when thus described, has good claim to be counted

aesthetic. These actions performed deftly, economically and adroitly, and therefore moving surely toward their goal, free from the gratuitous effort that would retard or impede attainment of it. Such conversational rejoinder, the outfielder's catch, the movements of the sandwich maker in the cafeteria are engaging even if we are indifferent, possibly hostile, to the goals the agent thereby attains.[29]

What Stolnitz is maintaining here is first, that aesthetic experience of skills is not confined to the arts and second, that skills, including sporting ones can be experienced in terms of themselves and that an aesthetic appreciation of them can take place regardless of whether or not the purpose of the activity is one of which the percipient approves.

Stolnitz's comments, whilst written perhaps with the spectator in mind, are no less true of the performer. Although it would be possible to go on and discuss the distinctive nature of skills in different sporting activities from the aesthetic point of view for both spectator and performer I shall confine myself to some general points in connection with the standpoint of the latter.

It can perhaps be agreed that the skills of a sport are important not only for distinguishing it from other sports but more particularly for being able to engage in it successfully. Just as soccer requires an ability to dribble, trap and pass; and tennis the ability to serve, volley, drop shot and lob, so other sports have their distinctive and necessary skills. Now although these can be appreciated by the spectator in a *detached* way for their temporal, complex or expressive qualities, they have to be learned by the performer in a participant acquaintance way. In learning *how* to do them he experiences them in terms of the direct demands they put upon him as a person. In the same way that the dancer as artist is able to attend to and enjoy the kinaesthetic flow patterns by which he experiences the expression of form so the skill-equipped sportsman is able to kinaesthetically enjoy the skills and techniques that he has mastered. It is because a skill *is* mastered and under control that he is able to deliberately dwell upon it, if he so chooses, as an intentional aesthetic object. The aesthetic pleasure that can derive from a mastered sport's skill by attending to its identifiable but fluid gestalts of feeling is of course intrinsic to and logically dependent upon the motions the performer as agent makes. As a master of his chosen sport the first-class sportsman is able both to utilize his skills when required and, if he wishes, to attentively dwell upon them as sources of kinaesthetic pleasure. The sportsman's skills of course are primarily acquired for their use in competition and when actually competing it is unlikely that he will choose to dwell upon their kinaesthetic feel since for much of the time his attention will be taken up with 'outer' events and situations that are constantly changing and need to be dealt with. This is especially so in the case of 'open' skills where the performer must adjust his actions according to unpredictable environmental circumstances. The hockey player, for example, whether in attack or defence, must always be attentive to the 'field of play' anticipating, deciding and reacting all the time to unforeseeable factors. Skills in open contests, such as games, have to be adjusted and modified in response to the exigent need of the fleeting moment. Invariably there is something in the performer's perceptual field that compels his attention 'outwards' and away from an 'inward' dwelling upon the motions that he is making. With 'closed' skills on the other hand where what is performed is not nearly so dependent upon the external cues, the sportsman may find within limits that the more he attends to the familiarity of his established and successful kinaesthetic flow patterns the more successful he will be. The shot putter, for example, has to perform within the confines of the circle. There is not nearly the same call upon him to be attentive to external considerations and those that it would pay him to take notice of, such as the wind and the weather, can be taken into account before the performance starts. The 'closed' skill performer will often find it helpful to concentrate on the discrete motions of the movement itself. In learning them he will have learned *how* to do them. They will in other words be technically correct. This being so he will also have had the opportunity to acquaint himself with the experience of his own skilled motions by attending to them in terms of the differentiable kinaesthetic feelings they generate. It is by a return to the familiarity of these 'inner' but consciously felt flow patterns that the competitor is often best able to help himself. The competitive golfer quickly learns that what he wants is more likely to be forthcoming by attending to the reproduction of the easy, relaxed 'feeling' of the swing than by being preoccupied in the course of it by events or happenings that are extraneous to it. A bad last shot, an opponent's good score, a feeling of self-consciousness are just some of the things that can adversely affect the consummacy of the golfer's swing.

Outside of competitive situations, of course, sport skills, whether 'open' or 'closed' can more easily be, and often are, enjoyed in a kinaesthetically pleasurable way. In this lies their intrinsic value. They are returned to and practised not only because of hoped for improvement in terms of effectiveness but because aesthetic experience is found in the lived-body motions of their performance. What the *spectator* may appreciate as rhythm in the performer the *performer* himself enjoys as the perceptual harmony of his kinaesthetic feelings. For the performer a sports skill is a particular type of athletic *oeuvre* which has its own complex set of sensitively felt qualities. In this respect it is not unlike the experience of playing a distinctive and well loved melody in music or returning to look at a particularly appealing colour composition in art. Curl clearly had something of this sort in mind when he wrote:

> The highly skilled performer becomes the possessor of a new and expanded range of perceptions, new perceptions of his own movements and powers. . . . His total experience as a skilled performer has a qualitative range and dimensions denied to the unskilled—and much of this qualitative experience is aesthetically perceived and grasped.[30]

Skills in sport arise from particular 'frames of reference'. It is by these frames or separate sports that skills are recognized by the spectator and practised by the performer. In sport, skills occur in the context of rules and an agreed manner of proceeding. Whereas, however, for the spectator it is possible for them to be aesthetically appreciated, in a relatively detached, even perhaps contemplative way, for the performer involved in the doing of them this is a very much more difficult matter. Although it is theoretically possible for him to appreciate the aesthetic qualities objectively entailed in his own movements by looking at them in a mirror-image like manner, it is more natural for him to gain aesthetic satisfaction by attending to the qualitative feelings that are immanent in the motions as they are being made. When they are reflected upon as they occur, rather than retrospectively looked back upon after they have stopped, they can be said to be intrinsic to and embodied in the skill as it is performed. It is by attending to the familiarized kinaesthetic patterns of his own skilled actions that the agent as performer can, and often does, derive aesthetic satisfaction. For the performer skilled movements can be not only a source of aesthetic experience which can be transiently enjoyed but can also become constituted entities of meaning which can be appreciated and valued in retrospect.

The Dramatic. Sport is not drama. In the reality of struggle and contest there is no *mimesis*. Although the contrived and the spurious—like those wrestling matches that sometimes occur on television to entertain us—appear under the guise of sport, they are not examples of sport at all in any authentic sense. They are sham occasions and mock at the notions of effort and contest that are at the heart of genuine sport. To say, however, that sport is not drama in no way suggests that it cannot be dramatic or spectacular. On the contrary, what could be more dramatic than the manner of the win of Russia over the United States in the closing seconds of the Olympic Basketball final of 1972? Similarly, who having witnessed the skiing achievements of Jean Claude Killy in the 1968 Winter Olympics would deny that they were spectacular? On neither occasion, however, did the performers *set out* to dramatize or spectacularize. Rather what occurred was fortuitous and not planned for in advance. The basketball players did not intentionally bring about dramatic tensions as actors might in a production of King Lear, any more than Killy was aiming to be impressive as a drum-major is at the head of a military parade. What arose then arose naturally and was not staged or rehearsed; nor did it involve the impersonation of anybody else.

Although sport is not drama it can nonetheless be looked upon by the disinterested spectator *as if* it were. A spectator might look upon the arena as a theatre; regard the players as actors; and the run of play, with its patterned exchanges, as the plot. Indeed it is along these lines that Keenan[31] has attempted to show that Aristotle's model of dramatic tragedy has implications for the way in which sport as athletic contest can be viewed.

Interesting and possible though it is, however, to look upon sport as if it were drama and in doing so gain something in the process, I want to suggest that it is by being involved in an 'ordinary' way that aesthetic experience in sport is perhaps more poignantly realized. If in rugby the disinterested spectator is able to be *contemplatively appreciative* of the full-back's judgement in catching, side-stepping and kicking the ball into a safe touch in the face of charging forwards, the 'fan' by contrast will first *feel* the threat of a breakthrough, then *relief* at its passing. The spectator may see *a* full-back who plays his part well. The fan will see a saviour who has thwarted an enemy attack. The disinterested spectator is able to maintain 'psychical distance' and abstract from the episode, the 'fan' by contrast lives through the action and breathes a sigh of deliverance.

But what of the full-back himself? It is he who has to attack and be attacked. It is he who has 'to do or die'. As a one-time full-back I remember well the full-out run for the line, the satisfaction of a well-timed pass, the joy of a try scored. In defence I often felt the menace of marauding forwards. Sometimes by kicking or jinking it was possible to avoid them. At others, however, it was necessary to be caught in order to make play secure. At such times their savagery was alarming. It was as if they had gone wild and nothing mattered but the possession of the ball. If you were unable to escape from their clutches you would be thrown to the ground, fought over, trampled upon, pulled and kicked until miraculously it would suddenly end and like hounds they would turn and search for prey elsewhere. All the time whilst beneath these mauls there was the terrible weight of their bodies to bear and the helpless fear that an arm or leg might snap.

Such aspects of play, of course, are real enough; danger is present and felt to be so. Yet paradoxically in the reality of what transpires there is often an element of 'inner' drama going on. In *being* a full-back one is also conscious that one is playing in the *role* of full-back. As a player occupying this position one attempts to live up to the skills and attributes associated with it. In addition to being able to 'read play', run swiftly, catch reliably, and kick accurately other qualities are demanded. These include keeping a level head under pressure, being resolute in making tackles and having the ability to perceive when to join in an attacking three-quarter movement effectively. The full-back, in common with other players in the team, feels himself to be representative of a particular category of player and therefore wants to play well in accordance with this category. If in a match he is able to meet the requirements of 'good' full-back play considerable satisfaction is likely to follow. He knows he has *performed* well.

In many sports there is often a craftsmanlike pride in doing properly what has to be done especially when the circumstances are difficult or dangerous. The reality of role then to the performer involves him in a kind of 'inner' or 'private' drama whereby he tries to act out not only what others expect of him in an ascribed sense but more personally what he expects of himself. It is perhaps best described as a form of 'symbolic interaction' and is capable of providing its own form of aesthetic experience. A mountaineer, for example, may carry with him an ideal of what a mountaineer should be. He is concerned perhaps not only with *what* he achieves but with the *manner* of it. Getting to the summit is one thing but to get there in an approved of way is another. Arriving by an already charted and undemanding route is not enough. The unwritten part of what it is to be a mountaineer entails more than this. It involves entering into a kind of chivalric order which is marked by self-imposed hardships and challenges. Hence what matters and what can be a source of gratification to him is if he is able occasionally to be a mountaineer in a way that both he and his fellow mountaineers would extol. It is the living out of a particular order of perfection. Unless the mountaineer on reaching the summit feels that he has been extended and that his techniques, nerve, strength, fortitude and stamina have been put to the test it is unlikely that he will have much sense of achievement. The true mountaineer is not deluded by arrogance or conceit. There is no *hubris*. Rather he knows that if there is conquest at all it is of himself, not of the mountain. In the mastery of self there is reward enough.

It has been argued that although sport is not *mimesis* there is often within sport a kind of acting going on as the performer attempts literally to bring to life the role that he has created for himself. In this respect the sportsman in whichever role he has chosen to cast himself is in many ways no different from the doctor or the dentist or other players who also have roles to play in the ordinary world. The role of the sportsman, however, differs from most others in that it involves physical prowess, contest and risk. In the psycho-symbolic drama of performance there is often too, a deliberate seeking out of the quixotic and the exciting. The appeal of sport for many is that in contrast to most areas of existence it allows life to be lived more extravagantly and with a greater degree of intensity. Sport demands of the sportsman that he put himself to the test and find out whether his dreams can be turned into reality. Dignity, composure, courage and gallantry remain fantasies until they are willed into becoming actual and living events. The abstract can be made concrete. *Thoughts* of heroism can be transformed into *acts* of heroism. Even a tragic event can be idealized. In sport, as in drama, the boundaries between the real and the imagined are not always that distinct. Donald Campbell was both a tragic hero and sportsman.* He both knew that conditions on Coniston Water in 1967 for his attempt on the world's water speed record were ominous and fateful yet he also knew that the risk had to be taken. The attempt had to go on. He died knowing that for him what he did had to be done. The racing driver, the climber, the bob-sledder all know, just as soldiers come to know, that only in the shadow of death can life be fully known. High risk sportsmen know, sometimes almost as a matter of relish, that they do not always live to fight another day. They know in their

* See for example his comments in Scorecard 1967, p. 7.
'You boys (newspaper reporters) will see me carried away in a box one of these days. That's what you're all really here for.'
Again:
'There are things in life you must do—it's darned difficult to get inside yourself and find out why. All you know is that there is a fire burning inside.'

hearts that 'All life is coloured by the expectation of impending death.'[32]

If any one artistic yet symbolic performance brings together the things about which we have been talking it is perhaps that of the bullfight. Although many would contend that bullfighting is not a sport it does exemplify much of that which goes on in sport.* Here reality comes close to being a ritualistic drama. Whatever one's *moral* attitude to it may be there is no doubt about its *aesthetic* potential. In the *Teatro des Tauros* the performance is divided into three acts—the trial, the sentencing and the execution. In the bull-ring the matador with the aid of an accompanying cast symbolizes man living in scorn of death. The matador both dramatizes and yet lives out in reality with all its possible consequences the role that he has chosen to play. As Lea observes, the bullfight 'is the only art in which the artist deals actual death and risks actual death that gives the art its particular power....'[34] The matador in his encounter with the bull (a symbol of power and courage) is expected to conform to the accepted conventions showing not only knowledge of the tradition but style and grace in posture and movement. Even when danger is most threatening the artistic integrity of the performance must be maintained. Not to do so would not only offend his own pride but be judged a poor performance by the spectators. On this last point Hemingway writes:

> The matador must perform a series of classic passes before he kills if the bull is still able to charge. In these passes the bull must pass the body of the matador within hooking range of the horn. The closer the bull passes the man at the man's invitation and direction the greater the thrill the spectator receives.[35]

---

* It is a moot point whether or not bullfighting is a sport. One at first is not inclined to regard it as such yet it seems to fulfil most criteria. The one, however, which I think must ultimately lead to its exclusion, is that its proponents do not actively subscribe to the notion of 'sportsmanship'. Another objection which is based upon its lack of 'contest' with other people does not in my view exclude it. On this last point Hemingway has this to say:

Bullfighting is worthless without rivalry. But with two great bullfighters it becomes a deadly rivalry. Because when one does something, and can do it regularly, that no one else can do and it is not a trick but a deadly dangerous performance only made possible by perfect nerves, judgement, courage and art and this one increases its deadliness steadily, then the other, if he has any temporary failure of nerves or of judgement, will be gravely wounded or killed if he tries to equal or surpass it. He will have to resort to tricks and when the public learns to tell the tricks from the true things he will be beaten in the rivalry and he will be very lucky if he is still alive or in business.

See Hemingway, E., 'The Dangerous Summer', *Life*, 5 September 1960, pp. 91–2.

Elsewhere Hemingway comments:

> Bullfighting is the only art in which the artist is in danger of death and in which the degree of brilliance in the performance is *left to the fighter's honour*.[36]*

It is important to understand that the matador in Latin society, as to a lesser extent the athlete, the mountaineer and the racing driver is in ours, is a symbol of masculinity. In the bullring a matador's masculinity is bound up with his honour. In his confrontation with the bull he must not only demonstrate probity and courage but live them out in himself as a matter of pride and self-respect—just perhaps as Donald Campbell did and no doubt nameless others in sport have done.

What is at stake in sport as symbolic interaction is not always clear or easy to articulate. Again, Hemingway in connection with the bullfight recognizes this:

> Any man could face death but to be committed to bring it as close as . . . possible while performing certain classic movements and do this again and again and then deal it out with a sword to an animal weighing half a ton, which you love, is more complicated than just facing death.[37]

Whatever import a performance has for a matador or a sportsman it is clear that the *manner* of what he does and *his own feeling towards it* are no less important than its doing. Unless what he does is satisfying to himself it may not be regarded by him as an achievement at all no matter how impressed the spectators may be. In all forms of sport at one time or another as in the bullfight there is a 'moment of truth'. Either the part one has chosen is lived out to the full and if necessary to the death, or, there is withdrawal and compromise. Herein for the performer lies the true drama of sport. Although it is enacted in public, the characterization and playing of his part is judged ultimately by himself. Only the performer knows the difficulties, the joys, the anguish, the tragedies that are experienced by having and attempting to match up to a personalized ideal in the reality that is sport, a reality that brings the sportsman face to face with himself as well as with the world.

The Good Contest. It would be a mistake to think that fulfilment in sport comes only with victory. Victory can be 'hollow' just as some defeats can be 'glorious'. What matters more to the true sportsman

---

* My italicization.

is not so much who wins or loses as the manner and nature of the struggle. Whereas the disinterested spectator may derive enjoyment by looking at a game in terms of its configurational movement pattern, its cohesiveness and balance between teams, or the deftness and style of its individual players, the contestant is more taken up by the activity itself as he experiences it from the 'inside'.

In speaking of what I shall call the 'good contest' I am not then concerned with spectatorial criticism. Nor am I concerned with that type of confrontation where 'to win' is sometimes characterized by its kill-joy, bare-faced brutishness. Rather I shall be concerned with some of its uplifting elements as experienced by the involved participant.

One aspect of the good contest is best illustrated perhaps by what Metheny has referred to as 'the good strife'. She writes of it as follows:

> In 'the good strife' men treat each other as partners in a common enterprise; in 'the bad strife' they treat each other as animals or things. . . . The concept of 'the good strife' is implicit in the word competition, as derived from cum and petere—literally to strive with rather than against. The word contest has similar implications, being derived from con and testare—to testify with another rather than against him. The concept of 'the bad strife' is implicit in the idea of 'beating the opponent' as distinguished from 'winning the contest'.[38]

The 'good strife', although moral, is not entered into *in order* to be moral. Rather the good strife is an exemplification of what it is *to be* moral. In the midst of struggle there is always present a proper respect and concern to the other, a tacit acceptance that in giving one's best there is no malice. D. H. Lawrence[39] touches upon this precious if intangible form of relationship in his book *Women in Love* when the two friends, Birkin and Gerald, strip naked and wrestle 'fullbloodedly' in front of the fire. After it their friendship was enhanced and each was filled with a contented 'oneness'. Regardless of its psycho-sexual overtones it was an instance of the 'good strife'. Neither had been destroyed, each had been edified. Each was grateful to the other, for each in striving with the other had fulfilled himself.

A second aspect of the 'good contest' is that of the generation and release of enjoyable tension. Sometimes, of course, tension can amount to stress and be painful and debilitating. In the 'good contest', however, the ebb and flow of tensions is such that it is excitatory and pleasurable. The whole organism is suffused with energy and expectation. The contestant feels prepared, vital and ready to be tested. He wants to realize himself in effort and achievement.

In a sense this tensional aspect of the 'good contest' starts before the contestants meet. The psycho-physical experience of the 'warm up' or the 'anticipatory stage' is in itself a rewarding kind of ritual. There is an art regardless of what follows in bringing oneself into a pitch of readiness. Some contestants know how to do this and take pride in being able to present themselves in a state of 'set to go'. The 'engagement phase' is the contest itself. Each sport provides its own framework for the control, arousal and easement of tension. Its very rules and procedures to some extent determine what is experienced. The whole cycle of tension/release in tennis, for example, where the game is comprised of 'points', 'games' and 'sets' is very much more frequent than say in track cycle racing where it is largely focused on 'the break' for the finish. Each sport then because of its unique characteristics provides the competitor with distinctive opportunities for tensional experience. For many these structured excitatory rhythms become a part of a contest's intrinsic enjoyment. In this respect the 'good contest' is not unlike a kind of sexual encounter where a mounting of tension is followed by its pleasurable discharge. The cycle of tension/release can be regular or intermittent, mild or intense, sustained or short-lived but without this 'awakening' flow of psychosomatic energy the experience of a contest can be colourless and dull. When by contrast the 'good contest' is over and equilibrium is restored its 'euphoric phase' is entered into. Here the contestant feels both satisfied and spent.

Another feature of the 'good contest' is that it shall allow the contestants to exemplify the features and skills that are characteristic of that sport of which it is an instance. Although this may be of particular significance to the spectator the contestant too is affected by what he does and is permitted to perform. In squash, for example, it is unlikely that a contestant would feel the game to be a 'good one' in any aesthetic sense if the game were reduced to an infinite series of lobs.

The struggle and excitement may not be less real but the satisfaction that comes through using the court in a variety of ways would be lacking. In a sport like squash the 'good contest' is to some extent bound up with the notion of the 'well-played game'. Again its intrinsic interest lies in not so much who wins or loses but the manner in which the game is played. This applies as much to the explorations of its characteristic skills and strategies as to the way in which it is conducted. A squash match like other contests in sport is an instance of a particular type of human activity. It has its own art-form or *genre* as it were, and unless this dimension of play is entered into and profitably explored one aspect of the 'good contest' may never be fully discovered. When it has been, to have it denied or frustrated by negative or inexpert play detracts from the game's aesthetic potential and leaves the contestant in this respect unfulfilled.

It has been argued that the 'good contest' in sport involves three separate but interrelated aspects—the good strife, the creation and discharge of enjoyable tension and the aesthetic living out of the skills and strategies. It will be appreciated that the 'good contest' may not arise if the contestants or teams are not evenly matched or if there is ill-will or a feeling of 'bad faith' before the encounter takes place. Sometimes, of course, it is only after the contest is under way that its qualitative potential develops and is experienced. Even then there is no guarantee as to how long it will last. It remains always in balance. Cheating, fouling, underhand ploys, distraction, boredom as well as a temporary inability to perform skilfully are all likely to prove disruptive of the 'good contest'. With some contestants the threat of danger is likely to bring it to an end. With others, however, it is the very presence of risk and uncertainty that somehow adds thrill and exhilaration to the occasion.*

Although the good contest has been discussed as if it were a bringing together of differing aspects it is experienced as a unitary 'happening' into which one is sometimes privileged to enter. The experience of the good contest is 'good' because it is upheld by the performer as both fine and beautiful. It is lifted above ordinary experiences because it is absorbing, actualizing, ennobling and fulfilling. The 'good contest' has its own dynamic structure. It moves forward under its own momentum and does so in such a gripping and enthralling way that all else is forgotten. The 'good contest' can be thought of as an uplifting form of sporting experience, the full import of which is not registered until after it is over. It derives from the institutionalization of a human activity but transcends any form of its logically stateable purpose. For the contestant the worth of the 'good contest' lies in the intrinsic satisfaction it provides. The qualitative *process* of engagement comes to be held as more important than the extrinsic aim of victory. To participate in the 'good contest' is valuable in itself, and from the aesthetic point of view more meaningful than its 'objective' result.

---

* It is of interest that Jean Claude Killy on giving up competitive skiing took to the 'high-risk' sports of bullfighting, skydiving, car and motor cycle racing.

6. Education, Movement and the Curriculum

The Place of Movement in a Curriculum of General Education

The major concern in writing this book has been with an exploration of the concept of movement, especially that dimension of it which is to do with the person as agent engaged *in* movement. It is the task now to say something about movement in relation to education and in particular say something about its place in the curriculum. Before doing this, however, a preliminary comment needs to be made in order to understand in general terms what follows.

Underlying any serious attempt to characterize what education is or what should go into the curriculum are two fundamental questions: 'What is it to be a person?' and, 'How can what is being suggested help the person to actualize himself along lines that are in keeping with the good life?' Any programme of curricula activities is likely to founder, no matter how impressive its superstructure, unless it can provide satisfactory answers to these questions. It will be appreciated, for example, that the person who is conceived 'dualistically' as opposed to 'holistically' is likely to affect the very aims and content of the educational enterprise—separating, distorting, emphasizing, ignoring as the case may be. Many intellectualistically biased forms of education are not only based upon dualistic assumptions, even if they are not always acknowledged, but have difficulty in seeing that the good life is made up of more than the pursuit of truth. What then is needed in education and curriculum planning if persons are to fulfil themselves and change in some way for the better is a rounded and balanced programme of activities that call upon all those forms of life that have significance in human affairs.

At the present time there are two influential formulations of what the curricula should contain. The first is the one constructed by Phenix;[1] the second is the one largely based upon the work of Hirst.[2] It is the former that I propose to look at further whilst at the same time making some comments about the latter.

In his *Realms of Meaning*, Phenix recognizes that a curriculum for general education must take account of the idea of logical patterns of disciplined understanding but at the same time not be exclusively bound by them. He sets out by stating that he wishes to avoid two temptations.

(i) To return to a traditional subject-matter curriculum related neither to the needs or ability of the individual learner nor to the social and psychological factors affecting education;

(ii) To construe knowledge too narrowly in purely intellectualistic terms.[3]

The full development of human beings, he maintains, 'requires education in a variety of realms of meaning rather than in a single type of rationality'.[4] Certainly on this point he has the support of Reid[5] who has argued that man comes to know and experience in a variety of ways and that not all of them are reducible to a propositional formulation of them.

What makes Phenix's approach to the curriculum particularly commendable is that he recognizes that it should be based upon a conception of the person that is holistic and not 'just a collection of parts'.[6] Also, instead of placing rational autonomy at the centre of the educational enterprise he emphasizes more the notion of *meaning*. If such ideas as 'reason' and 'mind' are too narrowly construed as referring to the processes of logical thinking, he contends, the life of feeling, conscience and imagination suffer, the outcome of which is a one-sided and emasculated form of development. By adopting the word meaning he hopes to overcome some of the criticisms that I have laid against some of the more traditional approaches to education.

Meaning, Phenix suggests, has four dimensions.[7] The first is that of *experience* which pertains to human consciousness and its peculiar quality of reflectiveness, or self-awareness. It recognizes that the inner life of testimony and direct objectification are no less valuable in our knowledge of what it is to be human than the knowledge about man which arises from scientific interpretations based upon inference. The second is that of *rule, logic or principle* which helps characterize and differentiate between the various

kinds of meaning.* The third is *selective elaboration*. Here reference
is made to those areas of meaning which in the long history of
mankind have demonstrated their actual fecundity and have not
arisen from an *a priori* analysis of possible classes of meaning.
Meanings in this third dimension have arisen from and have been
elaborated by particular groups of scholars. They incorporate those
meanings which have been explicated by the traditional disciplines
but are by no means confined to them. The fourth dimension of
meaning is *expression*. Here the concern is the effective communication of meanings through the use of appropriate symbolic forms.
Symbolization presupposes self-transcendence in the awareness of a
common world, for the symbols are taken as having the same or
similar connotation to oneself as to others into whose being one
imaginatively projects oneself. All in all it will be seen that meaning
for Phenix is a more embracing notion than Hirst's characterization
of 'knowledge'. Clearly these are not identical or interchangeable.
What is found meaningful in human affairs ranges considerably
beyond those areas for which there are agreed procedures for the
establishment of truths. Existentially meaningful experiences, for
example, are not rendered less poignant or significant because they
cannot be validated or because they cannot be readily articulated
and shared within an already formulated and commonly shared
symbolic system.

Phenix's underlying thesis is that people have the power to
experience meanings. What characterizes human existence,
he maintains, is its distinctively different patterns of meaning.
·A curriculum of general education is therefore concerned with
'the process of engendering essential meanings'.[8] What then
are these realms of meaning that will help the person to live
his life in a unified, comprehensive and personally significant
fashion?

To list them they are:[9]

1   SYMBOLICS, under which realm he places (i) Ordinary language;
    (ii) Mathematics.

2   EMPIRICS, includes (i) Physical Science; (ii) Biology; (iii)
    Psychology; (iv) Social Science.

3   AESTHETICS, covers (i) Music; (ii) The Visual Arts; (iii) The Arts
    of Movement; (iv) Literature.

* It is this dimension of meaning with which Hirst is primarily concerned when he
speaks of the categorization of the different 'forms of knowledge'. Hirst sees knowledge as 'the domain of true propositions or statements'. See his *Knowledge and the
Curriculum* (Routledge and Kegan Paul, 1974), pp. 84–7.

4 SYNNOETICS invokes the significance of (i) Personal Knowledge.

5 ETHICS, which is really to do with (i) Moral Knowledge.

6 SYNOPTICS, which are integrative and interpretative realms. They serve to give a unified perspective about life. The disciplines here are (i) History; (ii) Religion; (iii) Philosophy.

It will be noticed that when Phenix's 'realms' are compared with Hirst's 'forms'[10] (Mathematics, Science – physical and social, Ethics, History, Religion, Aesthetics and Philosophy) that, despite the considerable agreement that exists between them, there remain two noticeable differences, which from the point of view of movement, are important. These are:

(i) That 'the arts of movement' are given explicit recognition as coming under the general heading of aesthetics;

(ii) That the whole area of 'personal knowledge' is given a place of its own in what is called the synnoetic realm.*

In connection with the first of these two points Phenix makes specific reference to dance and underlines what I have previously said about it—namely that dance is the primordial art in that the human body itself is the source, instrument and object of aesthetic experience. Furthermore, Phenix acknowledges, again in common with what has been maintained earlier, that the arts of movement, because they involve the person as a unitary totality, help bring together in a distinctive way his thoughts, feelings and actions. The arts of movement then may be regarded as an important area of holistic education.

The synnoetic realm also represents an attempt to bring attention to and highlight precisely those dimensions of living which are to do with the articulation, significance and interpretation of personal meanings. It recognizes that a person lives in a private and existential world as well as a public and objectively shared one. Synnoetics is perhaps best described as a realm of meaning which is personal, direct and relational and which arises out of the concrete existence of individuals in the experience of a personal encounter with one's self, with others or with things. Put another way synnoesis or personal knowledge is concerned with those somewhat abstruse but nonetheless crucial aspects of what it is to be a person. It emphasizes

* Hirst in the modified version of his original thesis now recognizes that a mode of awareness 'of our own and other people's minds' exists, but despite talking about such concepts as 'wanting', 'intending' and 'believing' etc. fails to get to grips with what Phenix is essentially referring to in his synnoetic realm. See P. H. Hirst and R. S. Peters, *The Logic of Education* (Routledge and Kegan Paul, 1970), p. 63.

subjectivity not *objectivity*; the *concrete* and not the *abstract*; *engagement* and not *detachment*. It is not concerned with *essences* as in language and science, for instance, but with the *existential* in which *being* and the *freedom to become* are held as important. In broad terms it will be seen to incorporate much of what has been discussed in relation to movement when dealing with such themes as the phenomenology of action and meaning, perceiving and knowing in movement, aesthetic experience, inter-personal perception as well as such notions as the lived-body, and self-actualization. In other words a good deal of what has been discussed under the general heading of movement as a source of meaning and significance could be suitably accommodated under what Phenix has designated as the synnoetic realm of meaning.

All in all, although it can perhaps be said that Phenix's 'realms' are less rigorously formulated than Hirst's 'forms', they do have the merit of attempting to produce a curriculum structure that has as its fundamental concern the unitary person rather than that aspect of him which is predominantly to do with the intellectual aspects of 'mind'. It is worth pointing out that despite the difference in what they take to be the central purpose of education both Hirst and Phenix each take as their baseline the common rooting of experience in the different forms of life or systems of meaning that make up what is most characteristic of human culture. Whereas, however, Hirst sees education as principally to do with the acquisition of knowledge, Phenix sees education as something more than just this. It is perhaps because Phenix is conscious that education as rational autonomy* is important but somewhat limiting and distorting in relation to what it is to *be* a person, that he calls his scheme a curriculum for general education. Be that as it may the fact is that Phenix's realms, especially the two called 'aesthetics' and 'synnoetics', are very much more sympathetic to and in accord with what has been said previously about the person as an embodied consciousness. Nonetheless the question remains 'Should movement be left assimilated under the two realms that are able to accommodate much of what the concept involves, or is movement best considered as an independent element in curriculum design'? The straightforward answer to this question is that movement should be regarded as an independently viable yet necessary element in any curriculum of general education. To omit it altogether from the

---

* Being 'rational' Hirst sees 'as a matter of developing conceptual schemes by means of public language in which *words* are related to our form of life, so that we make objective judgements in relation to that form of life'. See *Knowledge and the Curriculum* (Routledge and Kegan Paul, 1974, p. 93).

'serious curriculum as the Initiation Model does*, or to detract from its coherent and distinctive character by seeing it in a limited way by subsuming it under the aesthetic realm, as Phenix does, is to leave unrecognized the full import of its conceptual implications. With regard to the synnoetic realm of meaning, although as has been pointed out it has a number of the major themes in common with the concept of movement, it is by no means commensurate with it. Synnoetics in the writings of Phenix is more associated with certain aspects of philosophy, psychology, literature and religion than with movement, to which he makes no explicit reference. There is no reason, however, why movement should not remain partially associated with the synnoetic realm in the same way that the other disciplines mentioned are, yet at the same time have recognition of its own.

Among the arguments that can be made for movement as 'subject', apart from practical and administrative ones, are the following. First, recent advances in the articulation of movement as a 'field of study' are now sufficiently well established for it to be regarded as an area of scholarly interest and worthy of study in its own right. Second, it should be acknowledged more readily that sometimes it is possible to justify movement on instrumental grounds if it can be shown in so doing that educative ends are being served. Third, there are good grounds for claiming that certain physical activities (e.g. sport and dance), called here for convenience, movement, together constitute a traditionally related system of culturally shared meanings which should be transmitted from one generation to the next. These, it is contended, are no less worthwhile than the different 'forms of knowledge'. Fourth, movement, apart from the provision of distinct types of whole-bodied, action-based contextual meanings, is the only area of the curriculum which is directly concerned with those experiences of moving that can be entered into and enjoyed for their own sake. It should not be forgotten either that kinaesthetic perception is a unique form of awareness and that to deny movement is to deny one aspect of the growth of consciousness.

It is the task now to take up these themes and look at movement as an element in curriculum design which is as much to do with the all-round and balanced education of the person as such other elements as mathematics, science, languages, religion, art and history. Because movement is the only subject that takes as its central focus those aspects of the culture that are to do with meaningful whole-bodied action it has a strong claim for inclusion in any core curriculum of general education.

* See Peters, R. S., *Ethics and Education* (Allen and Unwin, 1966) pp. 145–66.

Education and the Three Dimensions of the Concept of Movement

During the past hundred years or so the place of physical activity in the curriculum, when it has found a place at all, has undergone many vicissitudes and several changes of direction. What has gone on has been called successively 'drill', 'training', 'physical education' and more recently by some people, 'movement'. Each label connotes in turn a different emphasis, a new stage of enlightenment. Whilst to the lay person and perhaps even to some teachers, all may seem calm and orderly, there has been in fact, within what has been called 'the movement movement',[11] considerable confusion and bewilderment.

The literature in this area, it seems to me, has been troubled by two main problems: one, conceptual; the other, professional. The major part of this book has been concerned with attempting to help unravel the first of these. It remains now to say something about the second.

The purpose of this final section then is to look at what has been said about movement as a concept and see how and to what extent it can be constituted as a 'subject' in a curriculum of general education. This task will be undertaken by looking at the three 'dimensions' of movement as I shall call them, and see how they relate to what has been said about education and curriculum design. The three dimensions I propose to discuss in turn are

Dimension I.   Education *about* movement;
Dimension II. Education *through* movement;
Dimension III. Education *in* movement.

It should be stressed that these three dimensions of movement are not mutually exclusive. On the contrary, they are overlapping and interdependent. In the context of education this should not only be recognized but whenever possible brought about by a structured programme of work.

Dimension I. Education 'about' Movement

Education *about* movement can be looked upon as a rational form of enquiry, concerned with the answering of such questions as: What effect does movement have on the living organism? How is growth related to motor control? How does man best learn to move in different ways? What factors determine man's potential for achievement in movement? In what ways does movement, or lack of it, influence the development of the personality? What part does movement play, if at all, in facilitating interaction and communication? What place does movement have in the cultural study of man? What are the best ways of classifying, analysing, and notating movement? What are the questions that should be raised and what are the methods that should be adopted in attempting to evaluate movement?

As a *subject to be studied* movement takes an interest in human motion in all its richness and diversity. By calling upon such areas as anatomy, physiology, physics, psychology, sociology, anthropology, aesthetics and philosophy it can be regarded as comprising a composite area of study and research. In principle, the study of human movement is as much to do with work and industry, the theatre and arts, medical services and the armed forces, as with education, sport and recreation. It therefore spills over into areas of life the school as an institution cannot ignore.

Apart from studying movement as a theoretical body of knowledge that is of interest in its own right, it can be studied in order to apply it to practical situations. How best to lift and carry? How best to train in order to delay the onset of fatigue? These are questions to which one can find answers in the disciplines of bio-mechanics and physiology. 'Moment of inertia' and 'oxygen debt' are terms or concepts associated with the provision of intelligible and rational answers to matters of practical concern. Movement study and research then can (a) be entered into for its own sake or intrinsic value; or (b) taken up for its usefulness or instrumental value. It should be pointed out, of course, that the one need not preclude the other. Both as a 'field of study' and a 'practical theory' movement can be found to be intrinsically worthwhile as well as useful.

Although movement as a body of knowledge draws upon such concepts, processes and procedures as embodiment, kinaesthetic perception, knowing-how, interaction, communication, aesthetic experience, intention and action that are not exclusively its own, together with some it has been suggested that are its own, such as movistruct, movicept and movisymbol, it uses them in such a collective and family-like way that when taken together they constitute a network of meanings that help characterize movement as an important psycho-social and cultural aspect of life. Movement forms like games, play, sport and dance, incorporate and provide instances of some of those facets of life without which the nature of what it is to be a person could not be fully grasped. Sport and dance, particularly perhaps, incorporate within their differing instances, beliefs, values, norms, signs and symbols which make them peculiarly what they are as sources of meaning and expression. In this respect they are no different from such other cultural forms of music, poetry or painting. As 'objects' of study they are no less rewarding.

Movement as a 'field of study', it is being claimed, is a composite 'discipline' and as such is concerned with the understanding of a 'portion of reality—that is its description, its explanation and sometimes its prediction'.[12] Since movement in this academic or theoretical sense is 'professionally' orientated towards education, it must necessarily be selective in its content and attentive to changing people in some way for the better in a coherent course of study. This highlights what can be said about movement in a rational way and be capable of providing satisfactory answers to such questions as: What is its purpose? What subject matter is to be used? What learning experiences is it hoped to bring about? How is the planned for knowledge and understanding to be assessed?

The rational study of movement as one dimension of the subject in the curriculum can take many forms. Although it can and does relate to the other dimensions of movement, as will be made clear, it can be studied as a theme or project on its own, rather as 'roads' or 'ships' might be. In Primary Education this type of approach has much to commend it. In the later stages of Secondary Education, however, by which time a good deal of general background knowledge will have been assimilated, there is no reason why education 'about' movement should not become more differentiated and broken down into such sub-components as human developmental patterns; motor learning and skill development; social-cultural aspects of human development; history and development of sport and dance. The content of such sub-components readily lend themselves to some sort of examination structure if this is desired.

It will be appreciated then that education 'about' movement is predominantly concerned with the transmission of what might be called rational movement knowledge. It is largely of a propositional kind and is capable of being presented in a discursive way. It is public and objective, in principle shareable, and therefore communicable. It has the merit of providing a theoretical background of understanding which helps make coherent and meaningful that which is performed. In this respect knowing 'about' movement can act as an analytical as well as a critical and evaluative aspect of movement education.

Dimension II. Education 'through' Movement

The idea of education *through* movement is perhaps most easily associated with the term physical education. To say, however, that physical education is to learn by means of the 'physical' is to say little for as has been argued the learning of a person as an embodied consciousness is largely if not exclusively bound up with and dependent upon the use of his sensory organs. Nonetheless as Wunderlich[13] says of movement: 'It provides sensory data. It broadens the perceptive horizon. It stimulates function and structure of all bodily organs. It is the means by which an individual learns about himself in relation to his ambient environment.' What in addition, however, education 'through' movement more particularly entails is the taking of that culture-based family of activities and processes—games, dance, gymnastics, athletics, swimming, outdoor pursuits, etc.—as a means 'through' which the teacher can help effect desirable outcomes, regardless of whether or not those activities have intrinsic worth of their own.

When 'physical education' or education 'through' movement is conceived of in instrumental terms it is looked upon as being able to assist in the fulfilment of certain useful purposes. It is concerned not so much with any intrinsic values the activities might have but with the extrinsic or functional values with which they are associated. Such values are sometimes spoken of in terms of 'spin offs', 'by-products' or 'outcomes'. When activities are expressly taught with a view to promoting their extrinsic, rather than their intrinsic, values, they can be justified as being worthy of inclusion in the curriculum if it can be shown that they are a good means in the promotion of other ends that are considered worthwhile.

A brief acquaintance with the history of physical education will show that what was done was invariably done for what were regarded as good extrinsic reasons. Thus in classical Greece physical education was concerned not only with hygiene, medicine, aesthetics, and ethics but was seen in addition as a means of recreation. In ultimate terms, however, it was regarded as a necessary element in the balance and harmony of the soul.[14*] In Roman times physical education was tied more to notions of health and military training, but by the Middle Ages with the establishment of Christianity it had become a part of the chivalric order of which both dancing and the martial arts formed a part. In the 19th century under the influence of such patriots as P. H. Ling in Sweden and F. Jahn in Germany it became an effective force in the forging of a national identity.[15] In the public schools of Victorian England it became a strong influence in the movement which led to the theory and practice of 'muscular Christianity'[16] in which the notion of character featured strongly. It was not until the present century that physical education once more began to be seen as a means of bringing about the 'goals' of general education as they related to the developing 'total person'. It was left to Williams[17] who had been influenced considerably by Dewey, to sound a more contemporary note and state unequivocably that:

> Education through the physical will be judged, therefore, even as education of life will be judged—by the contribution it makes to fine living.

Since 1930, when these words were written, the idea of education 'through' movement has continued to gather ground. Kane,[18] in an examination of the literature to do with physical education found that among the 'purposes' most frequently mentioned in connection with it were emotional stability, self-realization, leisure-time pursuits, social competence, moral development, organic development, motor skills, aesthetic appreciation and cognitive development. It will be seen that these findings are somewhat divers and range from the broadest of 'aims' to the narrowest of 'objectives'. The important question for the instrumentalist, however, is not to ask whether activities are done for their own intrinsic values, but whether as a result of them being done in a certain way and with appropriate guidance, they do or can be made to assist in the bringing about of ends which are considered desirable. If in other words movement activities in the form of extrinsic values can be shown to be a good means of helping to further educational endeavours then there is good reason for including them in the curriculum apart from whatever intrinsic values they may have of their own.

Andrews in arguing along these lines through what he called the 'supportable' evidence, concluded that the following areas were tenable as curricula 'aims':[19]

1 The promotion of cognitive development;
2 The promotion of aesthetic education;
3 The promotion of moral education;
4 The promotion of social relationships;
5 The promotion of education for leisure;
6 The promotion of fitness for 'positive living'.

Although one may have some qualms in many instances about what can be claimed on behalf of physical education as an instrument of general education in view of the inconclusiveness of the relevant evidence available there is little doubt that in some of the more finite areas it is a good if not the best way of realizing them. In that health, for example, is a precondition of education and organic

---

* For a detailed account of physical education in the Hellenistic Age see Marrou, H. I. *A History of Education in Antiquity* (Mentor, 1956), pp. 165–86.

fitness contributes to its achievement, it is clear that there is no substitute for the taking of exercise[20] and that in the school situation physical education has responsibility for seeing that it is taken in a responsible and profitable way.

According to Jahoda,[21] 'positive' health too, not just the absence of disease, is bound up with the ability to play and to physically cope with the environment. This, as Jahoda recognizes, is associated not only with the acquisition of skills in order to do what has to be done but with the confidence that comes from their mastery. To the extent indeed that organic fitness and the development of motor skills are the *sine qua non* of most people's health and pleasure and that physical education activities can bring them about they should be pursued as instrumental values. As Barrow observes: 'It matters little whether we call such activity educational or not. What is of importance is the claim that this is something that we ought to be concerned with in relation to children.'[22]

It would be possible to expand upon the considerable empirical evidence assembled by writers like Arnold,[23] Rarick[24] and Cratty[25] that indicates how effective a means physical education *can* be in promoting desirable general outcomes to do with health, growth and development, but rather than do this—since as Taylor[26] points out what is actually accomplished is always dependent upon 'a set of transactions' between the teacher and learner—I propose instead to outline in principle how, even in those intellectual areas to do with knowledge and understanding, the dimension of education 'through' movement can be of value.

It has been suggested that the notion of education 'through' movement is an adaptable and flexible one. The purpose now is to indicate that even within academically orientated areas of the curriculum it can still be profitably employed. Here it will entail the intelligent utilization of those situations that arise, or can intentionally be made to arise, in the teaching of physical activities that can assist in being initiated into what are sometimes spoken of as the basic forms of awareness. Thus education 'through' movement can be made to relate to education in at least two main ways:

(i) It can be 'illustrative' of something that has arisen in another context;

(ii) It can throw up problems and issues of its own which are unlikely to be resolved unless they are 'referred back' to one or more of the basic forms of knowledge.

For the sake of convenience I will call respectively these two main ways of relating education 'through' movement to an academic type of curriculum based upon the forms of knowledge as the 'illustrative function' and the 'referent function'.

1 *The Illustrative Function*. The illustrative function is perhaps best understood in terms of the question 'How can I, the teacher, get children to better understand what they have learnt in the classroom through the active use of their bodies or through the concomitant activities that form a part of physical education?'

It may be, for example, that mechanical principles arising in science can be put to the test and made more meaningful by the pupils using themselves or their fellows as subjects. In such activities as athletics, diving, trampolining and gymnastics, theory can be transformed into practice. The track, pool and gymnasium can become an extension of the laboratory. Apart from the possibility of transforming something inert and abstract into something fresh and meaningful, the utilization of one's self in learning in the form of the body can have several other effects which can assist the growth of knowledge and understanding. It can help 'personalize' knowledge:[27] it can give a new perspective on the same material; it can help illuminate and give a greater insight into what in a sense is already 'known'; and it can act as a secondary reinforcing process.

2 *The Referent Function*. The referent function, like the illustrative function, is best understood in terms of a question. Let us take the activity of dance. It may be that at some stage in a lesson the question will arise 'What is it that makes dance dance?' It is not long before a host of other questions are raised to do with such notions as expression, rhythm, line, form, illusion, and so on. It is inevitable if such questions persist that one is led back into that branch of knowledge called aesthetics.

A second example of the referent function can arise in the case of games. In this situation it may happen that a question like 'Why is it necessary to have rules?' will be asked. If the educationist is to take the query seriously it may lead on to a consideration of the purpose of rules, their function and their justification or otherwise. Such concepts as freedom, equality and justice, it will be seen, are related to such notions as 'sportsmanship' and 'fairplay' and are as applicable on the field of play no less than off it. The point here is that when regarded instrumentally games and what goes on in them need not remain morally neutral, or as 'self-contained' activities which they are sometimes made out to be, and which have no bearing on the world outside them. Certainly it is unlikely that educators like Arnold of Rugby and Kurt Hähn would have viewed games and sports with such favour unless they were able to see in them an efficacious means whereby such character-building qualities as determination, self-reliance and courage could be brought about. It is possible that there is more in the claim than is generally acknowledged that the battle of Waterloo was won on the playing fields of Eton. Games then, it is being maintained, can be (but of course need not be) looked upon as a useful medium through which pupils can be encouraged to consider and act upon, ethical values. From the midst of sporting engagement can come the moral injunction 'What ought I to do?' The question calls for executive decision-making not armchair deliberation. The question is real, not hypothetical and has to be dealt with in concrete terms. The schoolboy touch-judge, desperate for his team to win, sees his wing three-quarter about to score after putting his foot out of play. To raise the flag or not to raise the flag? The choice is his. Action is required. Opportunities like this are many in physical education. They are important for moral development because they provide situations for thought and will to be combined with responsible action. Such factors, together with those of empathy and a consideration for others are, according to Wilson,[28] the necessary components without which a person cannot be said to be fully morally educated. Far then from being removed from reality, games, if intelligently handled, although physically 'bound' by time and space, need not be cognitively bound by the same factors. The lessons that can be learnt from them can be made to relate in an open ended way to the issues and problems that lie outside them. In the hands of a gifted teacher the activities of games need not be more self-contained *per se* than any other family or class of activities. This, it seems to me, can be upheld regardless of whether or not one accepts the arguments that have been put forward most recently by Keating[29] and Aspin[30] that sport and games are in and of themselves partially concerned with moral considerations.

It has been maintained that the instrumental use of physical activities in the curriculum can be justified if they can be shown to serve the interests and purposes of education. By capitalizing upon their 'illustrative' and 'referential' possibilities the teacher can contribute in new and exciting ways to the quality and coherence of what is learnt. Thus just as Caldwell Cook[31] transformed the teaching of English through play activities so other educationists such as Dienes[32] have found that a subject like mathematics can be better grasped by many pupils through the use of such activities as games and dance. Perhaps enough has been said to suggest that physical education or education 'through' movement in principle and in practice, can and frequently does serve, directly and indirectly, the purposes of education. The degree to which physical activities can be instrumentally used to effect desirable outcomes will always to one extent or another be dependent upon the intention, knowledge, imagination and skill of the teacher. All in all the dimension of education 'through' movement is best conceived of as being that part of the educational process which aims to enhance and harmonize the physical, intellectual, social and emotional aspects of a growing individual chiefly through professionally selected and directed physical activities.

Dimension III. Education 'in' Movement

Education 'about' movement has been characterized as being to do with movement as a field or theoretical body of knowledge that can be academically studied in a disinterested way, whereas education 'through' movement, it has been suggested, is to do with the justifiable utilization of that family of physical activities, known normally as physical education, which with intelligent teaching can be made to serve values which are not necessarily intrinsic to them. In this third dimension of education, *in* movement, the concern is with the values that are an inherent part of the activities themselves. To put the matter another way: education 'in' movement upholds the view that movement activities, especially when looked at from the 'inside' or participatory perspective of the moving agent, are in and of themselves worthwhile. What makes them educationally desirable is that they permit the person to actualize his self in a set of distinctive and bodily orientated contexts and thereby allow him to learn a great deal about himself and the world in which he lives.

Before going on to say something further in relation to the educative dimension of 'in' movement it will be appreciated that education, when employed in its evaluative sense, implies:

(i) That it concerns having respect for the person as an embodied consciousness;

(ii) That it involves becoming acquainted with a number of activities ('physical' as well as 'intellectual') that are in themselves worthwhile;

(iii) That the processes (or means) employed to bring about achievements (or capacities) are morally defensible.

It will be seen then that education like 'the good life' will be a 'mixed' life. It will comprise a plurality of inherently worthwhile activities which are not only recognized to be of value in an 'objective' sense but found to be so in a 'subjective' sense. They are both 'good-in-themselves' and 'good-for-me'. To be in an educative situation is to be caught up in a qualitative process of becoming. It is not just a question of pursuing activities considered valuable in a perfunctory or prudential way, but of entering into them for their own sakes as meaningful and satisfying enterprises. Although as Wilson[33] points out the process of education (in contrast to just learning or schooling) can only proceed through someone having interest, it should not be thought that interest exists as a sort of independent and free-ranging commodity. Always interest suggests an interest *in* something, and in terms of education it means having an interest in something that is worthwhile. Dewey helped clarify the nature of interest and the fact that, like consciousness, it is always 'intentive' towards something when he wrote:

> Interest is not some one thing; it is a name for the fact that a course of action, an occupation, or pursuit absorbs the powers of an individual in a thorough-going way. But an activity cannot go on in a void. It requires material, subject-matter, conditions upon which to operate. On the other hand, it requires certain tendencies, habits, powers on the part of the self. Wherever there is genuine interest, there is an identification of these two things. The person acting finds his own well-being bound up with the development of an object to its own issue. If the activity goes a certain way, then a subject-matter is carried to a certain result, and a person achieves a certain satisfaction.[34]

What should be made clear is that although education in relation to the concept of movement is partially explicated by reference to the dimensions of 'about' and 'through' movement, neither is centrally concerned with movement as a family of meaning laden activities and processes which are of interest in themselves and worth engaging in for the intrinsic values they contain and sources of satisfaction they offer. It is not that either of the dimensions of 'about' or 'through' are irrelevant to or out of keeping with the notion of 'in' movement. On the contrary both inevitably feed into it and in their different ways help illuminate it. The dimensions of the concept of movement then are conceptually discrete but functionally related. Each dimension is not exclusive of the others, but overlaps and merges into them. The concept of movement is a mutually reinforcing and inter-dependent one. Like a triangle, it has different points of emphasis which come into prominence at different times. If movement were conceived of only in intellectualistic terms or what can be propositionally stated about it, it would be but a hived-off and disembodied academic pursuit. Similarly, if movement was seen only as a means of serving ends other than its own it would remain purely instrumental in character and not worthy of being educative in its own right. For the curriculum implications of the concept of movement to be grasped in an adequate way it must be seen not only as a field of study, and as an instrumental value, but as a worthwhile group of physical activities to be engaged in for their own sake.

It will be seen that although 'in' movement is largely to do with 'knowing how' to engage in physical activities and in having a direct and lived-body 'acquaintance' of them, the mover who is the author of his movement actions can enrich and bring greater understanding to what he does by a knowledge of 'what is the case', just as he can help realize them by an informed appreciation of appropriate means. There is thus no artificial divide between the dimensions. The notion of 'in' movement without the employment of some rational knowledge would be intellectually vacuous just as without some utilization of movement as means it would fail to reach certain of its objectives.

The notion of education 'in' movement then is not a self-contained or distinct entity. Although it emphasizes the process of moving it relates to and draws upon the other dimensions at different times and in varying degrees according to the situation in hand. To acknowledge this, however, is in no way to detract from movement as a family of whole-bodied activities in which the person can meaningfully engage for no other reason than that he finds them intrinsically rewarding. They are, for everyone, potentially in and of themselves interesting and satisfying. They permit the person to actualize the physical dimensions of his being in the form of developed capacities, skilled accomplishments and objective achievements that are in themselves worthwhile. They provide consciously embodied exemplifications of a culture's sporting and dancing heritage that no other subject in the curriculum attempts. Movement in the meeting of its own internal rules, standards and traditions is in and of itself educative. It is in no need of a qualifying suffix as in the term 'physical education'. Just as it is redundant to speak of English education or mathematics education so it is equally redundant to speak of movement education. An initiation into the paradigm instances of movement whether sport, dance or outdoor activities, is inherently valuable and therefore should form a part of any humanistically based programme of education. What gives them their importance and distinctiveness is that they are 'body-orientated', culturally significant and synnoetically meaningful activities.

The dimension of education 'in' movement upholds the view that movement activities should be done for what they are. If they are only looked upon as 'objects' of study no matter how valuable this may prove to be, one is not entering into the nature of the activities themselves. If one studies muscle fatigue, one is doing physiology. If one studies body-mechanics, one is doing physics. If one studies games as an aspect of society, one is doing sociology. Somehow movement as an activity and as a process entered into for its own sake gets neglected. Locke, concerned by the growing tendency in America to study sport and use it as a means to other ends rather than participate in it for what it is, laments:

> To love and teach sport because it is human and beautiful, full of its own meanings and its own absurdity, has been denied us. We have had to struggle up-hill, like Sisyphus, to make sport something that it cannot be. Thus, sport seems sometimes to fail us, not because of what it is, but because of what we have asked it to become.[35]

Peters understands better than most the question of getting on the 'inside' of activities and the difficulties of the educator in getting children to take up activities for what they are. He writes:

> Now anyone who has managed to get on the inside of what is passed on in schools and universities, such as science, music, art, carpentry, literature, history, and athletics, will regard it as somehow ridiculous to be asked what the point of his activity is. The mastery of the 'language' carries with it its own delights, or 'intrinsic motivation,' to use the jargon. But for a person on the outside it may be difficult to see what point there is in the activity in question. Hence the incredulity of the uninitiated when confronted with the rhapsodies of the mountain-climber, musician, or golfer. Children are to a large extent in the position of such outsiders. The problem is to introduce them to a civilized outlook and activities for which they have aptitude.[36]

In conclusion it should be clear from what has been said that if movement is to be conceived of as being more than just a portion of reality to be studied or as a means to serve purposes extrinsic to itself, it must be entered into for its own sake. Only then can its intrinsic worth be experienced; its inherent values made manifest. The world of movement for the agent or the moving being, is a world of promise towards self-actualization. It can expand his conscious horizons. It is a world in which the mover can come to understand an aspect of his socio-cultural world and in doing so discover more perfectly his self and his existential circumstances. To deny this world of bodily action and meaning because of prejudice or neglect is to deny the possibility of becoming more fully human.

If, finally, there is need to state what unsought after advantages are possible or likely to accompany an education 'in' movement, I would, in the light of what has been discussed in this book suggest the following:

1   That the person's organic fitness and overall health will be improved;

2   That the person's range of physical skills and accomplishments will be increased as will his knowledge and understanding of them;

3   That the person's kinaesthetic perception will be extended and refined in such a way that this aspect of his consciousness will be considerably enriched;

4   That the person will be more aesthetically aware and more sensitized towards his own movements as distinctive sources of aesthetic experience;

5   That the person will be able to appreciate more fully the range, intricacy and subtlety of non-verbal interpersonal perception and communication;

6   That the person will because of the need for choice, involvement and commitment in movement situations become more firmly established in his identity;

7   That the person when engaged in authentic actional projects will be able to experience himself as a total, holistic and synthesized acting–thinking–feeling–willing–being: in short as a unitary embodied consciousness;

8   That the person because he has been touched by the spirit of 'sportsmanship' and all that this implies about fellowship and the quality of relations with others, will become more morally conscious and socially responsible;

9   That the person when caught up in and absorbed by what he is doing will be more open to the possibility of 'peak' moments, whereby he will be able to discover what it is to be self-actualized and thereby experience new and value-laden forms of existential meaning.

It will be seen then, somewhat paradoxically, that many of the benefits of an education 'in' movement can come about not because they are consciously formulated objectives but because they are fortuitous and invaluable by-products that arise as a natural consequence of what is done.

References

1. THE PERSON AS AN EMBODIED CONSCIOUSNESS

1. Marcel, G., *The Mystery of Being* (Regnery, 1960).
2. Sartre, J-P., *Being and Nothingness* (Methuen, 1969).
3. Merleau-Ponty, M., *Phenomenology of Perception* (Routledge and Kegan Paul, 1962).
4. Zaner, R. M., *The Problem of Embodiment* (Martinus Nijhoff, 1964), p. 249.
5. Sartre, *op. cit.*, p. 305.
6. Marcel, *op. cit.*, Vol. 1, p. 117.
7. Zaner, *op. cit.*, p. 48.
8. Stein, E., *On the Problem of Empathy* (Martinus Nijhoff, 1970), p. 43.
9. Sartre, *op. cit.*
10. Merleau-Ponty, *op. cit.*, p. 271.
11. *Ibid*. See Ref. 4 above, pp. 260-1.
12. Schrag, C. O., 'The Lived Body as a Phenomenological Datum', *The Modern Schoolman*, Vol. XXXIX (March, 1962), pp. 203-18.
13. Bannister, R., *First Four Minutes* (Corgi, 1957), pp. 11-12.
14. Pügge, H., 'Man and his Body' in S. F. Spicker, ed.), *The Philosophy of the Body* (Quadrangle, 1970), p. 294.
15. Schrag, *op. cit.*, p. 142.
16. *Ibid*. p. 143.
17. Jaspers, K., *Von der Wahrheit* (Piper, 1947), p. 329.
18. Sartre, J-P., *op. cit.*, pp. 368-431.
19. Van Den Berg, J. H., 'The Human Body and the Significance of Human Movement: a Phenomenological Study' in H. M. Ruitenbeck (ed.), *Psycho-analysis and Existential Philosophy* (Dutton, 1962), p. 108.
20. *Ibid*. p. 115.
21. *Ibid*. p. 127.
22. Natanson, M., *The Journeying Self: a Study in Philosophy and Social Role* (Addison-Wesley, 1970), p. 12.
23. Merleau-Ponty, M., *op. cit.*, p. 100.

24. R. May, E. Angel, and Ellenberger (eds.), *Existence: A New Dimension in Psychiatry and Psychology* (N.Y. Basic Books, 1958), p. 110.
25. *Ibid*. p. 110.

2. THE PHENOMENOLOGY OF ACTION AND MEANING

1. Husserl, E., *Formal and Transcendental Logic* (Nijmeyer, 1929), p. 149.
2. Dewey, J., *Human Nature and Conduct* (Holt, 1922).
3. Bergson, H., *Duree et Simultaneite* (Alcan, 1923).
4. Husserl, E., *The Phenomenology of Time Consciousness* (Indiana University Press, 1971), pp. 50–2.
5. *Ibid*. pp. 178–9.
6. Schutz, A., *On Phenomenology and Social Relations*. Selected writings edited by H. R. Wagner (University of Chicago Press, 1970), p. 52.
7. Maslow, A. H., 'Cognition of Being in the Peak Experiences', *Journal of Genetic Psychology*, Vol. 94, (1959), p. 45.
8. *Ibid*. p. 45.
9. Ravizza, K., 'A Study of the Peak-Experience in Sport', Unpublished article by courtesy of the author.
10. *Ibid*. p. 1.
11. Porot, M. A., *Alphabetical Manual of Psychiatry*.
12. Rogers, C. R., 'The Concept of the fully functioning Person', *Psychotherapy*, Vol. 1, (1963), pp. 17–26.
13. *Ibid*.
14. Maslow, A. H., *Toward a Psychology of Being* (Van Nostrand, 1968), p. 201.
15. Suits, B., 'What is a Game?', *Philosophy of Science*, Vol. 34, (June 1967), pp. 148–56.
16. Jaspers, K., *Philosophie*, Vol. II (Springer-Verlag, 1948), p. 182.
17. Macquarrie, J., *Existentialism* (Penguin, 1973), p. 145.
18. Heidegger, M., *Being and Time* (Harper and Row, 1962), p. 186.
19. Macmurray, J., *The Self as Agent* (Faber and Faber, 1957), p. 27.
20. Jaspers, K., *Man in the Modern Age* (Doubleday, 1956), pp. 69–70.
21. Metheny, E., 'The Symbolic Power of Sport' in E. W. Gerber, (ed.) 'Sport and the Body' (Lea and Febinger, 1972), p. 223.
22. Herzog, M., *Annapurna* (Dalton, 1953), p. 12.
23. Macquarrie, *ibid*., p. 170.

3. MOVEMENT AS SOCIAL INTERACTION AND COMMUNICATION

1. Sherif, M., and Sherif, C. W., *Social Psychology* (Harper and Row, 1969), p. 100.
2. Goffman, E., *Interaction Ritual* (Allen Lane, 1972), p. 1.
3. Asch, S. E., *Social Psychology* (Prentice-Hall, 1952), p. 41.

4. Shannon, C., and Weaver, W., *The Mathematical Theory of Communication* (University of Illinois Press, 1949), p. 95.
5. Ross, R. S., *Speech Communication: Fundamentals and Practice* (Prentice-Hall, 1965), p. 4.
6. Harrison, R. P., 'Non-Verbal Communication', in de Sola Pool, I and W. Schaam (eds.), *Handbook of Communication* (Rand McNally, 1973), p. 93.
7. Barker, L., and Collins, N. B., 'Non-Verbal and Kinesic Research' in P. Emmert and W. D.Brooks, (eds.) *Methods of Research in Communication* (Houghton Mifflin, 1970).
8. Applbaum, R. L., *et al. Fundamental Concepts in Human Communication* (Canfield Press, 1973).
9. McCroskey, J. C., 'A Summary of Experimental Research on the Effects of Evidence in Persuasive Communication', *Quarterly Journal of Speech*, Vol. 36 (1969), pp. 169–76.
10. Cohen, A., *Attitude Change and Social Influence* (N. Y. Basic Books, 1964).
11. Wilson, J., *Language and the Pursuit of Truth* (Cambridge University Press, 1969), p. 14.
12. Ogden, C. K., and Richards, I. A., *The Meaning of Meaning* (Routledge and Kegan Paul, 1969), p. 244.
13. Merleau-Ponty, M., *Phenomenology of Perception* (Paris: Gallimard, 1945), p. 406.
14. Simmel, G., 'Sociology of the senses: Visual Interactions' in R. E. Park and E. W. Burgess (eds.), *Introduction to the Science of Sociology* (Chicago University Press, 1921), p. 358.
15. Asch, S. E., *Social Psychology* (New York: Prentice-Hall, 1952), p. 139.
16. Strickland, L. H., 'Surveillance and Trust', *Journal of Personality*, Vol. 26 (1958), pp. 200–15.
17. Allport, G. W., *Pattern and Growth in Personality* (Holt, Rinehart and Winston, 1961), pp. 497–522.
18. Tagiuri, R., 'Person Perception' in G. Lindzey and E. Aronson (eds.), *Handbook of Social Psychology* (Addison-Wesley, 1969), p. 432.
19. Wagner, H. R., *Alfred Schutz on Phenomenology and Social Relations* (University of Chicago Press, 1970), pp. 14–15.
20. *Ibid.* p. 73.
21. James, William, *Principles of Psychology* (New York: Holt, 1890).
22. Wagner, *op. cit.*, p. 164.
23. Schutz, A., *The Phenomenology of the Social World* (Northwestern University Press, 1967), p. 101.
24. Salvan, J., *To Be and Not To Be* (Wayne State University Press, 1962), p. 66.
25. Amur, Neil, *The Fifth Down* (New York: Coward-McCann and Geoghegan, 1971), pp. 196–7.

4. PERCEIVING AND KNOWING IN MOVEMENT

 1. Merleau-Ponty, M., *The Structure of Behaviour*, trans. by Fisher, A. L. (Methuen, 1965), p. 166.
 2. *Ibid*. pp. 168–9.
 3. Scott, G., 'Measurement of Kinesthesis', *Research Quarterly*, Vol. 26, (1955), pp. 324–41.
 4. Hampshire, S., *Thought and Action* (Chatto and Windus, 1970), p. 47.
 5. *Ibid*.
 6. Macmurray, J., *The Self as Agent* (Faber and Faber, 1957), p. 111.
 7. Ricoeur, P., *Fallible Man*, trans. by Kelbley, C. (Regnery, 1965), p. 156.
 8. i) Ellfeldt, L. and Metheny, E., 'Movement and Meaning: Development of a General Theory', *Research Quarterly*, Vol. 29, No. 3., October 1958, pp. 264–73.
    ii) Metheny, E. and Ellfeldt, L., 'Dynamics of Human Performance', article in *Health and Fitness in the Modern World* (Athletic Institute, 1961), pp. 282–9.
    iii) Metheny, E., *Connotations of movement in Sport and Dance* (W. C. Brown, 1965), pp. 108–19.
    (iv) Metheny, E. with Ellfeldt, L., 'Symbolic Forms of Dance', in Nadel, M. H. and Nadel, C. G., *The Dance Experience* (Praeger, 1970), pp. 49–55.
 9. *Ibid*. See Ref. 8 ii) above, p. 285.
10. Cassirer, E., *An Essay on Man* (Doubleday Anchor, 1956).
11. Best, D., 'Meaning in Movement' in Conference Report on Human Movement Behaviour, Association of Principals of Women's Colleges of Physical Education (January, 1975), pp. 15–24.
12. Houts, J. A., 'Feeling and Perception in the Sport Experience', in *Journal of Health, Physical Education and Recreation*, Vol. 41 (October 1970), p. 72.
13. Ayer, A. J., *The Problem of Knowledge*, Penguin, 1969), p. 8.
14. Stace, W. T., *The Theory of Knowledge and Existence* (Greenwood, 1932), p. 7.
15. Polanyi, M., *The Tacit Dimension* (Anchor Book, Doubleday, 1967).
16. Hospers, J., *An Introduction to Philosophical Analysis* (Routledge and Kegan Paul, 1967), p. 79.
17. Scheffler, I., *Conditions of Knowledge* (Scott, Foresman and Co., 1965), p. 21.
18. Hamlyn, D. W., 'The Logical and Psychological Aspects of Learning' in R. S. Peters (ed.), *The Concept of Education* (Routledge and Kegan Paul, 1967), pp. 26–7.
19. Ryle, G., *The Concept of Mind* (Penguin, 1966).
20. *Ibid*. p. 30.
21. *Ibid* p. 30.
22. *Ibid*. p. 31.
23. Pears, D., *What is Knowledge?* (George Allen and Unwin, 1972), p. 29.

24. Ryle, *op. cit.*, p. 50.
25. *Ibid.* p. 32.
26. *Ibid* p. 32.
27. *Ibid.* p. 29.
28. *Ibid.* pp. 28–9.
29. Hampshire, *op. cit.,* p. 103.
30. Curtis, B. L., 'Teaching To and Teaching That' *Education Review* (February, 1977), pp. 83–96.
31. Kwant, R. C., *Encounter* (Duquesne University Press, 1960), pp. 25–32.
32. Russell, B., *The Problems of Philosophy* (Oxford University Press, 1970), pp. 25–32.
33. *Ibid.* p. 25.
34. Reid, L. A., *Meaning in Arts* (Allen and Unwin, 1969), p. 214.
35. Robertson, S., *Craft and Contemporary Culture* (Harrap, 1961), pp. 21–3.
36. Parks, B., 'Skiing'. Unpublished paper, University of Southern California (1966).
37. Polanyi, M., *Knowing and Being* (Routledge and Kegan Paul, 1969), p. 144.
38. Polanyi, M., *Personal Knowledge* (Routledge and Kegan Paul, 1958).
39. Polanyi, *Knowing and Being, op. cit.*, p. 132.
40. *Ibid.* p. 147.
41. Merleau-Ponty, M., *The Primacy of Perception* (North Western University Press, 1964).
42. Polanyi, *Knowing and Being, op. cit.*, p. 147.
43. *Ibid.*, p. 148.
44. Polanyi, M., *The Tacit Dimension,* (Anchor Book, Doubleday, 1967), p. 4.
45. *Ibid.*, pp. 141–2.

5. MOVEMENT AS A SOURCE OF AESTHETIC EXPERIENCE

1. Baumgarten, A. G., *Aesthetik* (Bonn: Leisig, 1907).
2. Bouet, M., *Les Motivations des Sportifs* (Editions Universitaires, 1969), pp. 37–41.
3. Bannister, R., *The Four Minute Mile* (Dodd, Mead & Co., 1956), pp. 11–12.
4. Dewey, J., 'Having and Experience' from 'Art and Experience' (1934) in M. Rader (ed.) *A Modern Book of Aesthetics* (Holt, Rinehart and Winston, 1973), p. 160.
5. Best, D., 'The Aesthetic in Sport' *British Journal of Aesthetics*, Vol. 14, No. 3 (Summer 1974), pp. 197–213.
6. Anthony, D. J., 'Sport and Physical Education as a Means of Aesthetic Education', *Physical Education*, Vol. 60, No. 179 (March, 1968), p. 2.
7. Turner, M. J., 'A Study of Modern Dance in Relation to Communication, Choreographic Structure and Elements of Composition', *Research Quarterly*, Vol. 34 (1963), pp. 219–27.

8. Osgood, L. E., Suci, G. J., and Tannerbaum, P. H., *The Measurement of Meaning* (University of Illinois Press, 1957).
9. Berndtson, A., 'Beauty, Embodiment and Art', *Philosophy and Phenomenological Research*, Vol. 21 (1960), p. 53.
10. Strawson, P. F., 'Aesthetic Appraisal and Works of Art' (*Oxford Review*, 1967), pp. 5–13.
11. Poole, R., 'Objective Sign and Subjective Meaning' in Benthall, J. and Polhemus, T., *The Body as Medium of Expressions* (Allen Lane, 1975), p. 78.
12. Best, D., *Expression in Movement and the Arts*, (Lepus Books, 1974), p. 150.
13. Bannister, R., 'The Four Minute Mile' (Dodd, Mead & Co. 1963), p. 12.
14. Palmer, A., *Radio Times* 15 September, 1973.
15. Herzog, M., 'Annapurna' (Dutton, 1952), pp. 208–9.
16. Atkinson, H., *The Games* (Cassell, 1967), p. 80.
17. Phenix, P. H., 'Relationship of Dance to Other Art Forms', in Haberman, M. and Meisel, T. G., *Dance: an Art in Academe*, (Teachers College Press, Columbia University, 1970), p. 10.
18. Sheets, M., *The Phenomenology of Dance* (University of Wisconsin, 1966), p. 83.
19. Jessup, B., 'Taste and Judgement', in M. H. Nadel and C. G. Nadel (eds.), *The Dance Experience* (Praeger, 1970), p. 198.
20. Wigman, M., *The Language of Dance* (Wesleyan University, 1966), pp. 37–8.
21. Fraleigh, S. H., 'Dance Creates Man', *Quest* (June, 1970), p. 66.
22. Fraleigh, S. H., 'Man Creates Dance', *Quest* (January, 1975), p. 21.
23. Fraleigh, S. H., 'Dance Creates Man', *op. cit.*, p. 67.
24. Keating, J. W., 'Sportsmanship as a Moral Category', *Ethics*, Vol. 75. (October, 1964), pp. 25–35.
25. Coubertin, P. de, 'The Olympic Idea' (Cologne High School for Sport, Carl-Diem Institute, 1966).
26. Maheu, R., 'Sport and Culture' in H. S. Slusher and A. S. Lockhart, (eds.), *An Introduction to Physical Education* (W. C. Brown, 1970), p. 190.
27. See entry on 'Gymnastics' in J. R. White (ed.), *Sports Rules Encyclopaedia*, (Palo Alto: National Press, 1966), pp. 293–4.
28. Elliott, R. K., 'Aesthetics and Sport', in Whiting, H. T. A. and Masterton, D. W., *Reading in the Aesthetics of Sport* (Lepus Books, 1974), p. 112.
29. Stolnitz, J., 'The Artistic Values in Aesthetic Experience' *Journal of Aesthetics and Art Criticism*, Vol. 32, No. 1 (1973), p. 7.
30. Curl, G. F., 'The Skilful—a Major Sector of the Aesthetic', *Momentum*, Vol. 1, No. 1 (Spring, 1976), p. 47.
31. Keenan, F., 'The Athletic Contest as a "Tragic" form of Art', in R. G. Osterhoudt (ed.), *The Philosophy of Sport* (Charles L. Thomas, 1973), pp. 309–26.

32. Kaufman, W., *Existentialism from Doestoevsky to Sartre* (Cleveland World Publishing Co., 1956), p. 87.
34. Lea, T., *The Brave Bulls* (Little Brown), pp. 193–200.
35. Hemingway, E., 'The Dangerous Summer', *Life* (5 September, 1960), p. 86.
36. Hemingway, E., *Death in the Afternoon* (Jonathan Cape, 1932), p. 91.
37. *Ibid.*, p. 76.
38. Metheny, E., *Connotations of Movement in Sport and Dance* (Dubuque: Broan, 1965), pp. 41–2.
39. Lawrence, D. H., *Women in Love* (Heinemann, 1966).

6. EDUCATION, MOVEMENT AND THE CURRICULUM

1. Phenix, P. H., *Realms of Meaning* (McGraw-Hill, 1964), p. x.
2. Hirst, P. H., *Knowledge and the Curriculum* (Routledge and Kegan Paul, 1974).
3. Phenix, *Realms of Meaning, op. cit.*, pp. x and xi.
4. *Ibid.*, p. xi.
5. Reid, L. A., a) 'Ways of Knowledge and Experience', Allen and Unwin, 1925. b) 'Feeling and Aesthetic Knowing', Journal of Aesthetic Education. Vol. 10. July–October, 1976. pp. 11–27. c) 'Feeling, Thinking and Knowing', Proceedings of the Aristotelian Society. March 1977. pp. 165–81.
6. Phenix, *Realms of Meaning, op. cit.*, p. 4.
7. *Ibid.*, pp. 21–5.
8. *Ibid.*, p. 5.
9. *Ibid.*, p. 28.
10. Hirst, P. H., 'Liberal Education and the Nature of Knowledge' in *Knowledge and the Curriculum, op. cit.*, p. 46.
11. Locke, L. F., 'The Movement Movement', *Journal of Health, Physical Education and Recreation* (January, 1966), pp. 26–33.
12. Kenyon, G. S., 'A Sociology of Sport: On Becoming a Sub-Discipline' in Brown, R. C. and Cratty, B. J. (eds.), *New Perspectives of Man in Action* (Prentice-Hall, 1968), p. 164.
13. Wunderlich, R. C., 'Hypokenetic Disease', *Academic Therapy Quarterly*, Vol. 2, No. 3 (1967), p. 188.
14. Plato, 'The Republic' Translated by H. D. P. Lee. Penguin, 1955. pp. 145–55.
15. McIntosh, P. C., *et al. Landmarks in the History of Physical Education* (Routledge and Kegan Paul, 1957).
16. McIntosh, P. C., *Physical Education in England since 1800* (Bell, 1952), pp. 42, 64, 68, 102.
17. Williams, J. F., 'Education Through the Physical', in *An Anthropology of Contemporary Readings*, by Slusher, H. S. and Lockhart, A. (eds.) (W. Brown, 1970), p. 3.
18. Kane, J., 'The Schools Council Enquiry—Interpretation and Social Context', in *Curriculum Development and Physical Education* by J. Kane (ed.) (Crosby, Lockwood Staples, 1976), p. 78.

19. Andrews, J. G., 'The Curricular Aims of Physical Education' in *A.T.C.D.E. Conference Reports on The Philosophy of Physical Education 1970 and 1971*, pp. 17–31.
20. Davis, E. C., *et al., Biophysical Values of Muscular Activity* (W. Brown, 1965), p. 121.
21. Jahoda, M., *Current Concepts of Positive Mental Health* (Basic Books, 1958).
22. Barrow, R., *Common Sense and the Curriculum* (Unwin, 1976), p. 110.
23. Arnold, P. J., *Education, Physical Education and Personality Development* (Heinemann, 1968).
24. Rarick, G. L., *Physical Activity: Human Growth and Development* (Academic Press, 1973).
25. Cratty, B. J., *Physical Expressions of Intelligence* (Prentice-Hall, 1972).
26. Taylor, P. H., *et al., Purpose, Power and Constraint in the Primary School Curriculum*, Schools Council Research Studies (Macmillan, 1974).
27. Polanyi, M., *Personal Knowledge, op. cit.*
28. Wilson, J., *et al., Introduction to Moral Education* (Penguin, 1967).
29. Keating, J. W., 'Sportsmanship as a Moral Category' in E. W. Gerber (ed.), *Sport and the Body* (Lea and Febinger, 1972), pp. 263–70.
30. Aspin, D., 'Ethical Aspects of Sport, Games and Physical Education' in *Proceedings of Philosophy of Education Society of Great Britain*, Vol. 9 (1975), pp. 49–71.
31. Cook, H. C., *The Play Way* (Heinemann, 1919).
32. Dienes, Z. P., *Mathematics through the Senses* (N.F.E.R., 1973).
33. Wilson, P. S., *Interest and Discipline in Education* (Routledge and Kegan Paul, 1971), p. 67.
34. Dewey, J., *Interest and Effort in Education* (Cedric Chivers Ltd., 1969), p. 65.
35. Locke, L., 'Are Sports Education' *Quest* (January, 1973), p. 90.
36. Peters, R. S., 'Reason and Habit: the Paradox of Moral Education' in J. Scheffler (ed.), *Philosophy and Education*. (Allyn and Bacon, 1966), p. 255.

Glossary of Phenomenological Terms

APPERCEPTION. The spontaneous interpretation of sensory perception in terms of past experiences and previously acquired knowledge of the perceived object.

ATTENTION.* Active attention rests in the full alertness and the sharpness of apperception connected with consciously turning toward an object, etc., combined with further considerations and anticipations, etc., of its characteristics and uses. An act of attention is a 'free act' of willfully and selectively turning toward, or alertly paying attention to, certain features, objects, etc., in the actual given environment at a specific moment.

ATTITUDE. A general posture or stance taken toward larger spheres of life and interest, including a particular 'style' of thinking, for example: the common-sense attitude; the scientific attitude.

BRACKETING.* A methodological device of phenomenological inquiry consisting in a deliberate effort to set all ontological judgements about the 'nature' and 'essence' of things, events, etc., aside. Thereby, the 'reality' of things and events is not denied but 'put into brackets'. This procedure makes the mental processes of experiencing into the central subject matter of phenomenology.

CONSTITUTION.* The term refers to the constitution of thought objects (cogitata) and indicates the processes of clarification of meaning, establishment of meaning context, and mobilization of prior knowledge concerning specific objects of the ongoing conscious life. It is a cumulative process in which the cognitive results of repeated experiences of the 'same object' are deposited ('sedimented') in the mind.

EIDETIC APPROACH. The main level of phenomenological inquiry. It serves the establishment of the 'essential' features and characteristics of concrete objects of apperception. Eidetic features of thought objects consist of general meanings as constituted by cognitive processes.

EPOCHÉ. The suspension of belief in the ontological characteristics of

---

* The thirteen definitions marked with an asterisk are the work of Helmut R. Wagner and are reproduced from *On Phenomenology and Social Relations* with his permission and that of the publishers, the University of Chicago Press.

experienced objects, etc. Each basic realm of human experience (everyday life, science, etc.) has its particular epoché.

EVIDENCE. That which, in the light of a person's accumulated experiences and knowledge, appears as unquestionably true.

EXPERIENCE.* The basic starting point of all phenomenological considerations is the essential actual, or immediately vivid, experience, that is, the subjective, spontaneously flowing stream of experience in which the individual lives and which, as a stream of consciousness, carries with it spontaneous linkages, memory traces, etc., of other, prior, experience. Experience becomes subjectively meaningful experience only by an act of reflection in which an essentially actual experience, in retrospect, is consciously apprehended and cognitively constituted. In the course of his life, a person compiles a stock of experience which enables him to define the situations in which he finds himself and to guide his conduct in them.

FOUNDED OBJECTS. Objects in the environment of a person upon which he bestows a specific intentional meaning.

IMMEDIACY. The fundamental characteristic of all actual experience, of experiencing. Immediacy is spatial and temporal: here and now.

INTENTIONALITY.* The most basic characteristic of consciousness: it is always the consciousness of something: it is directed toward something, and in turn is 'determined by the intentional object whereof it is a consciousness' (Wagner). The intentional object, then, is the object intended and meant by the individual, and singled out by him for apperceptional and cognitive attention. An intentional act is any act in and through which a person experiences an object, whether physical or ideal. Through it, the object itself is cognitively constituted.

INTERSUBJECTIVITY.* A category which, in general, refers to what is (especially cognitively) common to various individuals. In daily life, a person takes the existence of others for granted. He reasons and acts on the self-understood assumption that these others are basically persons like himself, endowed with consciousness and will, desires and emotions. The bulk of one's ongoing life experiences confirms and reinforces the conviction that, in principle and under 'normal' circumstances, persons in contact with one another 'understand' each other at least to the degree to which they are able to deal successfully with one another. Phenomenologists have posed the problem of intersubjectivity. In terms of phemomenological psychology, this problem may be subdivided into two questions: 1) How is the 'other Self' constituted in my mind as a Self of basically the same characteristics as my own Self? 2) How is the experience of a successful intercourse with another Self possible, or: how is the experience of my 'understanding' the other, and his 'understanding' me, constituted?

KNOWLEDGE. For a person in everyday life, knowledge is whatever he thinks is the case. Essentially, it concerns practical matters and, frequently, consists of recipes for all kinds of conduct and activity. Common-sense knowledge may range from near-expertness to extreme vagueness. What a person knows, *in toto*, is his stock of knowledge. As a whole, this stock is incoherent, inconsistent, and only partially clear. It serves its purposes adequately as long as its recipes yield satisfactory results in acting, and its tenets satisfactory explanations. By contrast, philosophical and scientific knowledge serves purely intellectual interests and is subject to controls, principles of coherence and consistency, etc.

LIFE-WORLD; also WORLD OF EVERYDAY LIFE.* The total sphere of experiences of an individual which is circumscribed by the objects, persons, and events encountered in the pursuit of the pragmatic objectives of living. It is a 'world' in which a person is 'wide-awake', and which asserts itself as the 'paramount reality' of his life.

MEANING.* The meaning of an experience is established, in retrospect through interpretation. Subjective meaning is that meaning which a person ascribes to his own experiences and actions. Objective meaning is the meaning imputed to the conduct of another person by an observer. All human conduct appears in a subjective meaning context. The meaningful self-interpretation of conduct consists in relating specific experiences to other experiences in the light of one's interests and motives involved. By contrast, interpretation of the conduct to another person consists in relating the observed conduct to an objective meaning context, consisting of preestablished generalized and typified conceptions.

NATURAL ATTITUDE.* The mental stance a person takes in the spontaneous and routine pursuits of his daily affairs, and the basis of his interpretation of the life world as a whole and in its various aspects. The life world is the world of the natural attitude. In it, things are taken for granted.

NOEMA AND NOESIS. The noema is the intentional object, the thing apperceived and experienced. Noesis is the process of experiencing.

OBJECTIVITY.* The mental stance of the disinterested onlooker. Basically, the objective point of view is the point of view of the detached observer.

PHENOMENOLOGICAL REDUCTION. The basic procedure of phenomenological method. Through 'bracketing' of all judgements about the ontological nature of the perceived objects, etc., and by disregarding their uniqueness, that which is given in cognitive experience is reduced to the 'essentials' of its form.

PROTENTION–RETENTION.* Protention designates an experience expected to follow immediately after 'he present experience. Retention refers to the remembrance of an experience which has just passed.

RELEVANCE. The importance ascribed by an individual to selected aspects, etc., of specific situations and of his activities and plans. In accordance with a person's multifarious interests and involvements, there exist various domains of relevance for him. Together, they form his system of relevances with its own priorities and preferences, not necessarily always clearly distinguished and not necessarily stable for longer periods. At any particular time, however, this system falls into specific zones of primary or minor relevances and of relative irrelevance. In so far as relevances spring from a person's own interests and motivations, they are volitional. If they are urged upon him either by situational conditions or by social imposition, they are imposed. Thus, social systems of relevance are imposed. Common relevances occur in direct interpersonal involvement (We-relations).

SEDIMENTATION.* The process by which elements of knowledge, their interpretations and implications are integrated into the layers of previously acquired knowledge. The sedimented items are fused with existing typifications, etc., or form the core of new ones. Either way they become a person's 'habitual possessions'. The 'experiencing activities' of the human consciousness, then constitute a person's stock of knowledge by way of sedimentation.

SPONTANEITY. The basic mode of immediate, essentially active, experience. It means being immersed in ongoing experience and excludes self-awareness.

SUBJECTIVITY.* In the immediate sense, the term refers exclusively to the experiences, cogitations, motives, etc., of a concrete individual. Strictly speaking, the subjective meaning inherent in conduct is always the meaning which the acting person ascribes to his own conduct: it consists of his motives, that is, both his reasons for acting and his objectives, his immediate or long-range plans, his definition of the situation and of other persons, his conception of his own role in the given situation, etc.

TENSION OF CONSCIOUSNESS. The attentive state of consciousness which varies in different realms of experience, ranging from 'full awakeness in the reality of everyday life to sleep in the world of dreams' (Wagner).

THOU ORIENTATION. The orientation upon another person with whom one is in direct, that is, face-to-face contact and of whom one conceives as a specific person.

UNDERSTANDING–VERSTEHEN. To understand, in general, means to comprehend the meaning of something. What is understood is meaningful. Understanding is the basis of all interactive intersubjectivity. Persons deal with one another successfully only to the degree to which they reciprocally understand each other's motives, intentions, etc., at least to the degree to which this is relevant to their purposes on hand. Understanding is 'the experimental form of common-sense knowledge of human affairs' (Wagner). Sociological understanding is the result of a sociologist's subjective interpretation of the phenomena of human conduct which he studies. As such, it belongs to the objective realm of sociological method and interpretative theory.

WE–RELATIONSHIP. The relationship which ensues when two persons, dealing with one another in a face-to-face situation, consider each other reciprocally in a Thou orientation. It is consumed in a period of participation in each other's life, however short. No emotional attachment is presupposed.

WORLD. The term refers to subjective experience and comprehension. It is, first, a world of somebody, namely the concretely experiencing individual, and second, the world of a more or less specific sphere of experience. In the directly subjective sense, a world is the totality of a specific sphere of experience as seen and understood by a specific individual at a particular time and under specific circumstances. Any individual may live successively, alternatively, or occasionally, in an indetermined number of worlds: the life world, the world of play and pretention, the world of dreams, etc. The application of the term world to these multiple spheres of experience is subjectively justified in that, for the experiencing individual, the sphere in which he finds himself at the moment is indeed the whole world. Objectively, for the phenomenological sociologist, each sphere is limited and of mere relative relevance. Therefore, he prefers to call it a 'finite province of meaning'.

Author Index

Allport, G. W., 69
Alvanez, A., 43, 47
Amur, N., 85
Anderson, B., 51
Andrews, J. G., 172
Angel, E., 12
Anthony, D. J., 125
Applbaum, R. L., 58
Arnold, P. J., 173
Asch, S. E., 54, 67
Aspin, D., 113, 175
Atkinson, H., 135
Ayer, A. J., 102

Bailey, C., 146
Bannister, R., 6, 45,
122, 134
Barker, L., 55
Barrow, R., 173
Baumgarten, A. G.,
120
Bergson, H., 20
Berndtson, A., 130
Best, D., 95, 124, 132
Best, G., 50
Bouet, M., 122
Brown, D. G., 108
Buber, M., 50

Caillois, R., 46
Campbell, C., 46
Campbell, D., 58,
156, 158
Cannon, W. B., 49
Cassirer, E., 95

Cleary, W., 47
Cohen, A., 59
Collins, N. B., 55
Cook, H. C., 175
Cope, E., 81
Coubertin, P. de, 147
Coutts, C. A., 43
Cratty, B. J., 173
Curl, G. F., 153
Curtis, B. L., 107

Davis, E. C., 173
Dewey, J., 18, 124,
177
Dickman, A. F., 136
Dienes, Z. P., 175
Dunphy, E., 45

Ellenberger, 12
Ellfeldt, L., 95
Elliott, R. K., 140,
149

Farrell, D., 47
Fast, J., 58
Fraleigh, S. H., 143
Furrel, D., 44

Gannon, R., 44
Goffman, E., 53

Hamlyn, D. W., 105
Hampshire, S., 92,
107
Harrison, R. P., 55

Hartland-Swann, J.,
108
Heidegger, M., 40
Heider, F., 69
Hemingway, E., 157
Herzog, M., 41, 46,
135
Herrigel, E., 50
Hill, T. E., 33
Hirst, P. H., 163, 164,
165, 166
Houts, J. A., 48, 101
Hospers, J., 104
Houston, C. S., 45
Huizingar, J., 146
Hunt, J., 47
Husserl, E., 2, 16, 20,
21

Jahoda, M., 173
James, W., 71
Jaspers, K., 8, 39, 40,
45
Jessup, B., 139
Jones, R. F., 52

Kane, J., 129, 172
Kaufman, W., 157
Kazantzakis, N., 143
Keating, J. W., 145,
175
Keenan, F., 154
Kenyon, G. S., 146,
170
Killy, J. C., 161

Kleinman, S., 85
Knight, H., 131
Kwant, R. C., 28, 109

Langer, S. M., 139
Lawrence, D. H., 159
Lea, T., 157
Locke, L. F., 168, 179
Lowen, A., 58
Luckman, T., 70

Macmurray, J., 40, 93
Macquarrie, J., 39, 41
McCroskey, J. C., 59
McDonnell, P., 48
McIntosh, P. C., 171
Maheu, R., 147
Marcel, G., 1, 2
Marcuse, H., 147
Marrou, H. I., 172
Maslow, A. H., 22, 31
May, R., 12
Merleau-Ponty, M., 1, 5, 12, 66, 89, 90, 116
Metheny, E., 41, 95, 159

Nansen, F., 47
Natanson, M., 11
Neal, P., 48, 50
Neitzsche, F., 46, 143

Ogden, C. K., 63
O'Malley, J. B., 10
Ornstein, R. E., 136
Osgood, L. E., 130
Ottum, R., 52
Owens, T. T., 74

Palmer, A., 134
Parks, B., 115

Pears, D., 105, 107
Peters, R. S., 167, 179
Phenix, P. H., 138, 163, 164
Pitcher, G., 108
Polanyi, M., 103, 116, 117, 174
Poole, R., 131
Porot, M. A., 27
Powell, B., 108
Plato, 171
Plugge, H., 6
Progen, J., 46

Quinn, C. H., 47, 51

Ralbavsky, M., 50
Rarick, G. L., 173
Ravizza, K., 23, 25
Reid, L. A., 113, 148, 163
Richards, I. A., 63
Ricoeur, P., 93
Robertson, S., 114
Rogers, C. R., 28, 29
Ross, R. S., 54
Russell, B., 110
Ryle, G., 105, 106, 107

Salvan, J., 83
Sandle, D., 129
Sartre, J-P., 1, 2, 4, 9
Scheffler, I., 104, 179
Schrag, C., 5, 6, 8
Schutz, A., 21, 70, 72
Scott, G., 90
Shannon, C., 54
Sheets, M., 138
Sherif, C. W., 53
Sherif, M., 53
Simmel, G., 67
Slavenko, R. and

Knight, J. A., 44, 45, 47, 51
Slusher, H., 43, 44, 50, 51
Stace, W. T., 103
Stein, E., 4
Stickland, L. H., 69
Stolnitz, J., 151
Strawson, P. F., 130
Suci, G. J., 130
Suits, B., 36
Swenson, E., 48

Tagiuri, R., 68, 69
Tannerbaum, P. H., 130
Taylor, P. H., 173
Turner, G., 45
Turner, M. J., 130

Van Den Berg, J. H., 9, 10, 11

Wagner, H. R., 70, 71, 72
Ward, P. M., 144
Weaver, W., 54
Weiss, P., 46, 49
Welter, G. H., 48
Wenkart, S., 51
White, J. R., 148
Wigman, M., 141
Wilde, O., 51
Williams, J. F., 172
Wilson, P. S., 177
Wilson, J., 62, 175
Wittgenstein, L., 102, 145
Wood, O. P., 108
Wunderlich, R. C., 171

Yates, J., 37, 38

Zaner, R. M., 1, 3, 5

Subject Index

Achievement, 49, 160
Action, 15, 88
  act, 19
  choice, 18
  concept of, 15
  and feeling, 93
  and habit, 17, 30
  kinaesthesia, 91
  as lived experience, 88
  and meaning, 15–22, 61–3
  non-rational, 17
  phenomenology of, 15
  and practical understanding, 87, 105–10
  project, 15
    actual, 16
    envisaged, 16
  protension-retention, 15
  rational, 17, 27
  and self, 91
  skill, 32
  unity of, 19
Aesthetic
  and artistic, 124–6
  attitude, 120–21, 123, 124
  experience, 120–21, 126–31
    performer, 126–36, 151–3
    spectator, 126–36
  feelings, 121–4
  meaning, 122, 131–7
  objects, 120–24
  perception, 120–24
  and skill, 150–53, 160–61
  and sport, 143–61
Agent
  as existent, 38, 88
  as performer, 126–8
Aloneness, 43

Authentic existence, 41
Autonomy, 43

Body, 87
  as being for itself, 9
  as being for the other, 9
  as known-by-the-other, 9
  see also Embodiment, Lived-body
Bullfighting, 157, 158

Challenge, 46
Communication, 54–5
  conceptual framework of, 59–61
  definitions of, 54–5
  and inter-personal perception, 65–85
  and interaction, 53–4
  meaning and expression, 56–9
  non-verbal, 55–6

Consciousness
  stream of, 73
Contest
  the good, 158–61
Co-operation, 81
Creating
  and becoming, 142–3

Dance, 137–43
  as an art form, 137–42
  creating and becoming in, 142–3
  the dancer as artistic performer, 137–43
Dancer
  as artistic performer, 137–43
  as embodiment of form, 141

Drama, 153, 157
  psycho, 156
  role, 155
Dramatic, the, 153–8
Dualism, 1, 86, 87

Education,
  and the concept of movement,
    168–80
  and the curriculum, 162–7
  and interest, 177
  and meaning, 163–7
  and movement dimensions
    'about', 168–70
    'through', 170–76
    'in', 176–80
Embodiment, 103, 141
  concept of, 1–14
  animate organism, 1–5
  see Lived-body, 5–14
Excitement, 46
Experience
  discrete, 20, 21
  meaningful, 20
  non-discrete, 20, 21
  peak, 22–5
Existent, 86
  as agent, 38, 87
  as knower, 86
Existential meaning, 38–40
  and sport, 40–52
Expression, 142, 143
  compositional form, 130
  expressive quality, 130

Feeling
  and thought, 93
  and language, 93–4
Fellowship, 81–3
  togetherness, 82, 83
Freedom, 43

Game
  the well played, 160–61
Gymnastics, 148

Habit
  and action, 17
  and skill, 30

Interaction
  and communication, 54–5
  non-verbal, 55

and the phenomenology of inter-
    personal perception, 71–85
  social, 53

Kinaesthetic
  see action
  feelings as intentional 'objects',
    121–4, 127–8, 151–3
  flow patterns, 98, 122, 151
  sense, 4
  see also Movicepts, Perception
Knowing
  by acquaintance, 110–15
  how, 34, 105–10
  in movement, 103
  and perceiving, 88–102, 116
  by tacit inference, 115–18
  that, 104–5
Knowledge
  acquaintance, 110–15
  forms of, 165
  about inter-personal perception,
    67–9
  and movement, 119
  practical understanding, 87, 88,
    104–10
  propositional, 104–5
  tacit, 115–18
  stock of, 70
  types of, 102–19

Language
  limitations of, 93–4
Life-world, 69–71
Lived-body, 5–14
  as self-referential, 7–8
  in reference to others, 8–11
  and human space, 11–13
  and human time, 13–14

Meaning
  action and, 15
  artistic, 124–6, 132–3
  contextual, 32–7, 85
  dimensions of, 163–4
  and education, 163–5, 177
  existential, 38–52
  and experience, 20
  and intention, 54, 61, 63, 69
  objective, 131
  and movement, 61–4
  non-artistic, 133–6

Meaning – *cont.*
  and peak experience, 22
  primordial, 25, 26–32
  realms of, 163
  and skills, 33–5
  subjective, 25, 75, 131
  symbolic, 62
  as symptom, 61
Mimesis, 153, 156
Movement
  concept of, xi–xiii, 168–80
  as aesthetic experience, 120–61
  and action, 15–22
  and dance, 137–43
  and education, 162–80
  ends and means, 124–6
  as a field of study, 168–70
  as an instrumental value, 123, 169, 170–76
  as instrumentally worthwhile, 123, 176–80
  as knowledge, 86–119
  and meaning, 25, 61–4, 177, 179
  as a perceptual form of consciousness, 88–94
  and the phenomenology of inter-personal relationships, 77–85
  qualitative, 129–31
  and skill, 29–31
  and sport, 29–31
  as social interaction and communication, 53–85
  spontaneous, 26
  three dimensions of
    'about', 104, 168–70
    'through', 170–76
    'in', 176–80
Moving
  conceptualisations of, 95–102
Movicept, 97–8
  moviceptualising, 98, 140
Movistruct, 96–7
  movistructuring, 97, 140
Movisymbol, 98–102
  movisymbolic, 99, 140

Natural attitude, 70–71
Nature, 50

Peak experience, 6, 22–5, 100
  in sport, 24, 41

Perceiver, 68
  two stances of, 75–7
Perception, 89
  aesthetic, 120–24, 147–62
  kinaesthetic, 90–91, 94, 122, 151–3
  inter-personal, 65–77
  phenomenology of, 71–85
  primacy of, 116
  process of, 66, 67
  and sensation, 89–91
  sensory basis of, 89–90
  and tacit knowing, 116
Perception, 49
Performer, 126, 155, 159
  and spectator, 126–36
Person
  as an embodied consciousness, 1
  fully functioning, 29
Play, 28, 147, 149
Power, 46
Practice, 109–10
  and skill, 109–10
Praxis, 3, 88
Project, 15–17
  collaborative, 36
  sub, 36
Protension/Retention, 15–17

Reflection, 21
  act of, 22
Relationships
  dyadic, 78–81
  I-Thou, 73, 74, 77, 79
  group, 81–5
  we, 73, 74, 77, 79
Remembrance, 16, 97
  primary, 98
  secondary, 98
Rugby, 154–5

Self
  actualisation, 28, 160, 179
  as agent, 39
  fulfilment, 28, 45, 161
  and kinaesthetic perception, 91–3
  knowledge, 103
  mastery, 45
  unity with, 50–51
Senses, 4
Skills, 29–32

Skills – *cont.*
  and action, 32
  capacities and needs, 31
  as contextual meanings, 33–5, 108, 160–61
  and habits, 30
  and kinaesthetic feelings, 31, 151–3
  and kinaesthetic flow patterns, 31, 151, 152
  knowing how, 105–10
  mastered, 109
  and perception, 153
  and practice, 109
  and sport, 151–2
Skilful, the, 150–53
Soccer, 89–90, 149
Social interaction, 53–4
Space, 11
  objective, 11, 72
  projectional, 13
  proximate, 12
  spatiality of position, 12
  spatiality of situation, 12
  subjective, 11, 72
Spectator, 126–36, 153
  and performer, 137
Spontaneity, 6
Sport(s)
  and art, 120–21, 143–4
  aesthetic aspects of, 143–61
  aesthetic perception of, 147–61

  and authentic existence, 40–52
  and the dramatic, 153–8
  ends and means, 124–6
  and the good contest, 158–61
  and existential meaning, 41
  nature of, 144–7, 157
  and the skilful, 150–53
  and skill, 33–7
  as rule-bound social realities, 35–7
Sportsman, 158
Sportsmanship, 145
Squash, 79–80
Symbolic form, 141
Symbolic interaction, 38, 158

Team, 83
  as a community, 83
  fellowship, 81
  togetherness, 82
Theoria, 3
Time
  as duree, 20, 22
  homogenous, 20
  inner duration, 20
  objective, 13, 72
  subjective, 13, 72

Unity, 161
  with self, 50
  with nature, 50